SHOW OFF

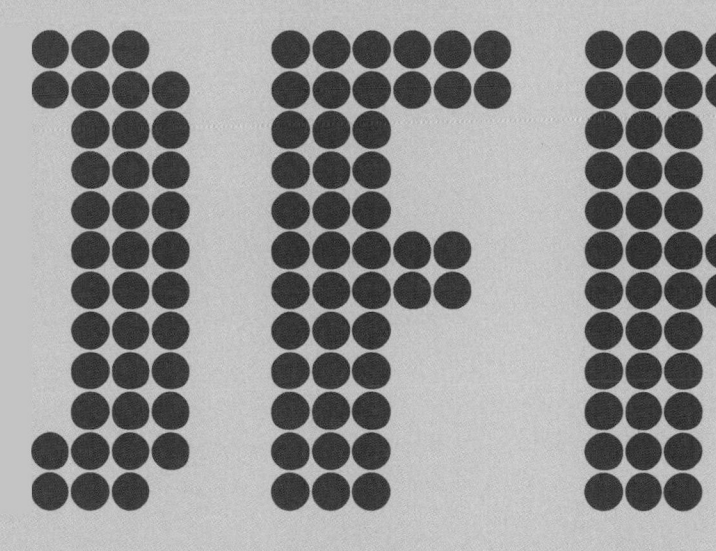

DIFF

How to Do
Absolutely Everything –
One Step at a Time

Sarah Hines Stephens
and Bethany Mann

templar publishing

contents

• how to use this book

investigate

52 erupt a fizzy fountain
53 squeeze an egg into a bottle
54 bend water with static
55 ring a bell with a TV
56 light a room with a ponytail
57 make tissue defy gravity
58 tell the time with a potato
59 mould a bouncy ball
60 grow a crystal initial
61 lift a friend's fingerprint
62 isolate DNA
63 encode notes with a scytale
64 send secrets by morse code
65 spy with a periscope
66 write in invisible ink
67 turn the world upside down
68 spin a mini kaleidoscope
69 view an eclipse
70 make a sun print
71 get cooking in a solar oven
72 make a light bulb
73 trap shadows
74 light up a lava lamp
75 flash a matchbook light
76 build a tiny robot
77 set off an exploding volcano
78 launch a rocket

create

79 take aim with a catapult
80 fire a pen crossbow
81 design a kite
82 fly a kite
83 fold a paper aeroplane
84 whip out a ninja star
85 marbleise pretty paper
86 cut festive papel picado
87 paste up a piñata
88 light paper-bag luminarias
89 fill a sea globe
90 pour a sand candle
91 weave a friendship bracelet
92 fold a gum-wrapper chain
93 link a daisy chain
94 tie-dye a stripy shirt
95 tie-dye a swirly shirt
96 cover an MP3 player
97 roll up a duct-tape rose
98 thread bead charms
99 mould clay monsters

100 create silhouette portraits
101 draw a cat
102 sketch a dog
103 draft a horse
104 draw awesome manga
105 flip out with a flip book
106 pop out a 3-D card
107 carry a comic-book bag
108 beautify trainers
109 punk up high-tops
110 stylise slip-ons
111 fashion a no-sew skirt
112 paint one-of-a-kind nails
113 make a crazy ponytail
114 ink a fake tattoo
115 annoy with a balloon horn
116 toot a straw horn
117 wire cereal-box speakers
118 screen-print a T-shirt
119 make a compact disc-o ball

explore

cook

move

how to use this book

Show Off is a brand-new type of book – one that uses pictures instead of words to show you how to do all sorts of activities. Sometimes, though, you may need a little extra info. In those cases, look for these symbols to help you out.

TOOLS The toolbar shows the items you'll need to do most projects. Follow the steps to see the amount or measurement that you'll need of each item.

⚠ You can make a kite with lots of things you find around your house. Decorate a garbage bag or old umbrella fabric for the sail, for instance, and use fabric strips for the tail.

35 in (90 cm)

40 in (100 cm)

1 Make a cross shape with the dowels.

2 Wrap string tightly at the joint. Tie.

3 Notch the ends of the shorter stick.

4 Wrap with string. Make loops at the top and bottom. Tie.

5 Trace an outline on the paper.

1 in (2½ cm)

6 Leaving loops free, fold over and glue.

7 Tie a string between the loops.

8 Tie a kite spool to the string, near the joint.

131   identify clouds

1 With the wind behind you, hand off the kite.

2 Unravel string as your friend backs away.

3 Your friend holds the kite high.

4 Signal your friend to toss the kite.

5 Walk into the wind with your arms up.

6 Let out the string to make the kite soar.

MATHS When measurements matter, they'll be written in the box – like in recipes, or when an item needs to be an exact length. Angle icons show you how far to tilt, and if it's a matter of ratio, icons like 1:1 show you how to get the perfect mix.

700 g (18 oz)   45°   1:1   100 cm (40 in)

ZOOMS These little circles, placed near or inside a larger frame, draw your attention to bonus information or important details about how to do a step – and sometimes how *not* to do a step.

CROSS REFERENCES Sometimes one thing just leads to another. Follow the cross reference to check out an activity that uses related ideas or tools.

131   **identify clouds**

listen up!

The activities in this book are designed for children aged ten and older. Please don't attempt anything that you think may be too difficult for you, and always make sure you ask a parent before starting messy activities, or where you need help to complete a project. If you can't find particular items for activities in high street shops, they are usually available on the Internet. We can't take responsibility for any unintended or unforeseen outcomes of the suggestions in this book, but we will take credit for increased awesomeness!

tool kit

Here are some basic items that you probably have at home, so they aren't listed in the toolbars. Pack a **Show Off** tool kit, and keep it handy!

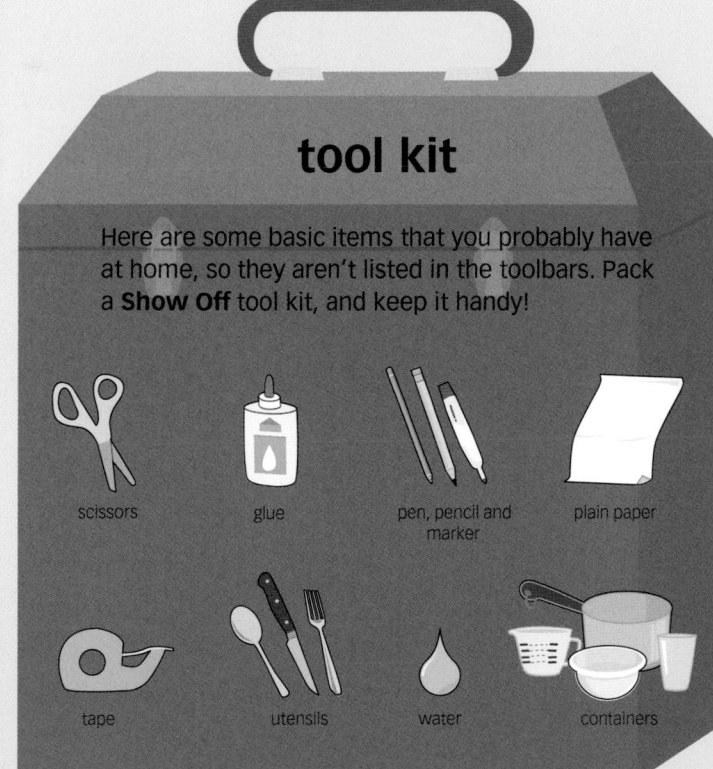

scissors

glue

pen, pencil and marker

plain paper

tape

utensils

water

containers

symbols

tell me more	Turn to the back of the book for extra info about this activity, including trivia, special techniques, history or the science that makes it all happen.
uses recyclables	This project helps you recycle old junk you probably have at your house. Go green!
messy	Wear old clothes, put down newspapers and warn your parents. This one will be messy!
science project	This activity makes for a great school project or a fun way to learn about basic scientific principles.
see our website	For additional resources – art, templates, late-breaking information and more – follow this icon to our website: www.showoffbook.com.
15 min	The timer shows the number of hours, minutes or seconds you should spend doing a step.
	The thermometer indicates the temperature to which you should heat or cool an ingredient.
×2	This symbol tells the number of times you should repeat a particular action.
XXX	The calendar's Xs show the number of days, weeks or months that a step requires.
*	Follow the little asterisk in a step to the larger one on the page for information about alternative methods or materials, or for tips.

amaze

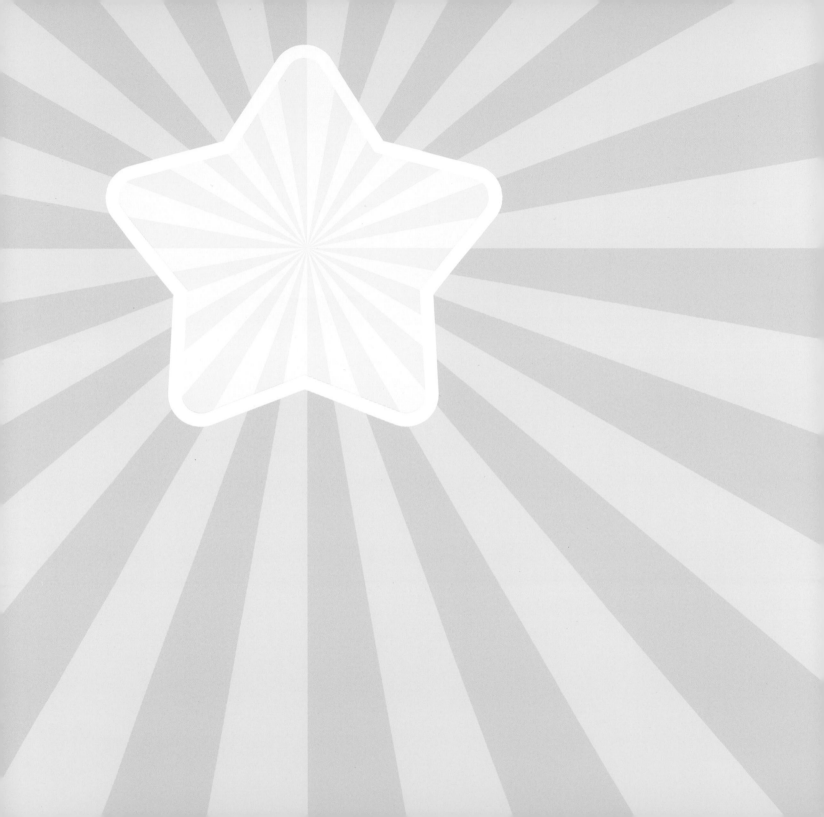

1 shimmy up walls

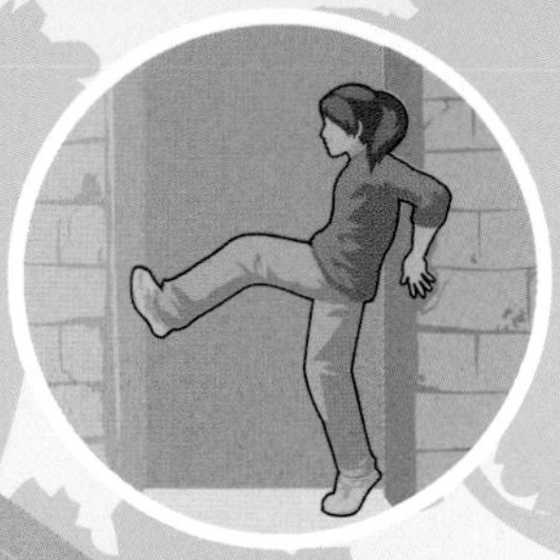

Place one leg up. Wedge yourself between walls.

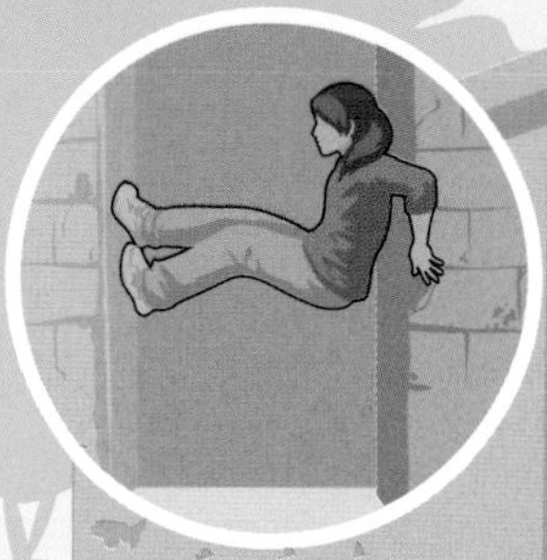

Bring up the other leg.

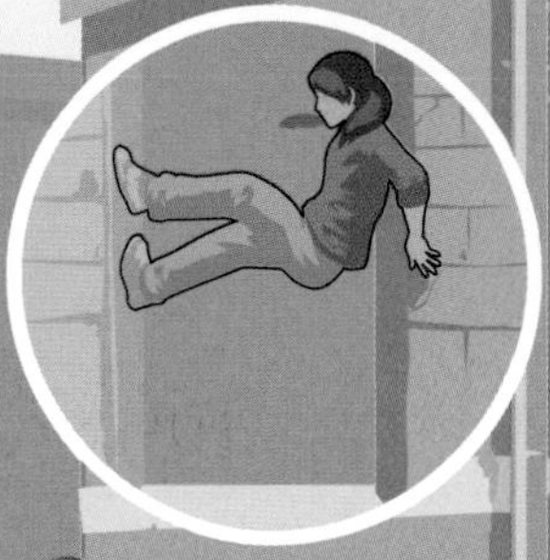

Straighten your arms to lift your torso. Step up. (Be sure not to climb too high!)

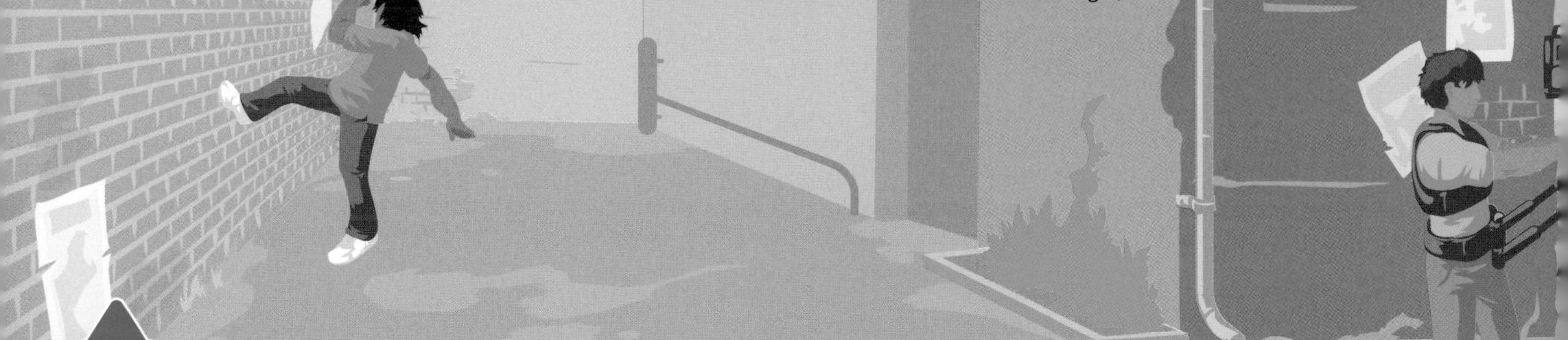

2 bounce off a wall

* Even the most fearless daredevil needs a soft landing sometimes. Start off doing these tricks over a mattress.

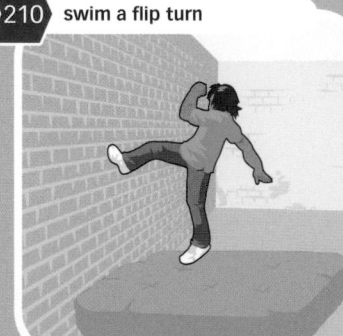

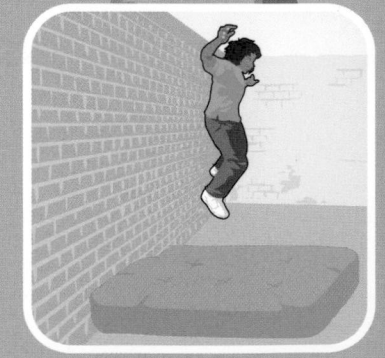

210 swim a flip turn

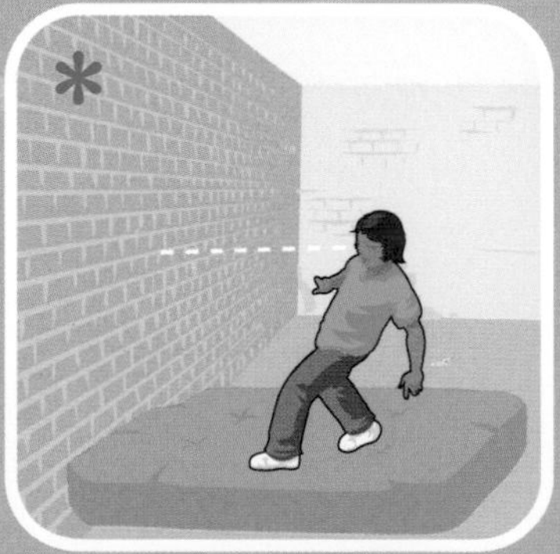

Run. Plan where to place your foot on the wall.

Put your right foot on the wall. Push off the ground.

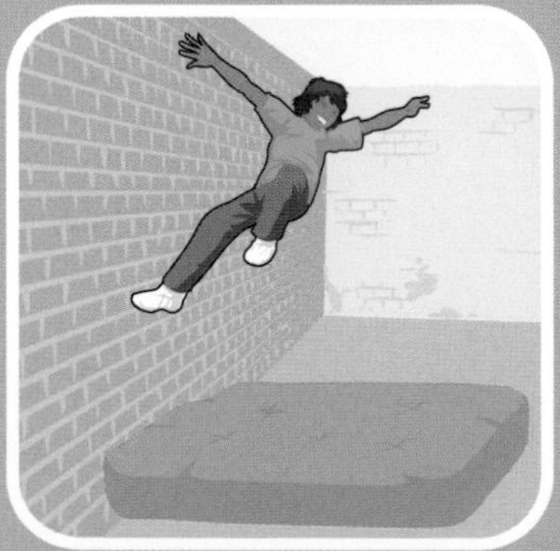

Swing your left leg around, turning your body.

Push off the wall and land with your knees bent.

do a stuntman vault 3

* Get a running start.

Plant your hand, then jump off the ground.

Swing your legs up and over.

Keep your knees loose as you land.

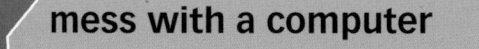

4 mess with a computer

Try these quick computer
pranks if you want to drive
someone crazy – without
causing permanent damage.

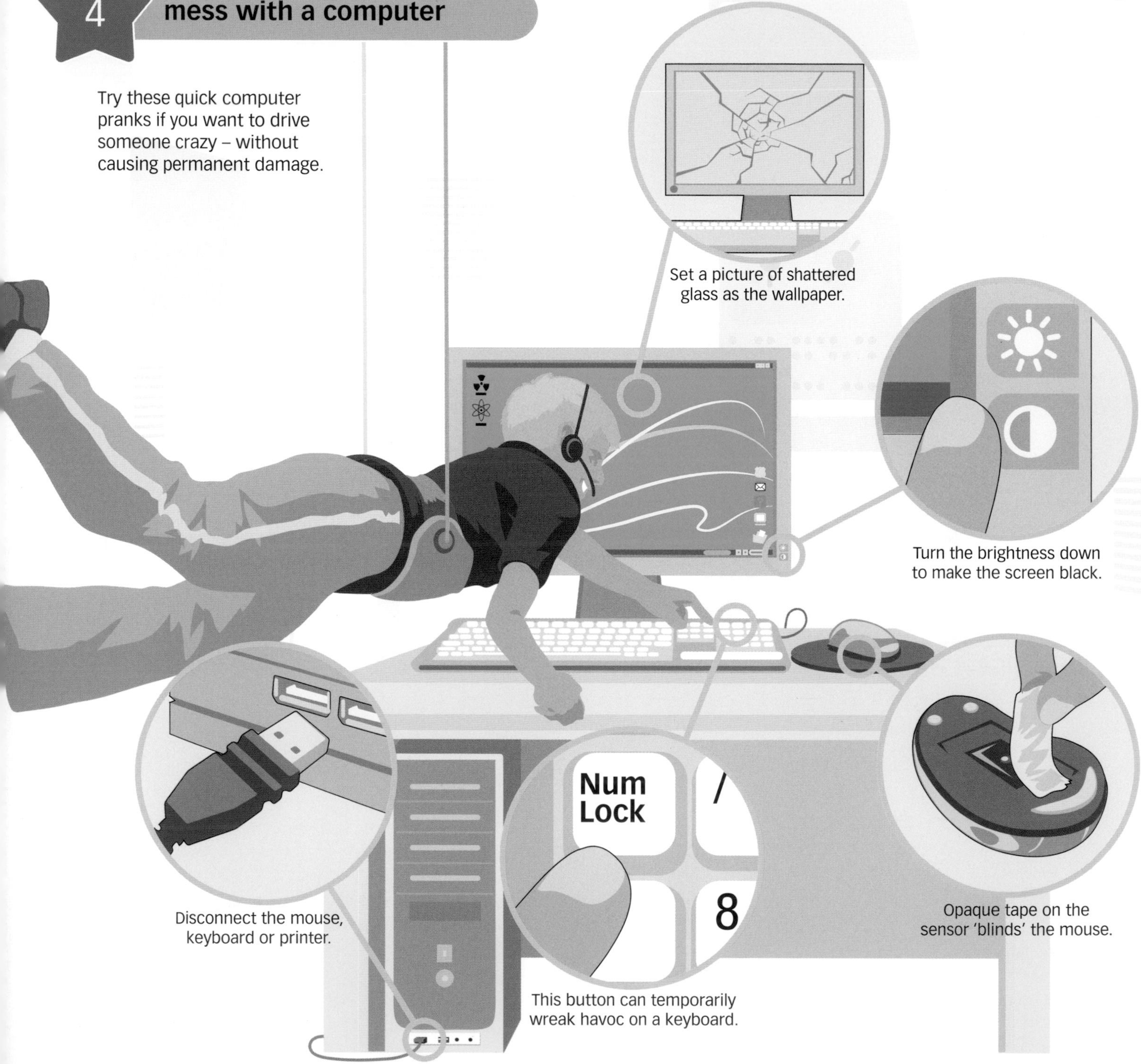

Set a picture of shattered
glass as the wallpaper.

Turn the brightness down
to make the screen black.

Disconnect the mouse,
keyboard or printer.

Num Lock / 8

This button can temporarily
wreak havoc on a keyboard.

Opaque tape on the
sensor 'blinds' the mouse.

Snap a photo while turning to follow a moving object.

blurry-background action shot

Take a picture with your camera on the ground.

ant's-eye view

Get one person to stand behind and higher than another.

tiny-friend illusion

alligator

bird

snake

boar

elephant

horse

standing dog

camel

llama

rabbit

human

deer

goat

turtle

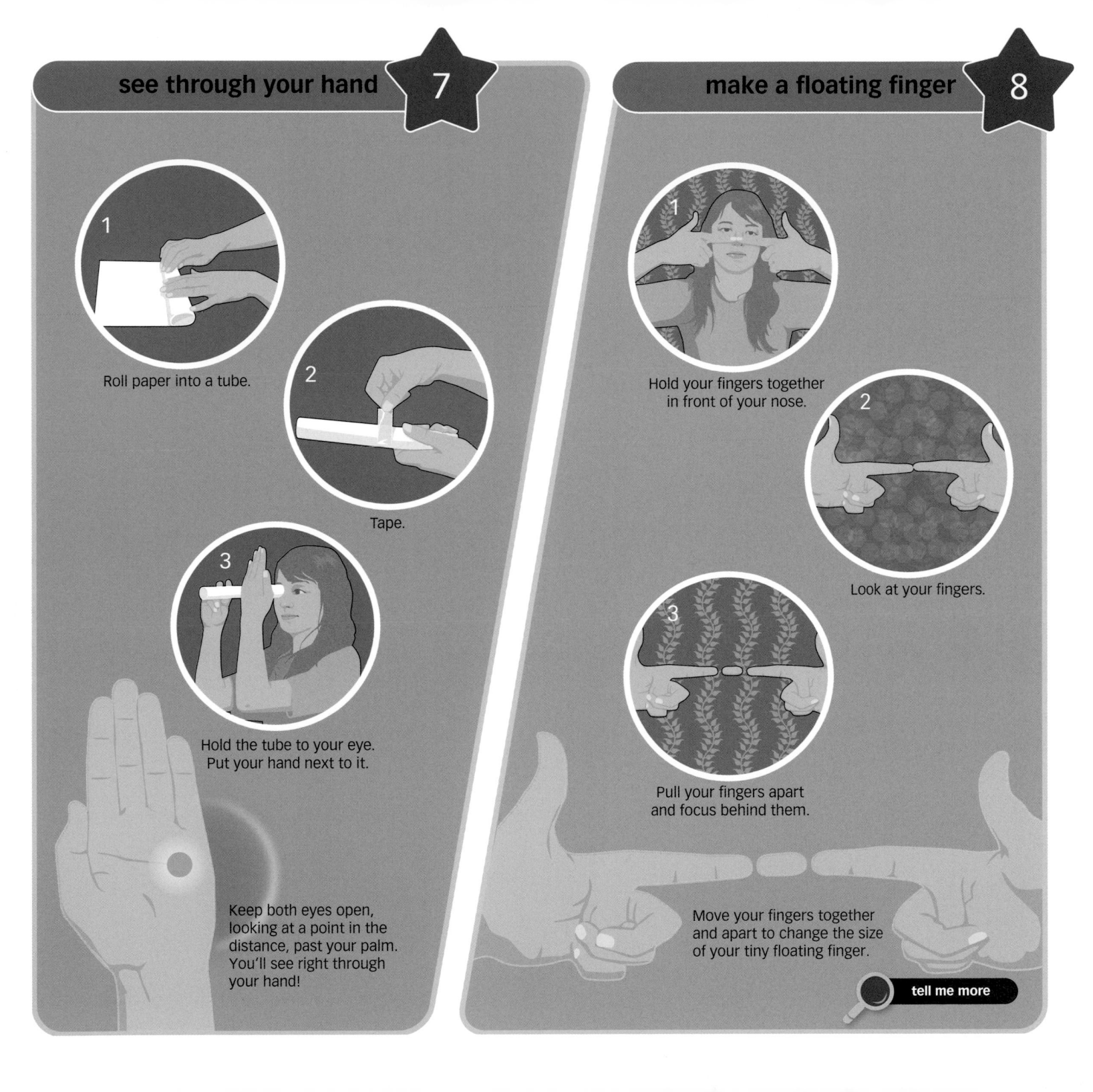

see through your hand 7

1 Roll paper into a tube.

2 Tape.

3 Hold the tube to your eye. Put your hand next to it.

Keep both eyes open, looking at a point in the distance, past your palm. You'll see right through your hand!

make a floating finger 8

1 Hold your fingers together in front of your nose.

2 Look at your fingers.

3 Pull your fingers apart and focus behind them.

Move your fingers together and apart to change the size of your tiny floating finger.

tell me more

1

2

3

4

5

6

7

8

9

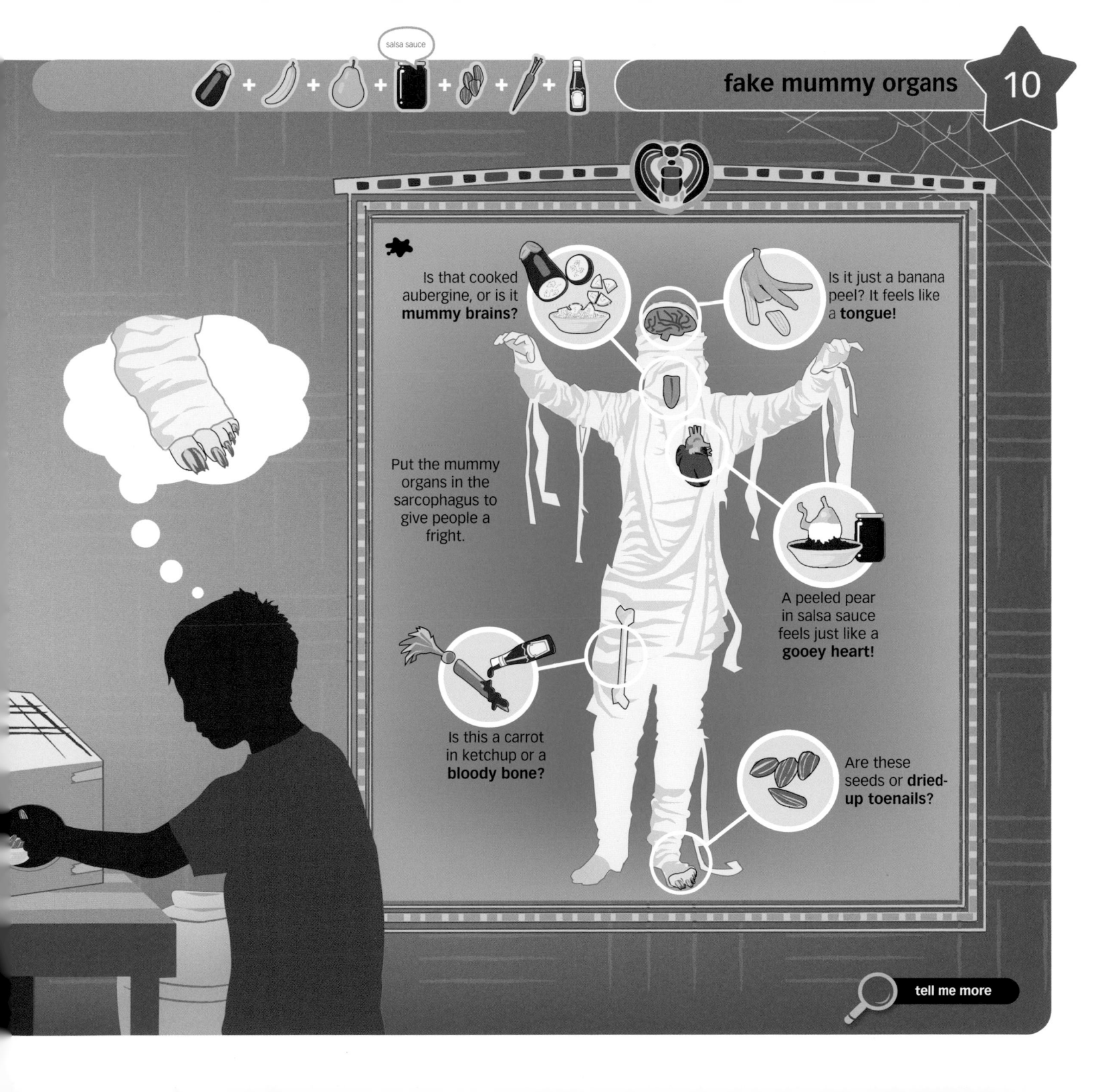

Make a torso with the chicken wire. Stuff it with newspaper, then cover with fake fur.

Cut features out of felt and glue in place.

Decorate overalls to look like chicken legs.

Sew the torso to the back of the overalls.

Put on the overalls, shirt and jacket.

Cut a slit up a jacket and shirt.

Glue the wings and trousers to the platter.

Cut out a space for your hips.

Stuff a pair of socks and the trousers of an old suit with newspaper. Sew the shoes to the socks, and the socks to the trousers.

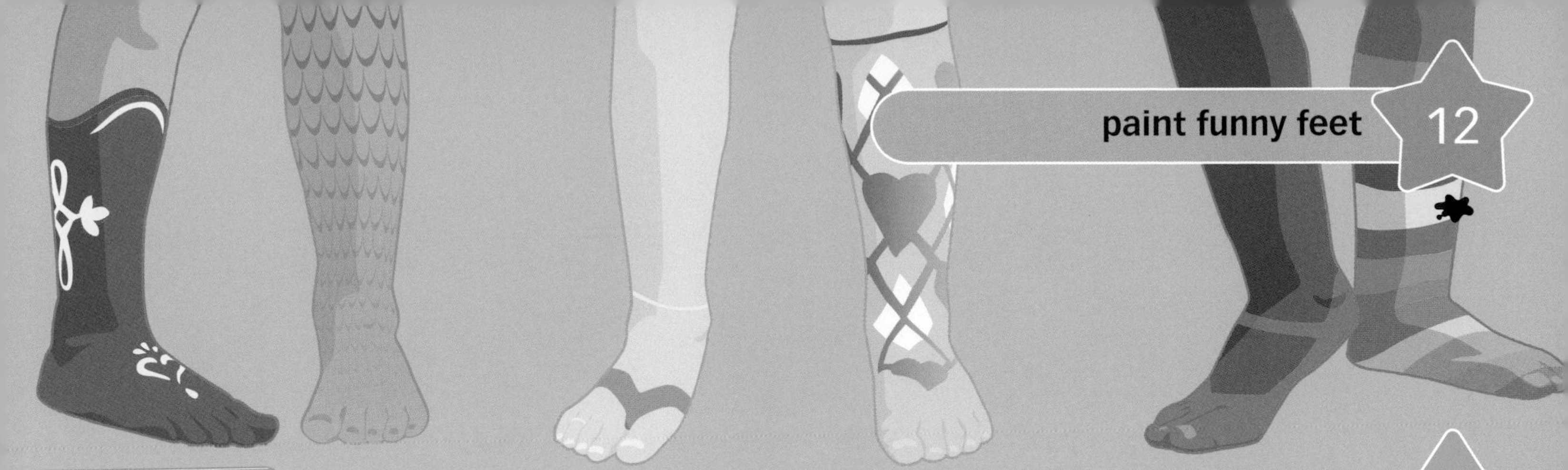

paint funny feet 12

draw hand costumes 13

create chin people 14

Freak out your friends with a topsy-turvy version of yourself. Turn upside down, and ask a friend to decorate your chin to look like a face. Then get them to take photos of you.

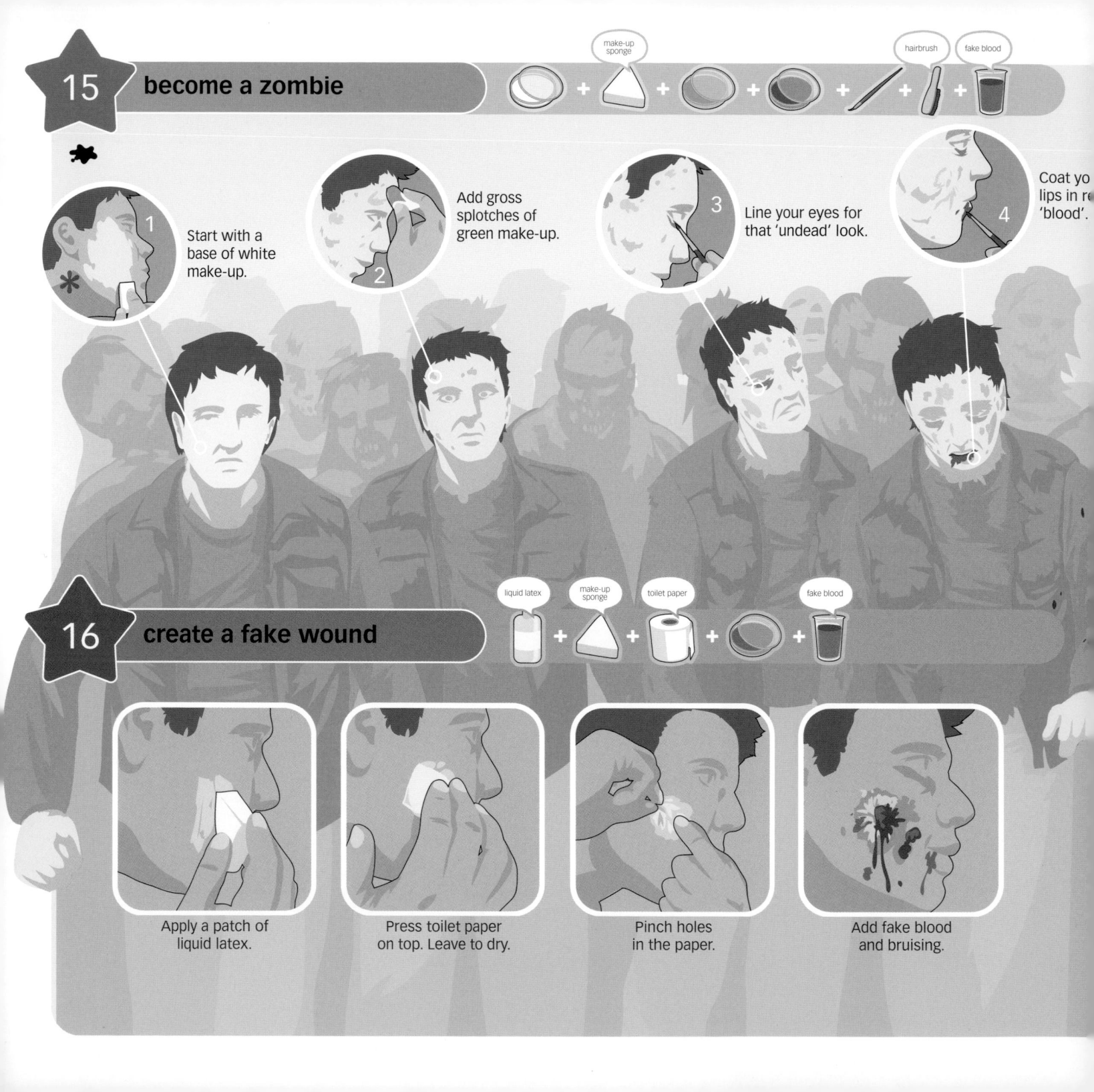

15 become a zombie

make-up sponge · hairbrush · fake blood

1. Start with a base of white make-up.
2. Add gross splotches of green make-up.
3. Line your eyes for that 'undead' look.
4. Coat yo lips in r 'blood'.

16 create a fake wound

liquid latex + make-up sponge + toilet paper + + fake blood

Apply a patch of liquid latex.

Press toilet paper on top. Leave to dry.

Pinch holes in the paper.

Add fake blood and bruising.

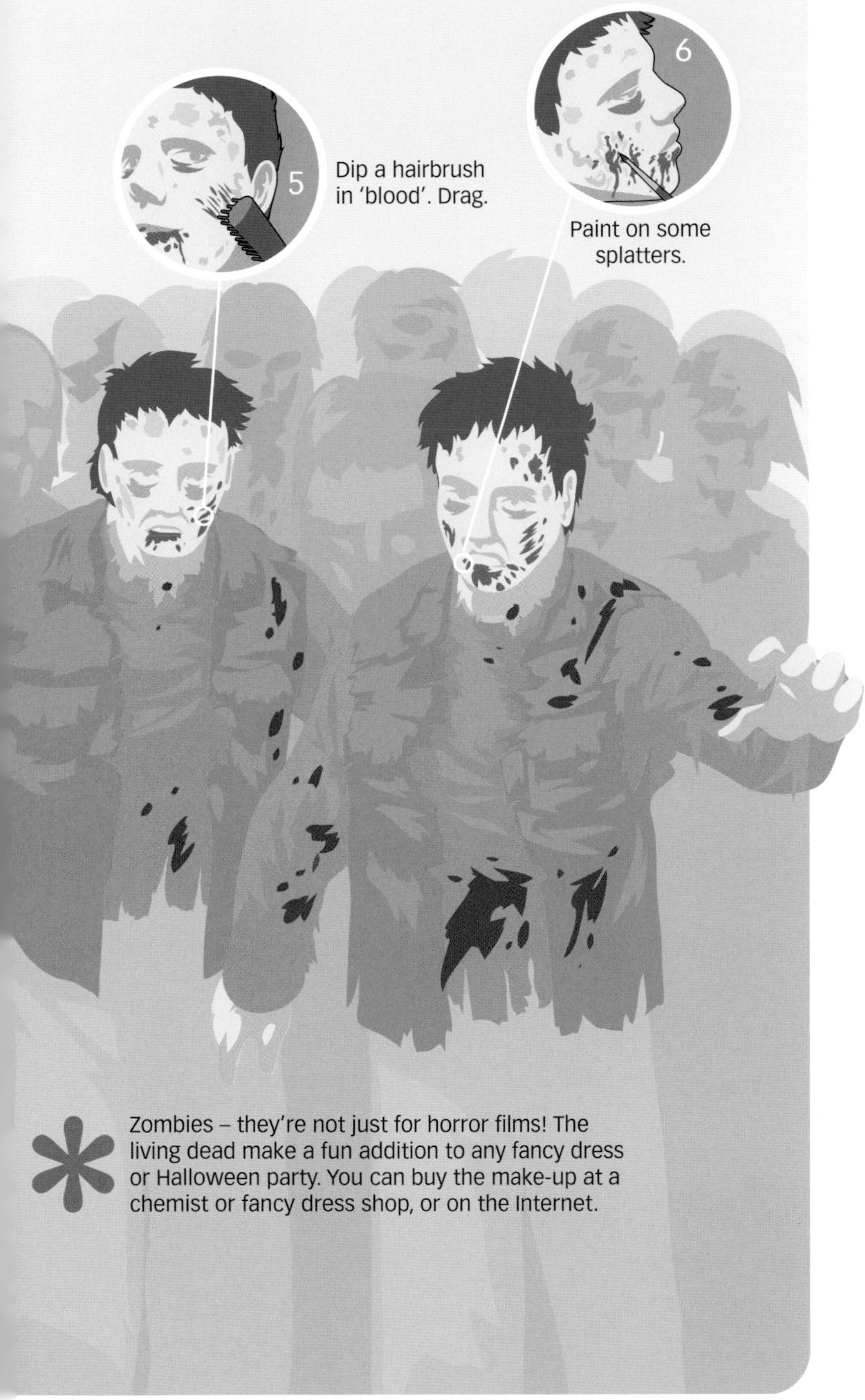

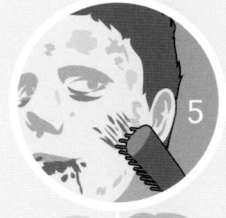

5
Dip a hairbrush in 'blood'. Drag.
6
Paint on some splatters.

Zombies – they're not just for horror films! The living dead make a fun addition to any fancy dress or Halloween party. You can buy the make-up at a chemist or fancy dress shop, or on the Internet.

17 spurt fake blood

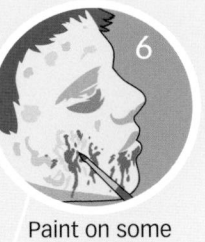

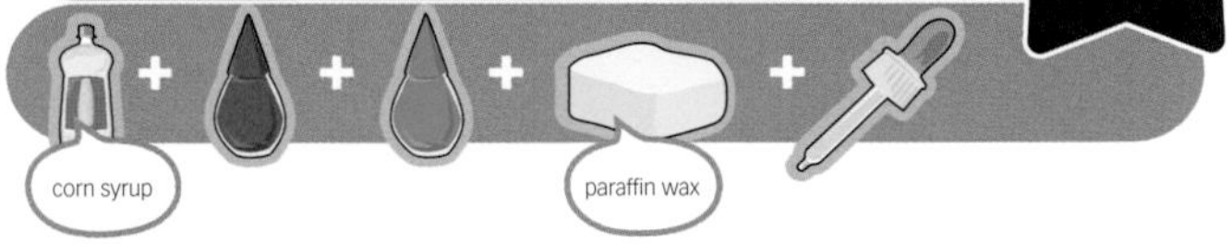

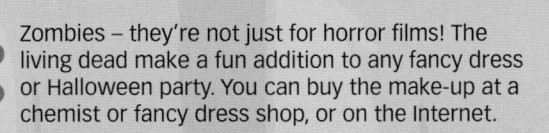

corn syrup
paraffin wax

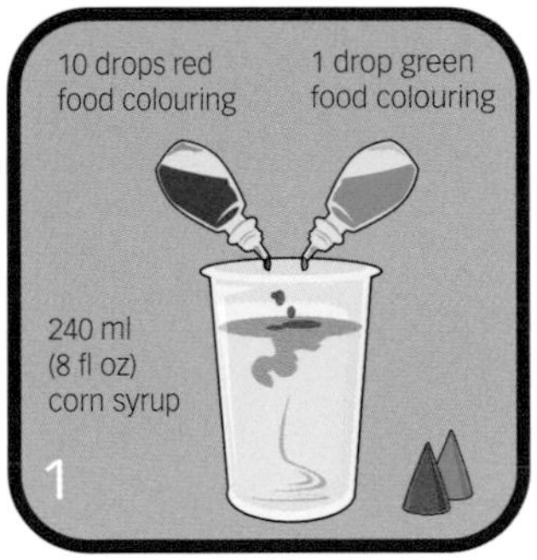

10 drops red food colouring
1 drop green food colouring
240 ml (8 fl oz) corn syrup
1

Combine.

10 sec
2

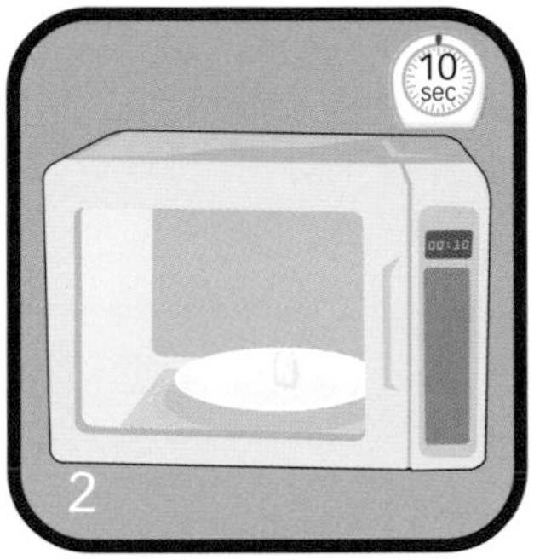

Soften a lump of paraffin wax.

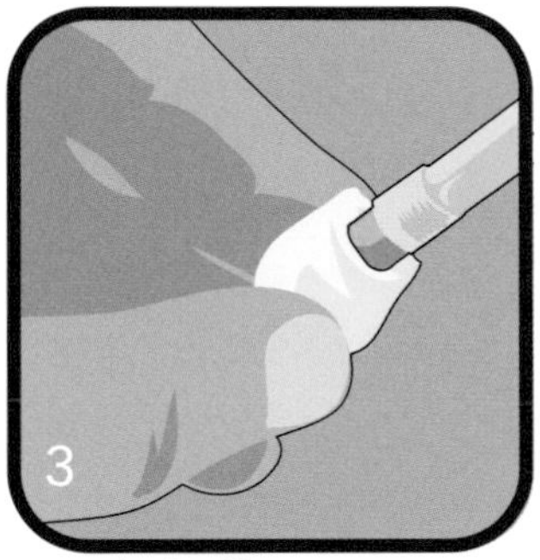

3

Pinch off some wax. Hollow out the inside.

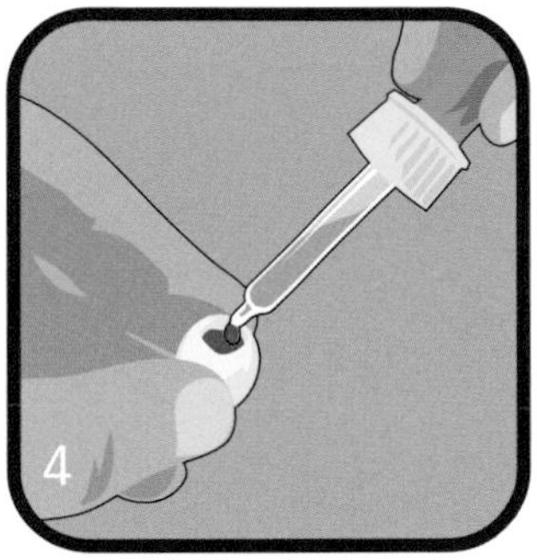

4

Fill with the corn syrup mixture.

5

Pinch the capsule closed.

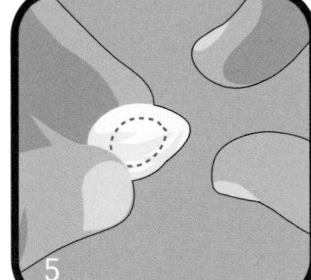

make edible fake vomit 185

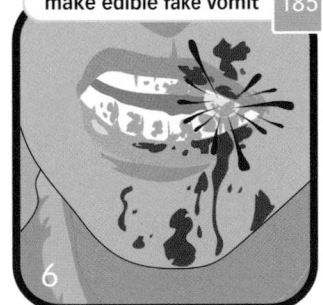

6

Bite down to spurt the 'blood'.

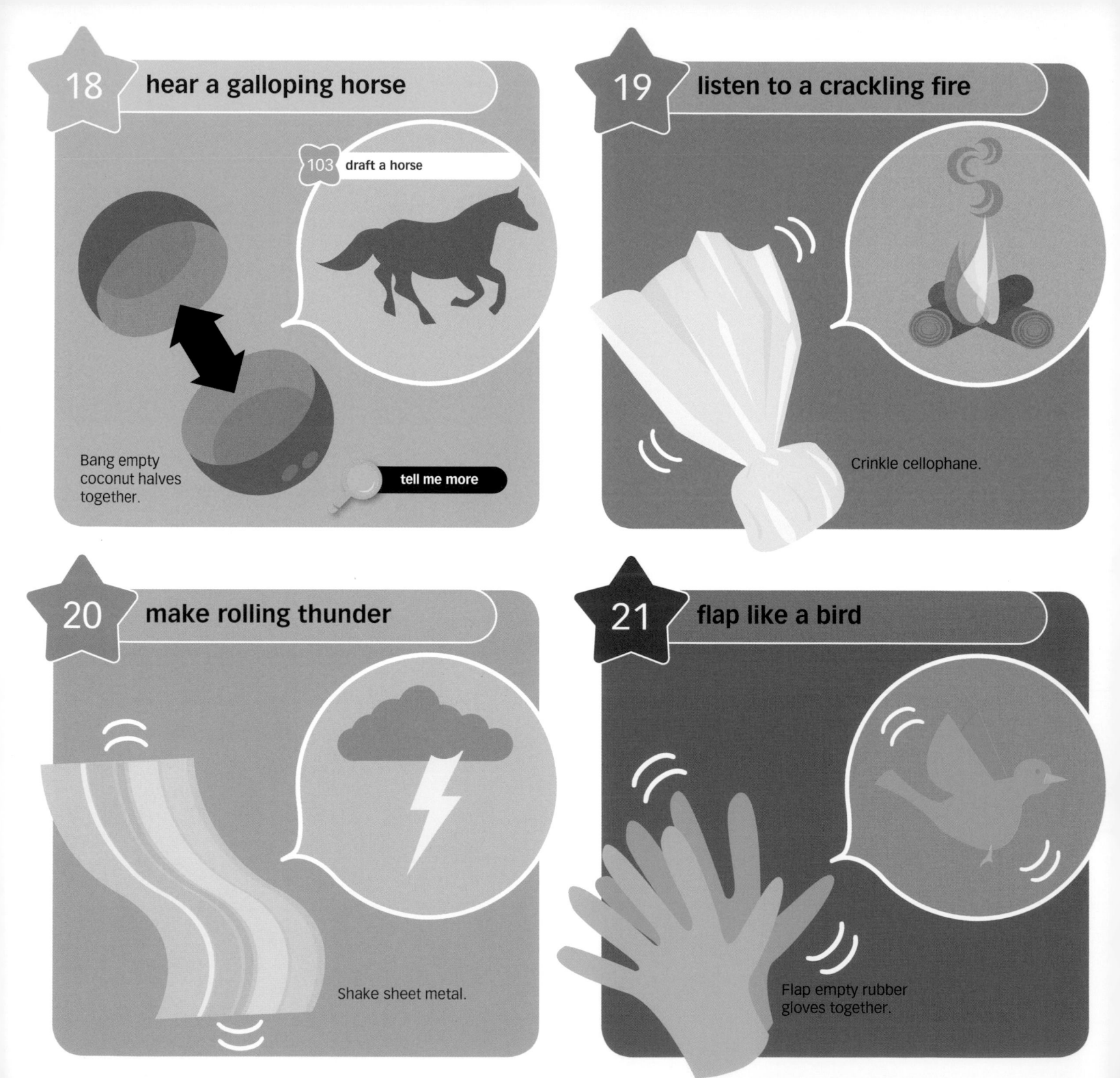

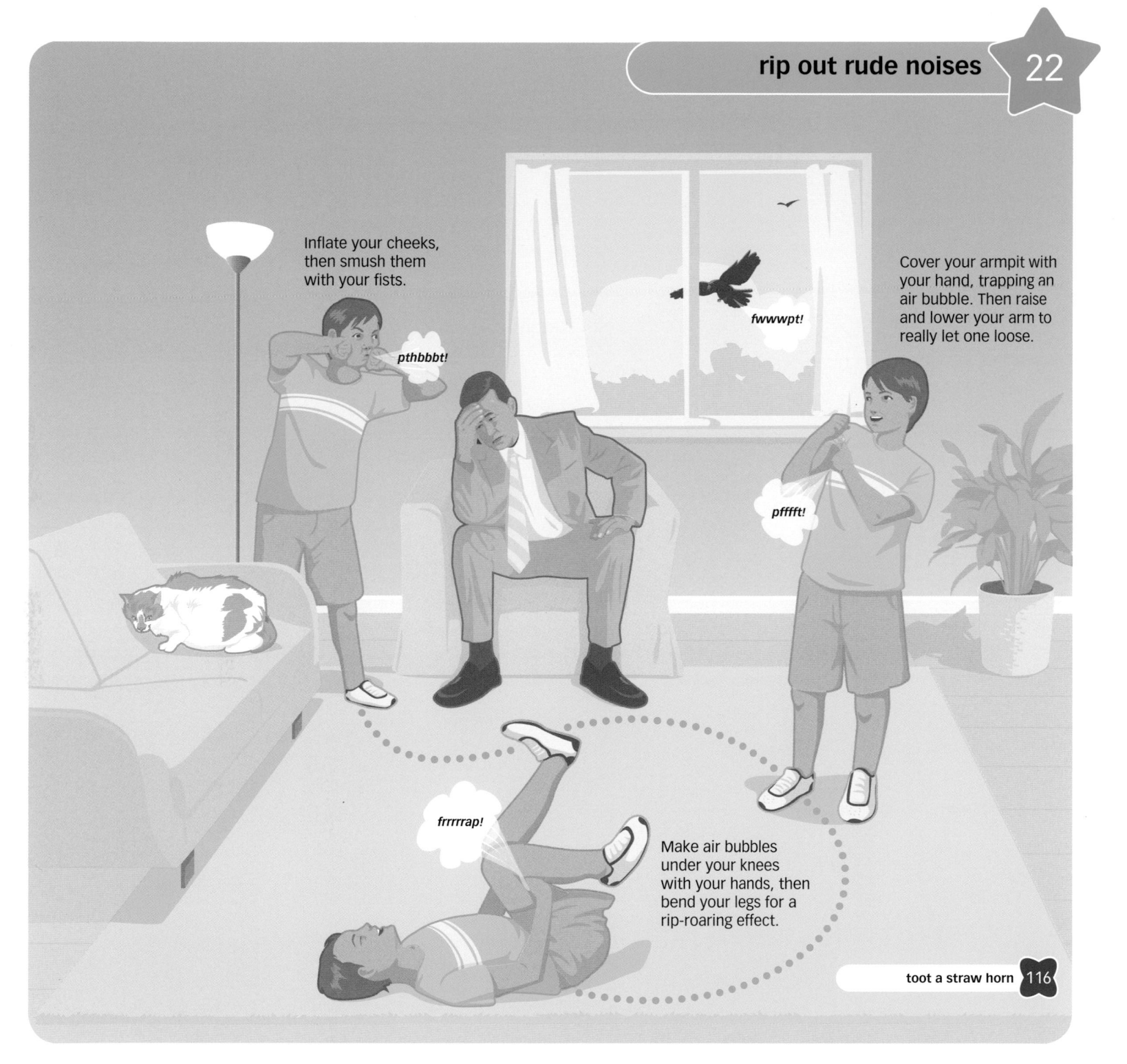

make a coin jump

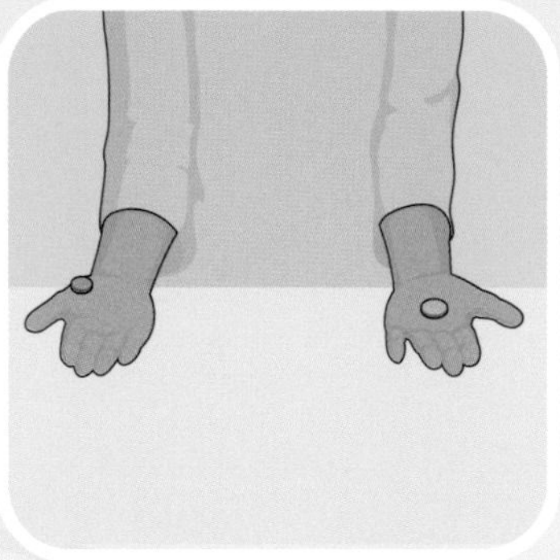

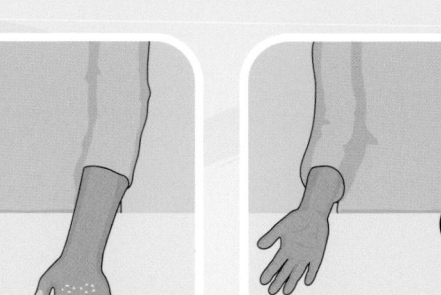

Put a coin on each palm, with one near your thumb.

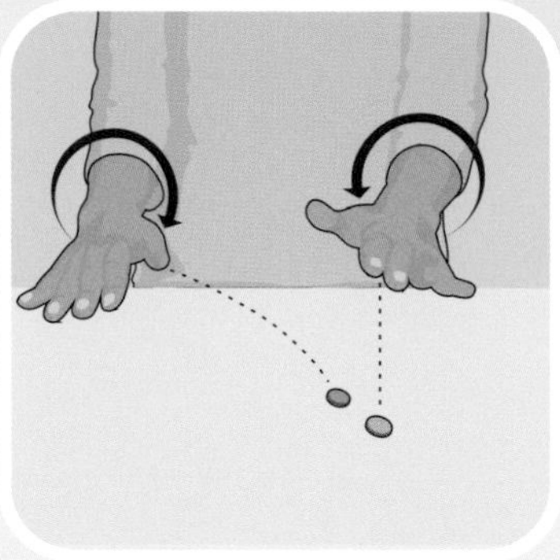

Flip your hands, shooting the coins under one hand.

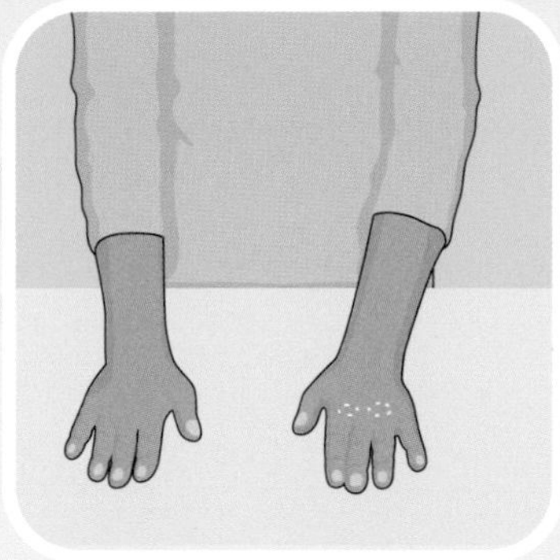

The audience will imagine there's a coin under each.

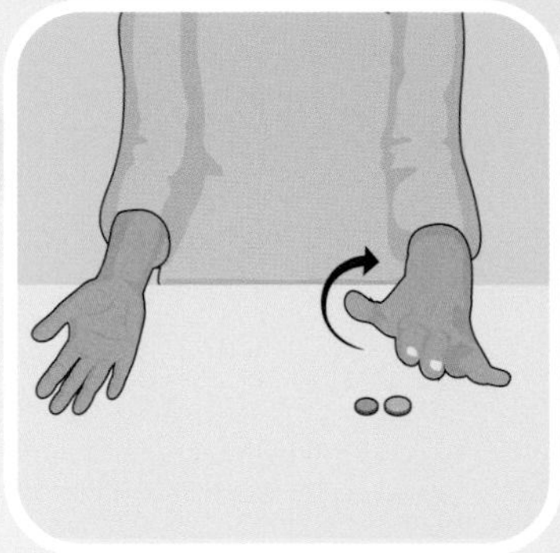

Show the empty palm, then the missing coin!

bring a dove back to life

Cut a head from a fake dove; decorate to match.

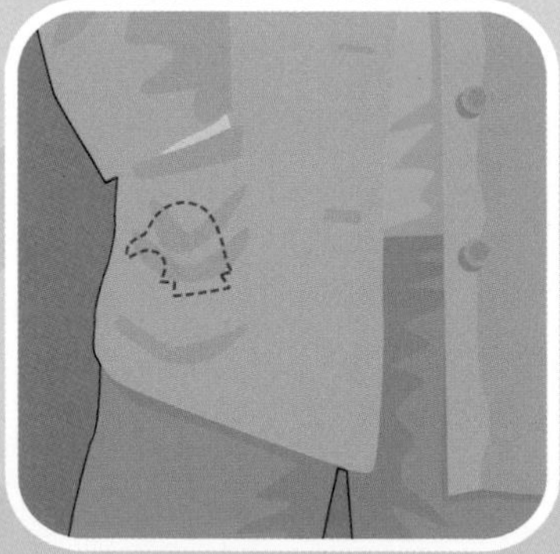

Hide the fake head in your pocket.

Stroke him. He's real!

Round up an audience. Show them the real dove.

Gently hide the real dove's head. Put the fake over it.

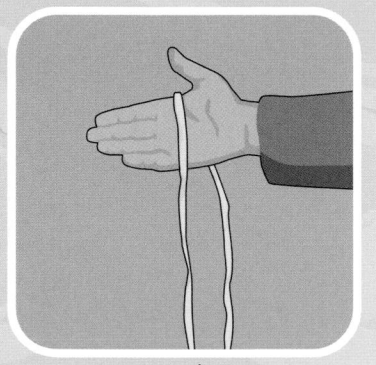

Hang a string over
your palm.

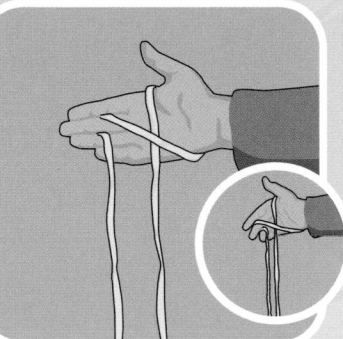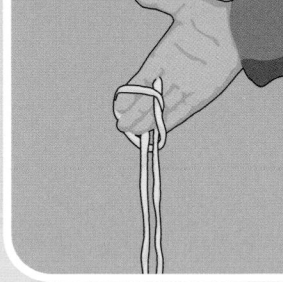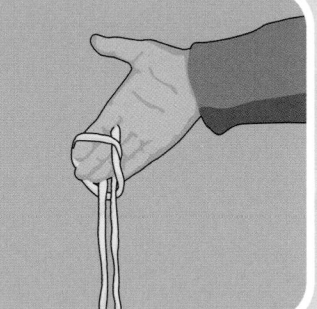

Loop the back end over
your middle finger.

Slide the loop down
around your knuckles.

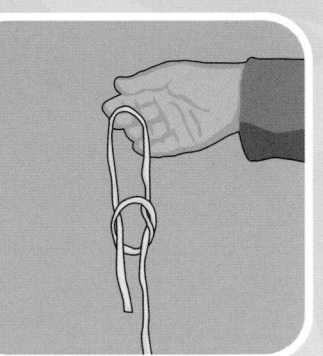

Pull the string between
your fingers up.

Pull the fake head
away suddenly.

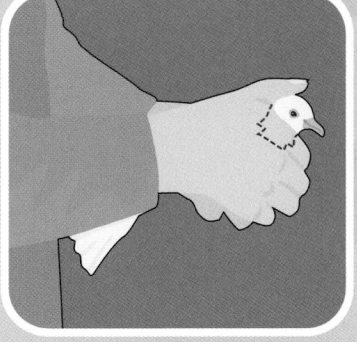

Cover the real dove
with the fake head.

149 **hollow out a bird house**

Hide the fake; blow on the
dove to raise his head.

Release, putting the fake
head back in your pocket.

fake a fall

Stroll along casually.

Hook your back foot behind your front foot.

'Trip' over your front foot, landing on your knees.

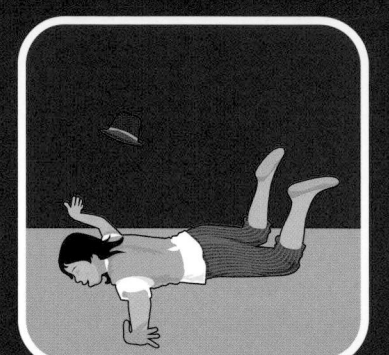

Fall from your knees to your hands, then onto your face.

Line up a hat brim with your outstretched arm.

Flick your wrist to roll it quickly down your arm.

Dip your arm to keep up the momentum.

Catch the hat once it reaches your hand.

spin a plate ★ 28

1 Put a stick under a plastic plate's rim.

2 Start rotating the stick, holding the bottom still.

3 When the plate is spinning fast, hold the stick still.

dowse for water

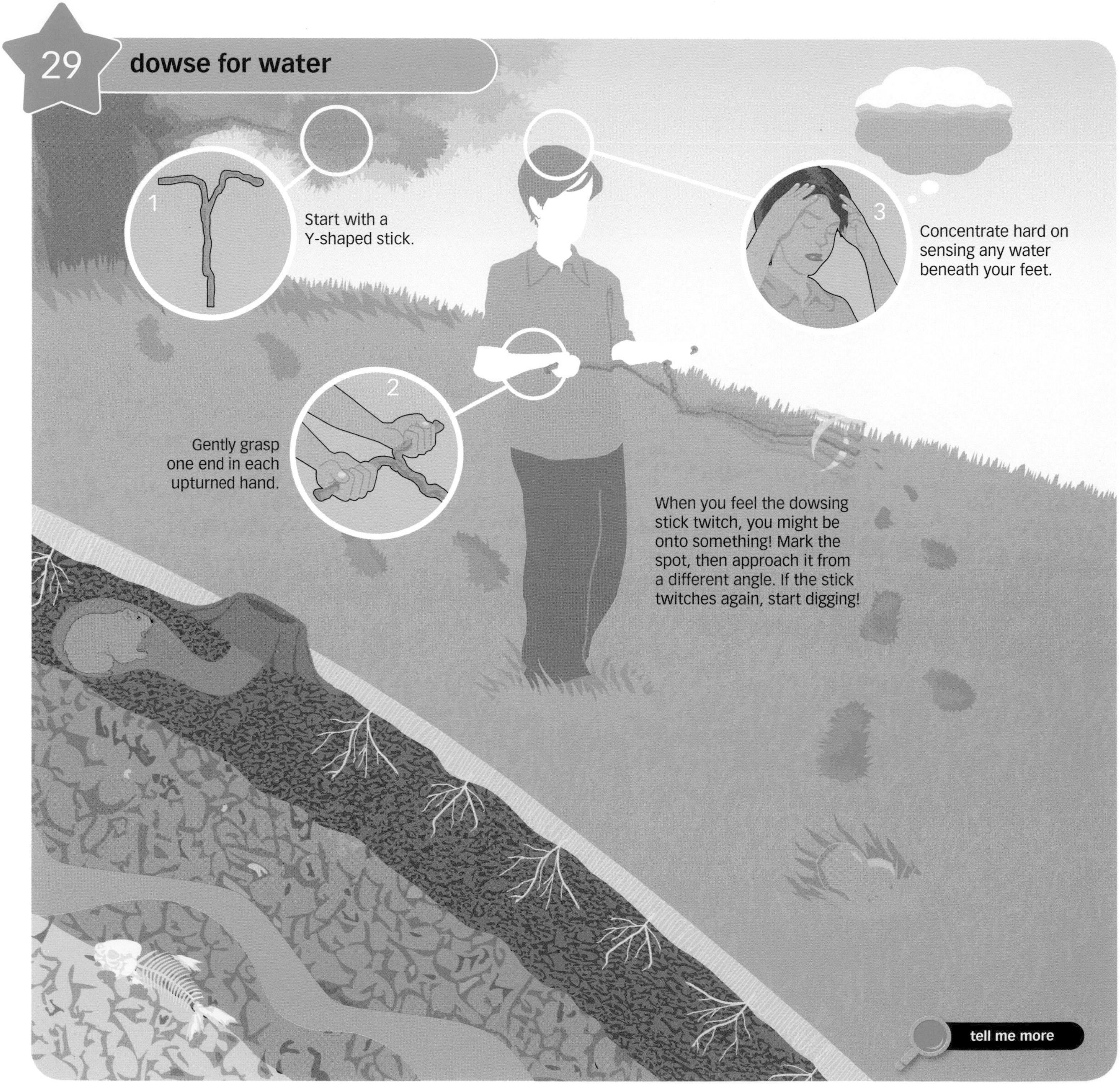

1 Start with a Y-shaped stick.

2 Gently grasp one end in each upturned hand.

3 Concentrate hard on sensing any water beneath your feet.

When you feel the dowsing stick twitch, you might be onto something! Mark the spot, then approach it from a different angle. If the stick twitches again, start digging!

tell me more

30 read a love line

tell me more

wavy = non-committal
broken = cloudy past
short = crushaholic
down-sloping = needy
long = romantic

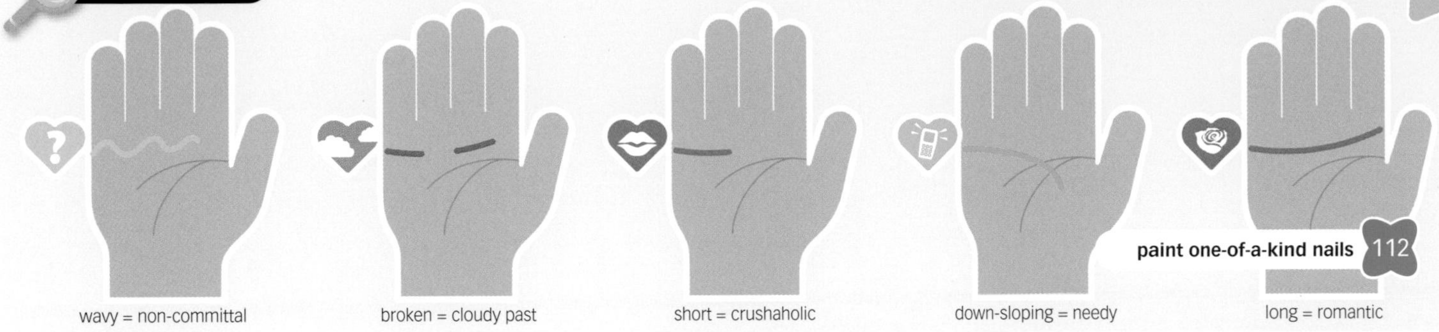

paint one-of-a-kind nails 112

31 interpret a head line

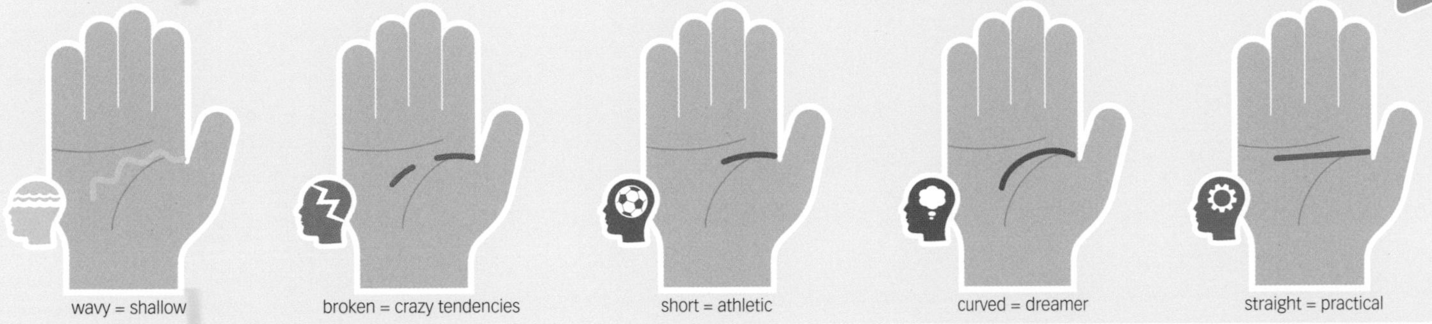

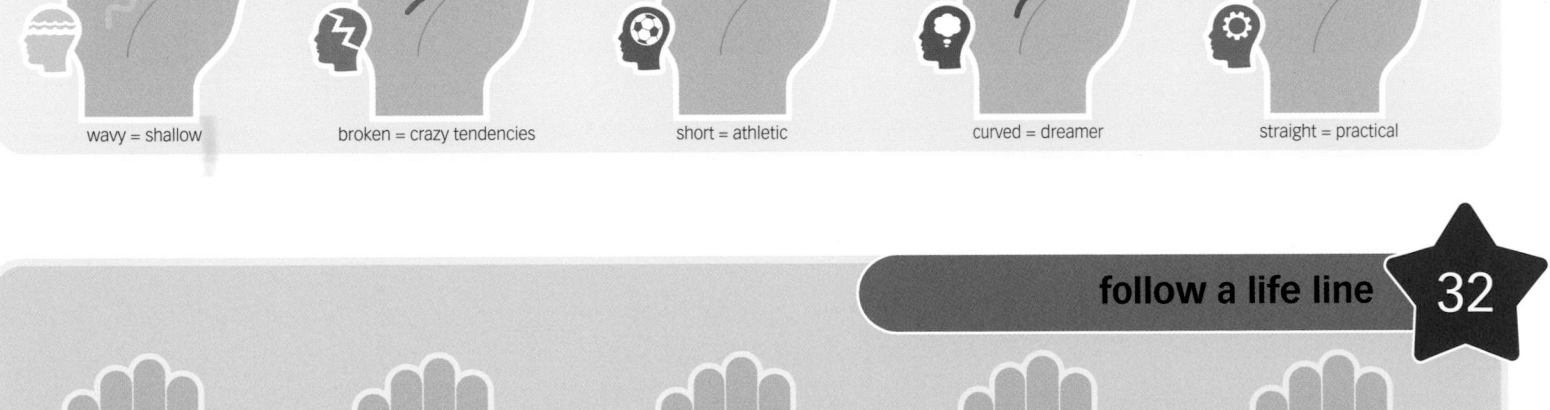

wavy = shallow
broken = crazy tendencies
short = athletic
curved = dreamer
straight = practical

32 follow a life line

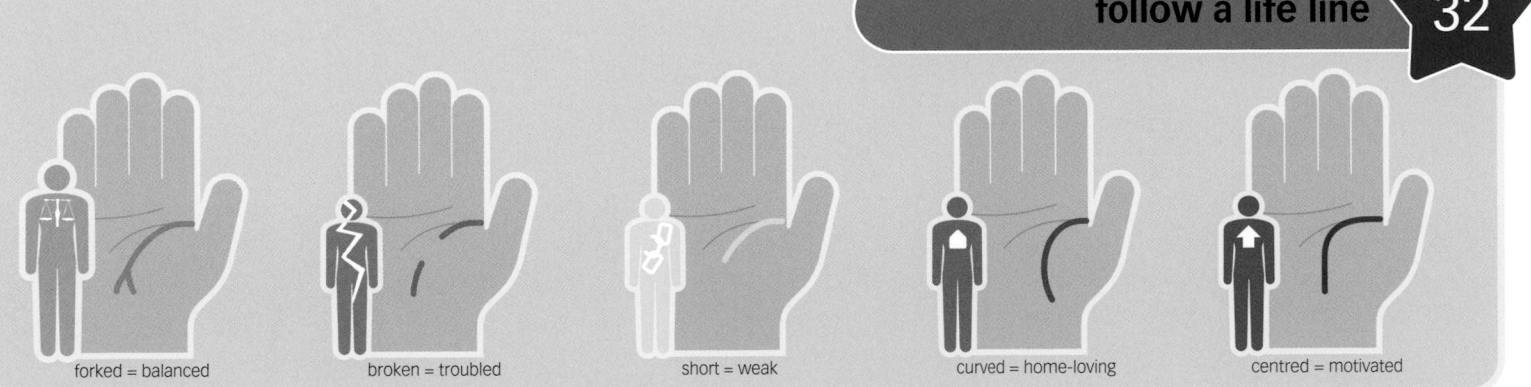

forked = balanced
broken = troubled
short = weak
curved = home-loving
centred = motivated

slice an unpeeled banana

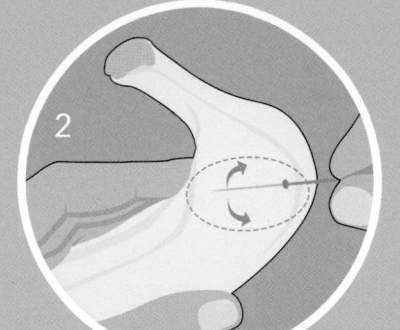

Slide the needle from side
to side inside the peel.

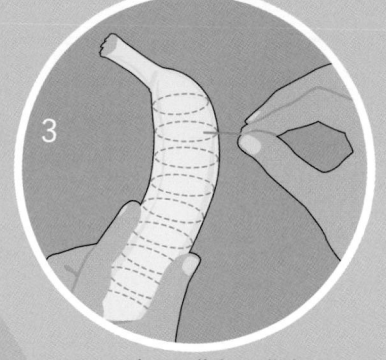

Continue slicing all the
way down the fruit.

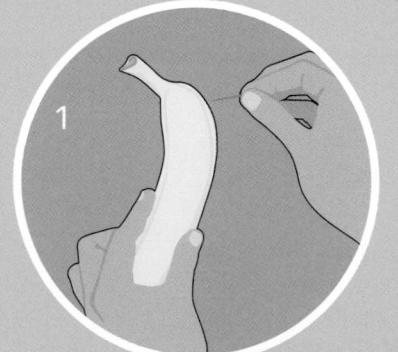

Poke a needle into a
banana along one seam.

Hand it to someone who
needs a surprise!

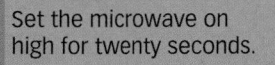

Set the microwave on high for twenty seconds.

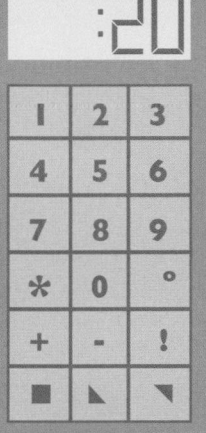

2.5 cm (1 in)

Arm each marshmallow by inserting a toothpick 'spear'. When the dust clears and the morphing, oozing and melting stop, the marshmallow in better shape is the winner.

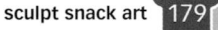
sculpt snack art 179

tell me more

blow a nose bubble

Chew bubblegum until it's soft.

Stretch out the gum. Press to make an airtight seal.

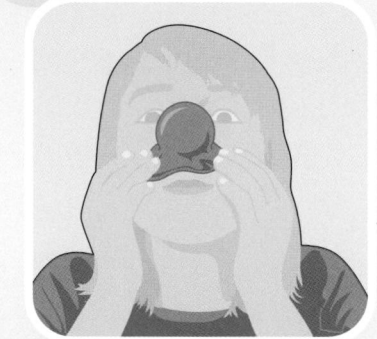

Blow through your nose, holding the gum's edges.

A good bubble-blower 'nose' when to stop!

* If you prefer to keep your gum in your mouth, try blowing a bubble inside a bubble! Blow a big bubble, seal it shut and use the excess gum to blow a small bubble inside the first one.

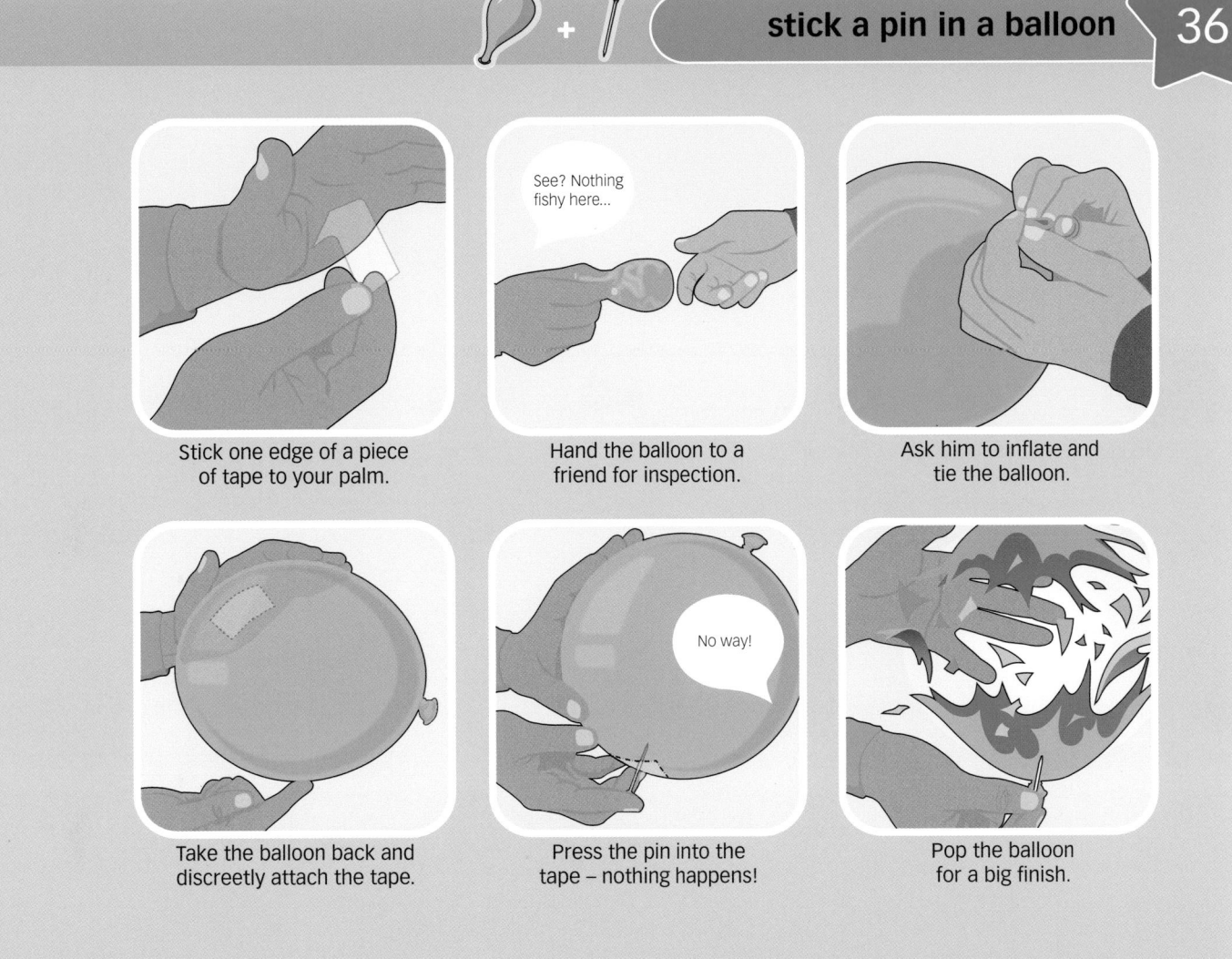

Stick one edge of a piece of tape to your palm.

Hand the balloon to a friend for inspection.

Ask him to inflate and tie the balloon.

Take the balloon back and discreetly attach the tape.

Press the pin into the tape – nothing happens!

Pop the balloon for a big finish.

37 walk the dog

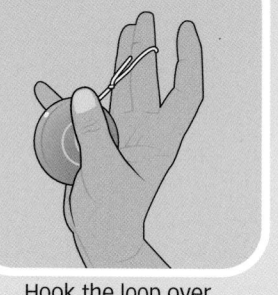

1. Hook the loop over your middle finger.

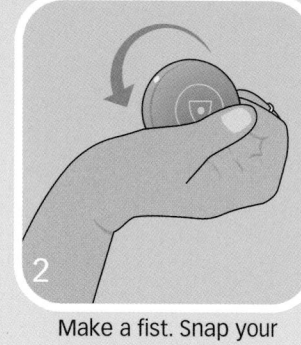

2. Make a fist. Snap your wrist down hard.

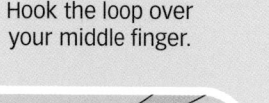

3. Gently let the yo-yo unwind.

4. Let it reach the floor.

102 sketch a dog

5. The yo-yo will 'walk' on its own.

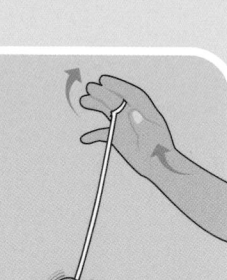

6. Jerk it back up to your hand.

38 rock the baby

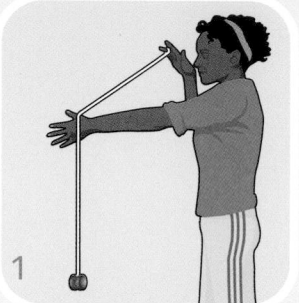

1. Toss the yo-yo over the back of your hand.

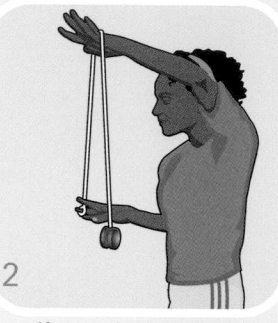

2. Lift your bottom hand to double the string.

3. Hook the string with your thumb.

4. Turn your top hand over so that it's palm up.

5. Lift your bottom hand. Pinch the string.

6. Let the baby 'rock' in the string triangle.

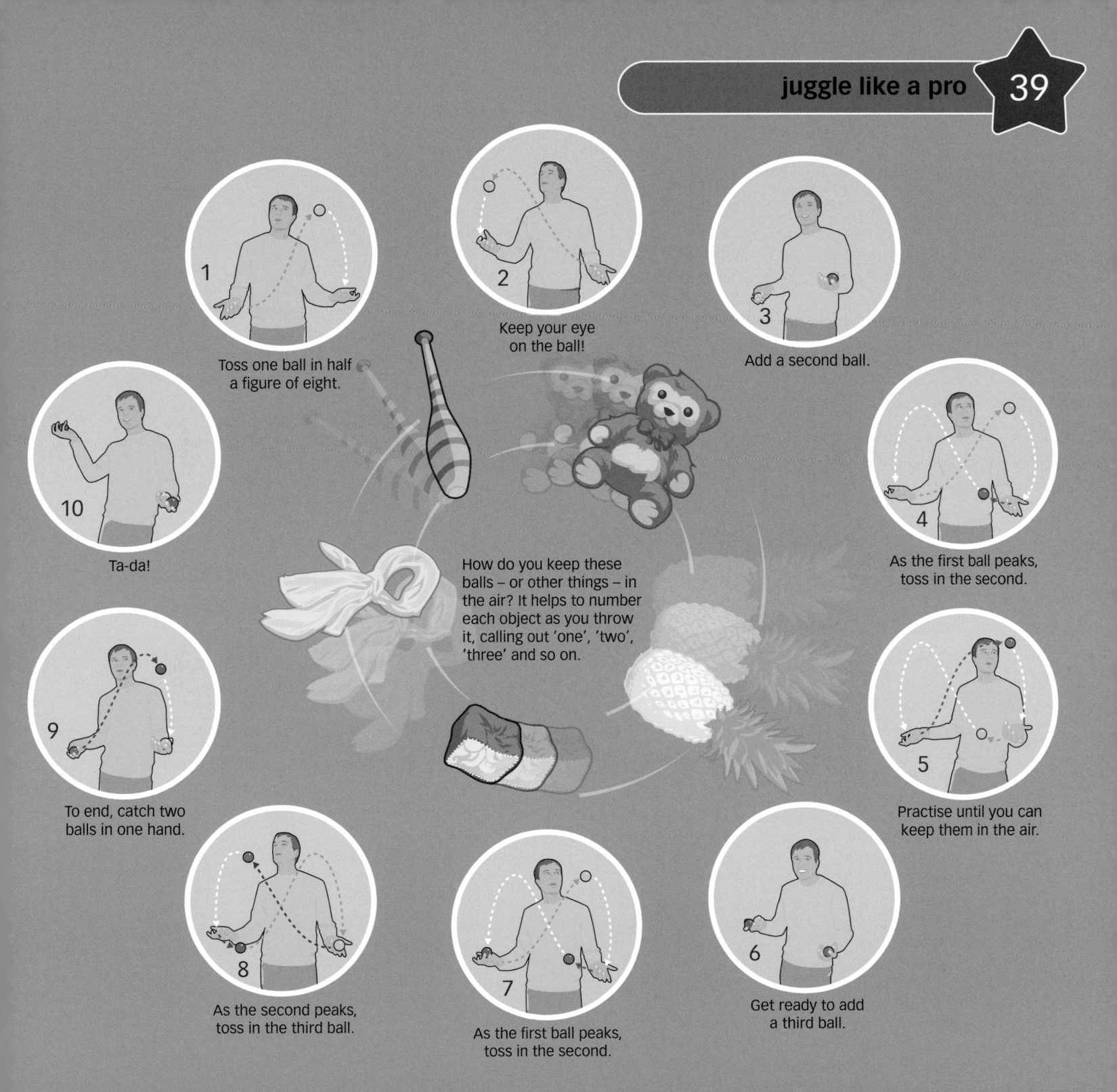

1. Toss one ball in half a figure of eight.

2. Keep your eye on the ball!

3. Add a second ball.

4. As the first ball peaks, toss in the second.

5. Practise until you can keep them in the air.

6. Get ready to add a third ball.

7. As the first ball peaks, toss in the second.

8. As the second peaks, toss in the third ball.

9. To end, catch two balls in one hand.

10. Ta-da!

How do you keep these balls – or other things – in the air? It helps to number each object as you throw it, calling out 'one', 'two', 'three' and so on.

40 spin a basketball

Hold the ball with just
your fingertips.

Spin it up onto
one fingertip.

Balance it on your finger
until it slows down.

204 sink a free throw

Switch to your other hand.
Brush to keep it spinning.

41 skim a stone

Pick a flat, smooth,
rounded stone.

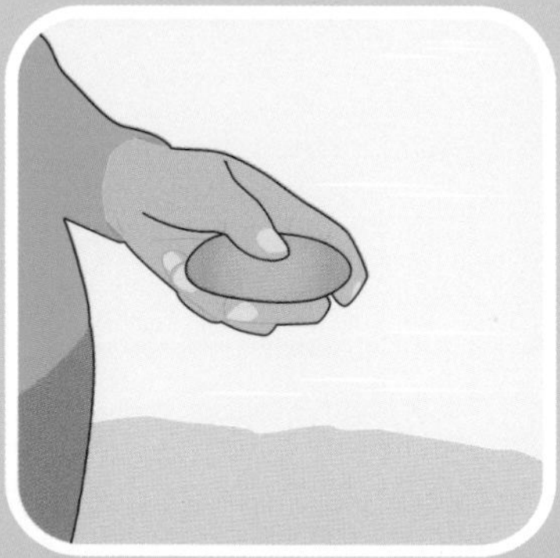

Curl your index finger
around it.

Aim to skim the stone
along the surface.

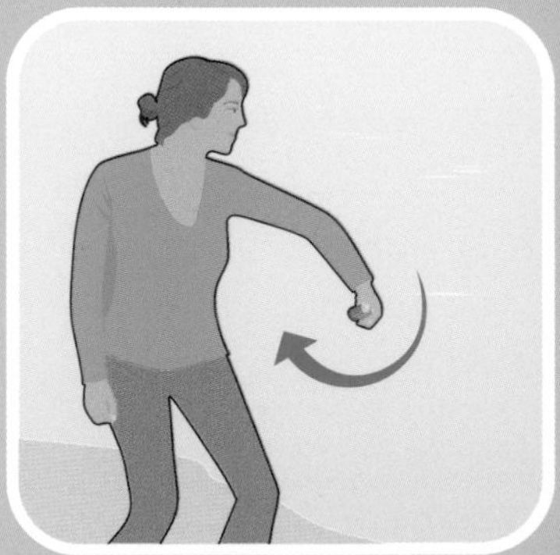

Crouch slightly, curling
your arm to your body.

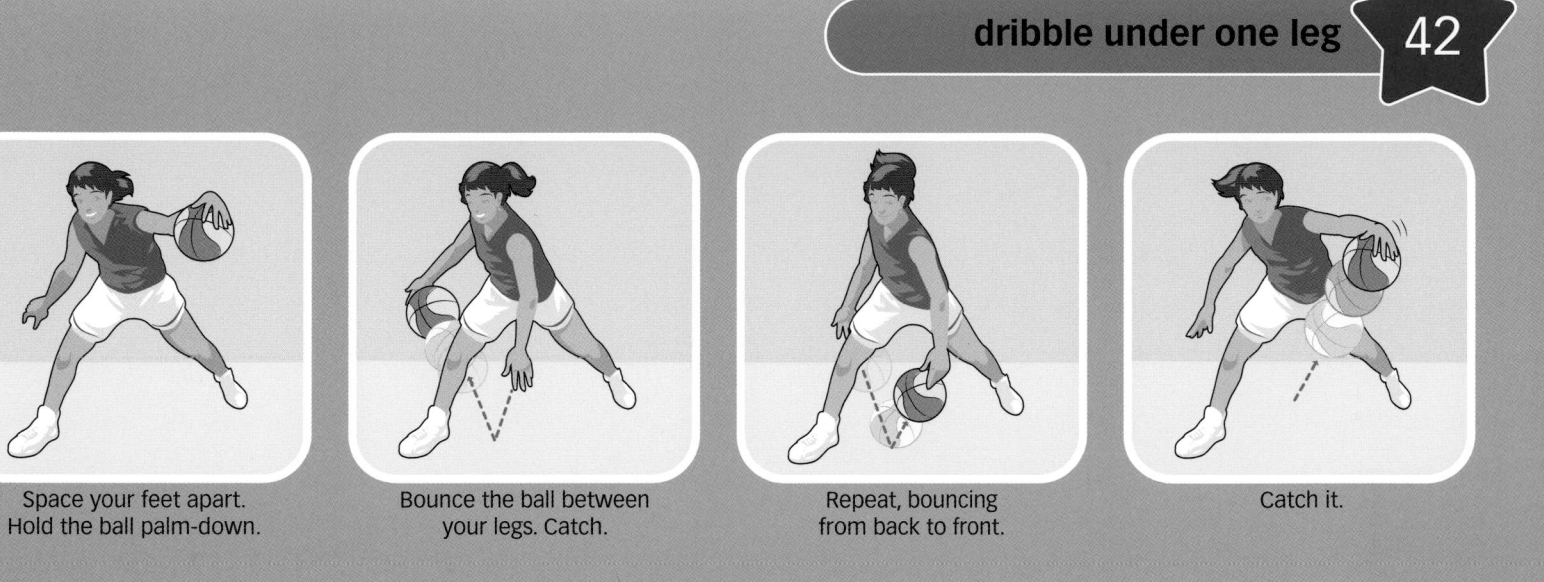

Space your feet apart.
Hold the ball palm-down.

Bounce the ball between
your legs. Catch.

Repeat, bouncing
from back to front.

Catch it.

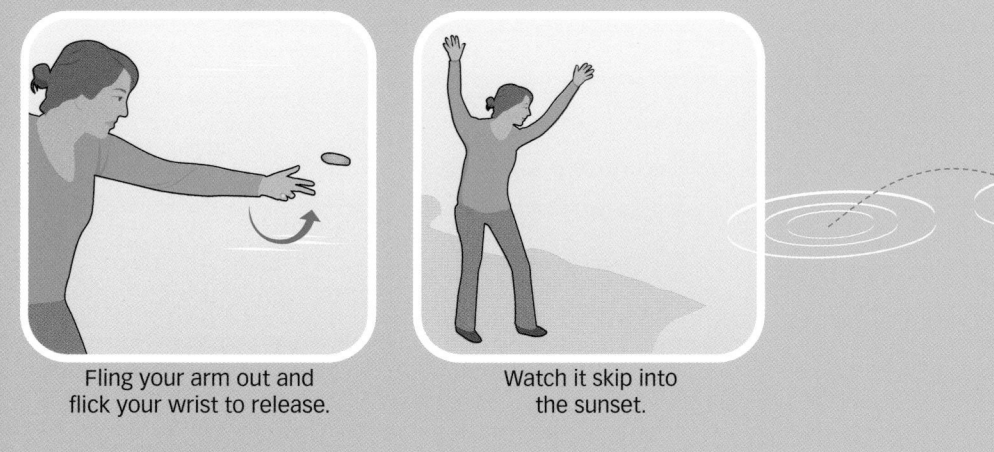

Fling your arm out and
flick your wrist to release.

Watch it skip into
the sunset.

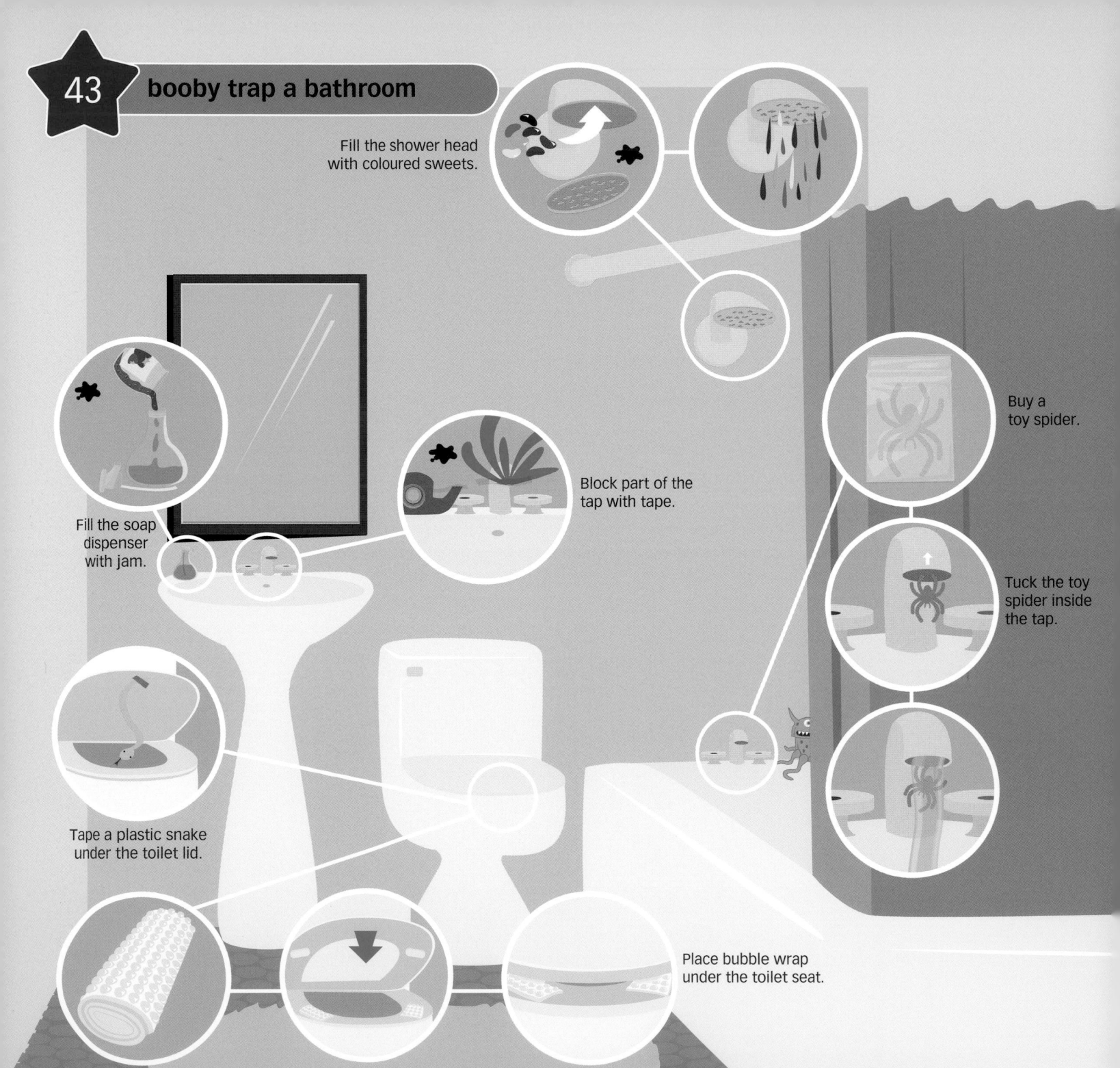

booby trap a bathroom

Fill the shower head with coloured sweets.

Fill the soap dispenser with jam.

Block part of the tap with tape.

Buy a toy spider.

Tuck the toy spider inside the tap.

Tape a plastic snake under the toilet lid.

Place bubble wrap under the toilet seat.

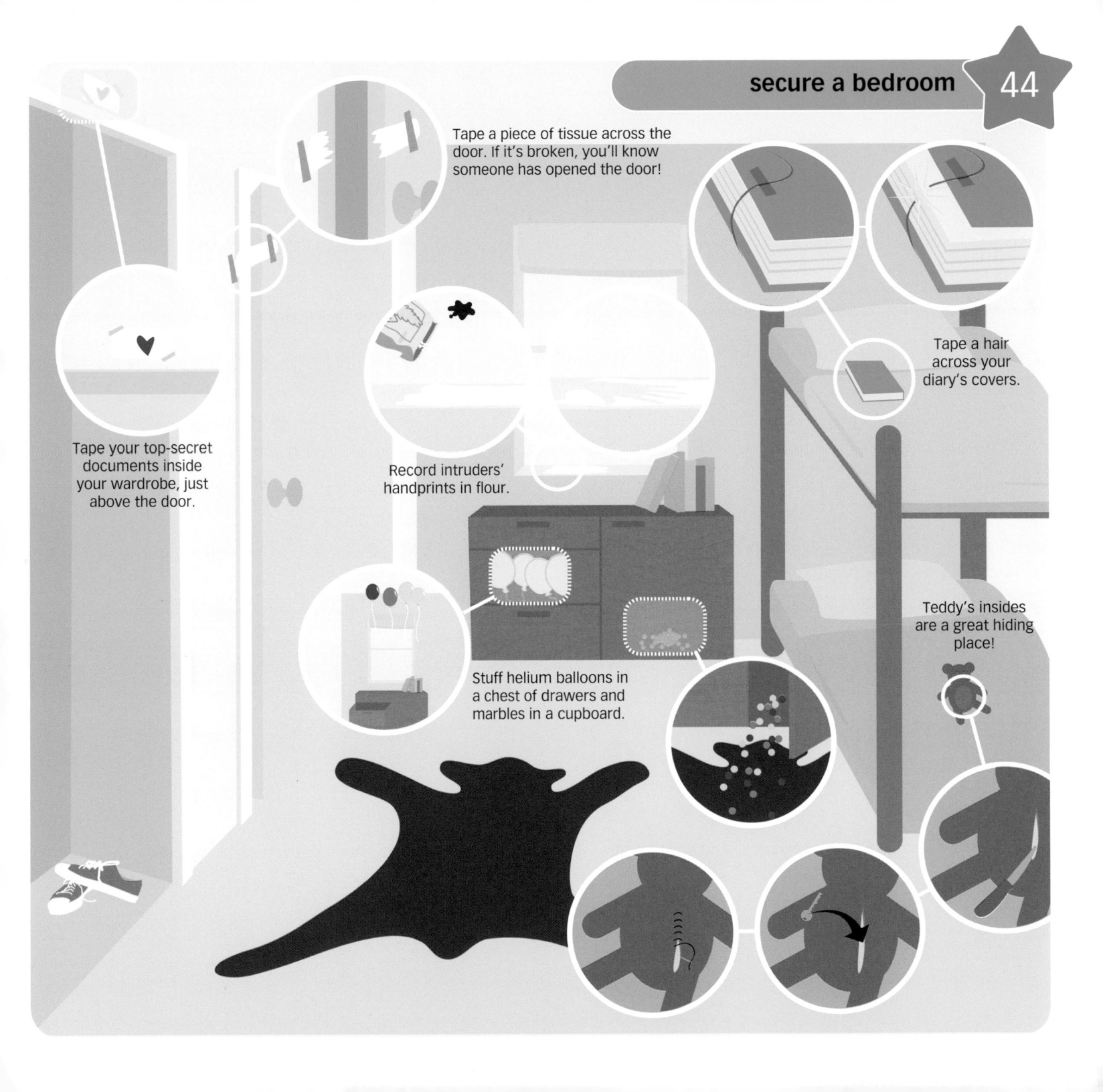

Tape a piece of tissue across the door. If it's broken, you'll know someone has opened the door!

Tape a hair across your diary's covers.

Tape your top-secret documents inside your wardrobe, just above the door.

Record intruders' handprints in flour.

Teddy's insides are a great hiding place!

Stuff helium balloons in a chest of drawers and marbles in a cupboard.

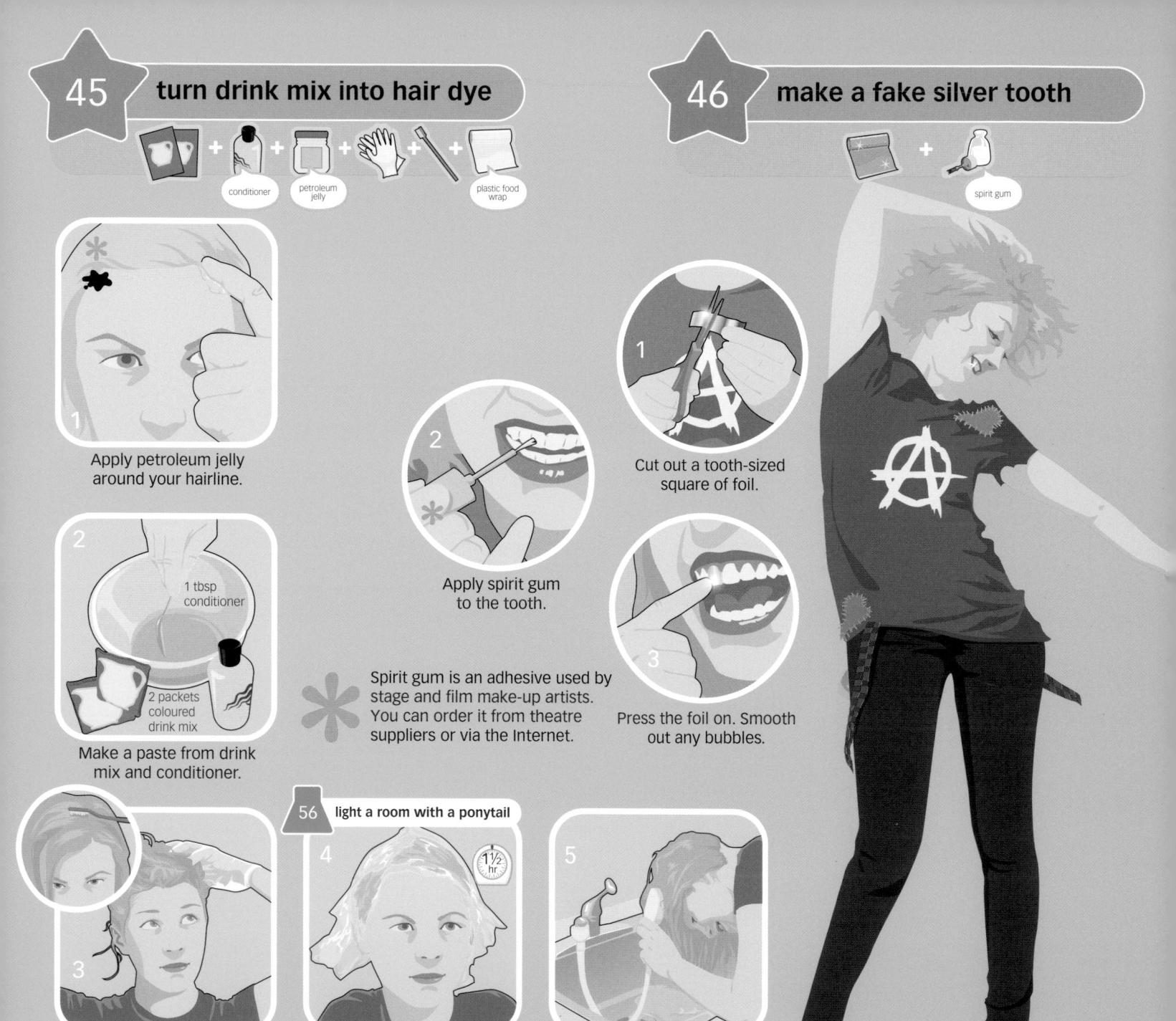

45 turn drink mix into hair dye

conditioner + petroleum jelly + [gloves] + [toothbrush] + plastic food wrap

1 Apply petroleum jelly around your hairline.

2 1 tbsp conditioner
2 packets coloured drink mix
Make a paste from drink mix and conditioner.

3 Work into hair with gloved hands and a toothbrush.

56 light a room with a ponytail

4 1½ hr
Cover with plastic food wrap. Wait.

5 Rinse.

This dye job will be subtle and should only last a few washes – unless you have fair hair. Colour will be brighter and last *much* longer on light hair.

46 make a fake silver tooth

+ spirit gum

1 Cut out a tooth-sized square of foil.

2 Apply spirit gum to the tooth.

3 Press the foil on. Smooth out any bubbles.

Spirit gum is an adhesive used by stage and film make-up artists. You can order it from theatre suppliers or via the Internet.

fake a cheek piercing 47

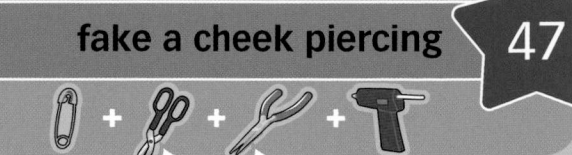

wire clippers   needle-nose pliers

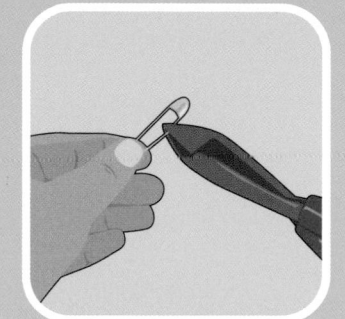

Clean a safety pin.
Snip the arm in half.

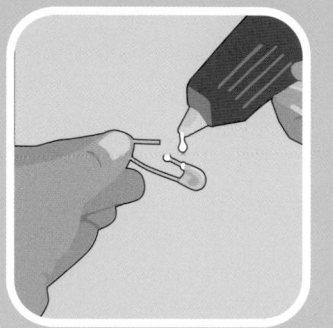

Put glue on the tip.
Secure the loose end.

Bend back the very
tip of the pin arm.

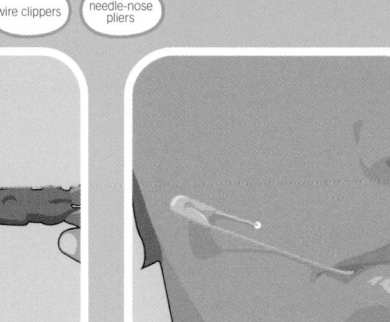

Put it in your mouth.
It's a 'piercing'!

sport spiky hair 48

hair gel   hairspray

1
Put gel in wet hair.
Twist into spikes.

2
Blow-dry on warm.

3
Set with hairspray.

49 twirl a drumstick

1 Hold the stick loosely.

2 Roll it over your middle finger.

3 Let it roll to an upright position.

4 Roll it over your ring finger.

5 Catch it and roll it over your little finger.

6 Catch it with your index finger. Repeat.

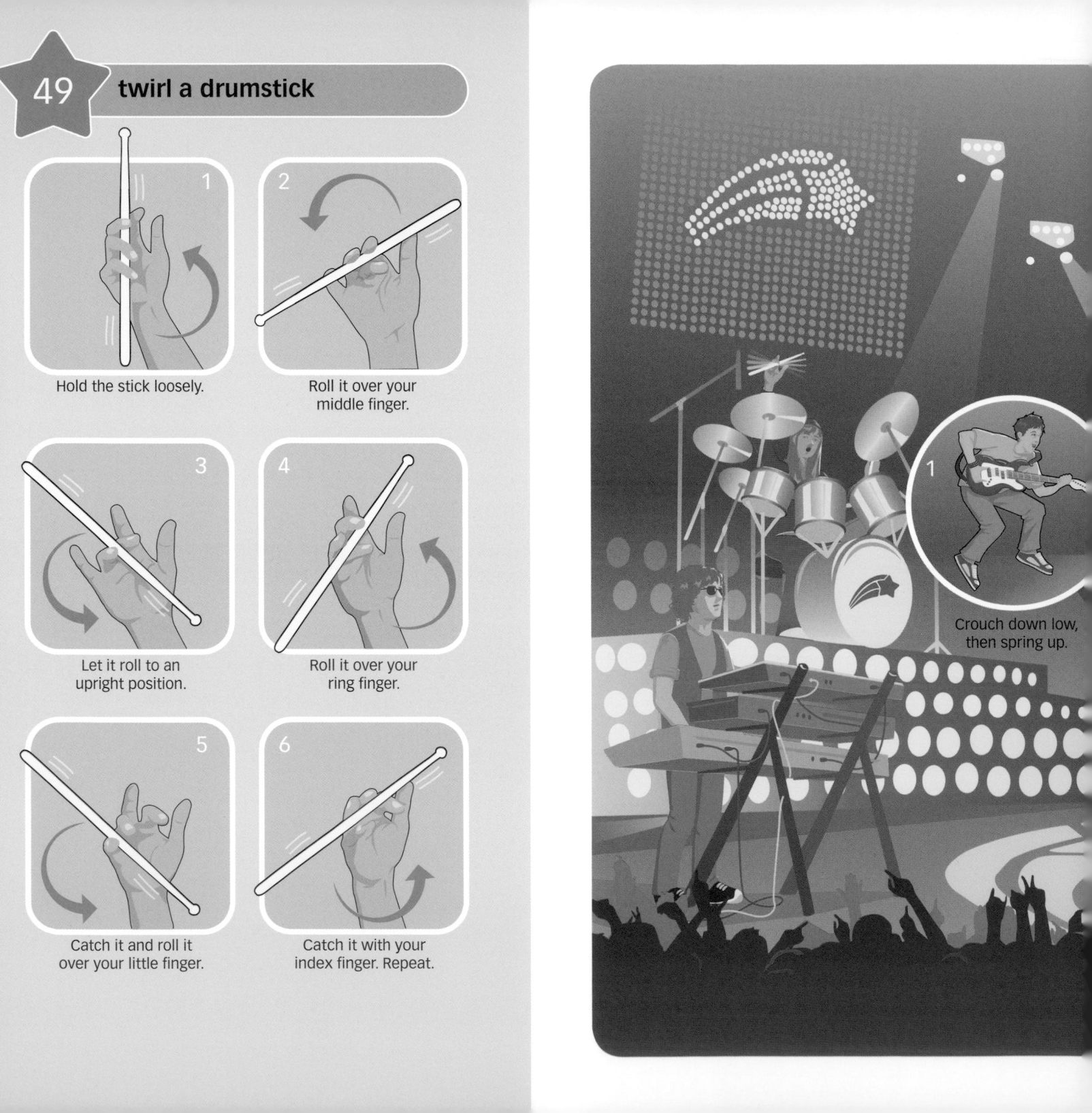

1 Crouch down low, then spring up.

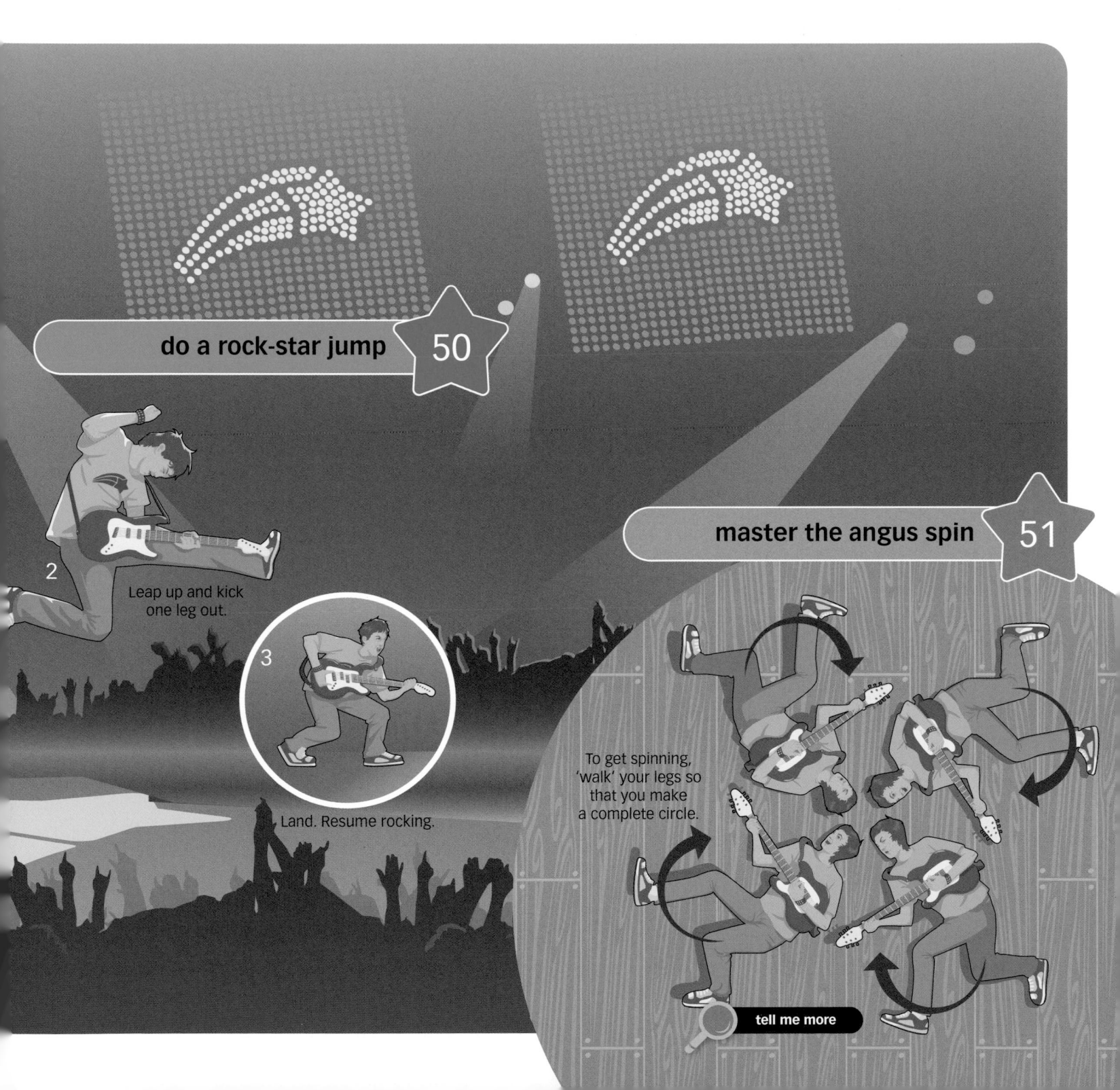

do a rock-star jump 50

2

Leap up and kick one leg out.

3

Land. Resume rocking.

master the angus spin 51

To get spinning, 'walk' your legs so that you make a complete circle.

tell me more

investigate

erupt a fizzy fountain

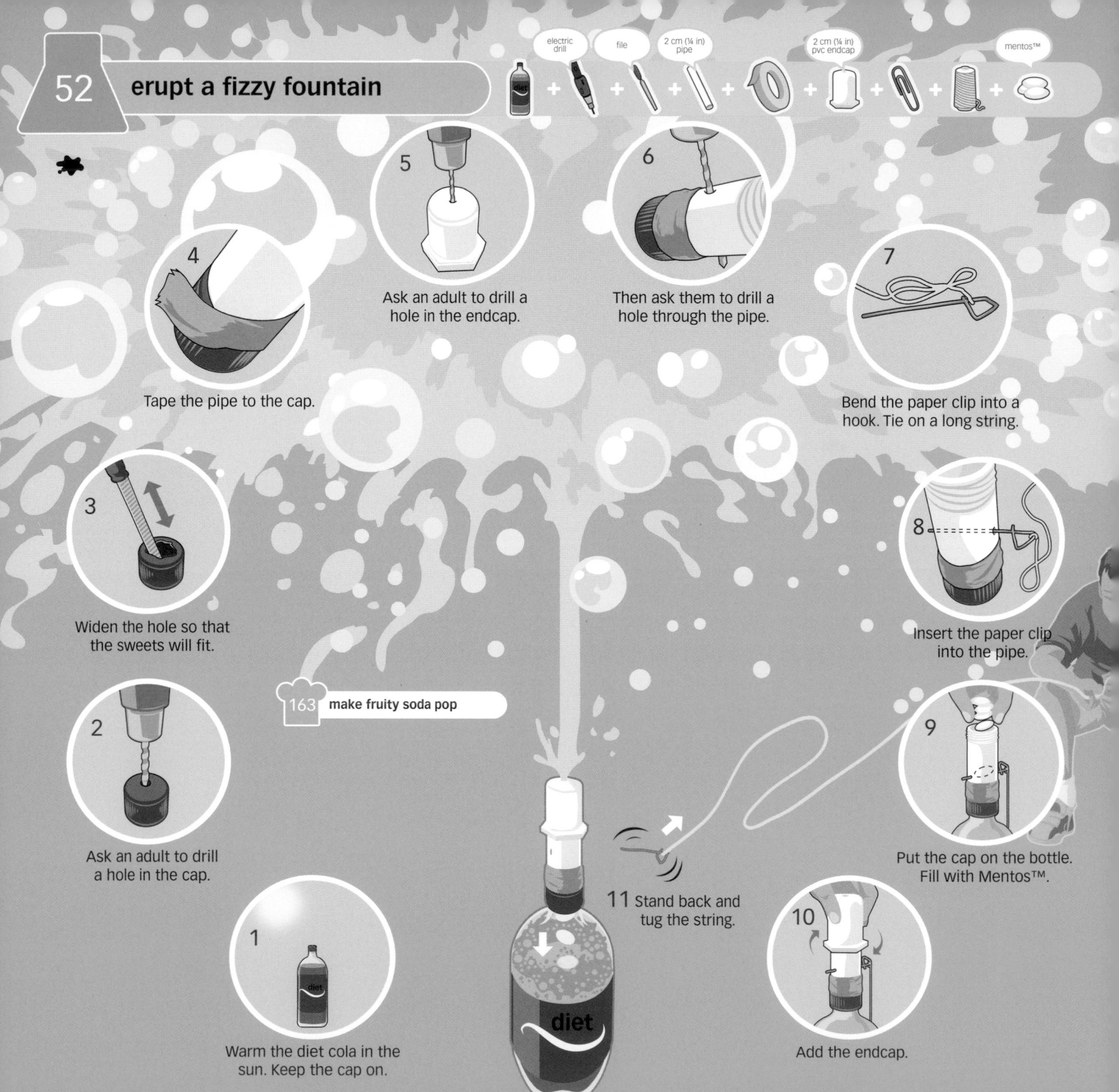

electric drill + file + 2 cm (¼ in) pipe + + 2 cm (¼ in) pvc endcap + + + mentos™

4 Tape the pipe to the cap.

5 Ask an adult to drill a hole in the endcap.

6 Then ask them to drill a hole through the pipe.

7 Bend the paper clip into a hook. Tie on a long string.

3 Widen the hole so that the sweets will fit.

163 make fruity soda pop

8 Insert the paper clip into the pipe.

2 Ask an adult to drill a hole in the cap.

1 Warm the diet cola in the sun. Keep the cap on.

11 Stand back and tug the string.

9 Put the cap on the bottle. Fill with Mentos™.

10 Add the endcap.

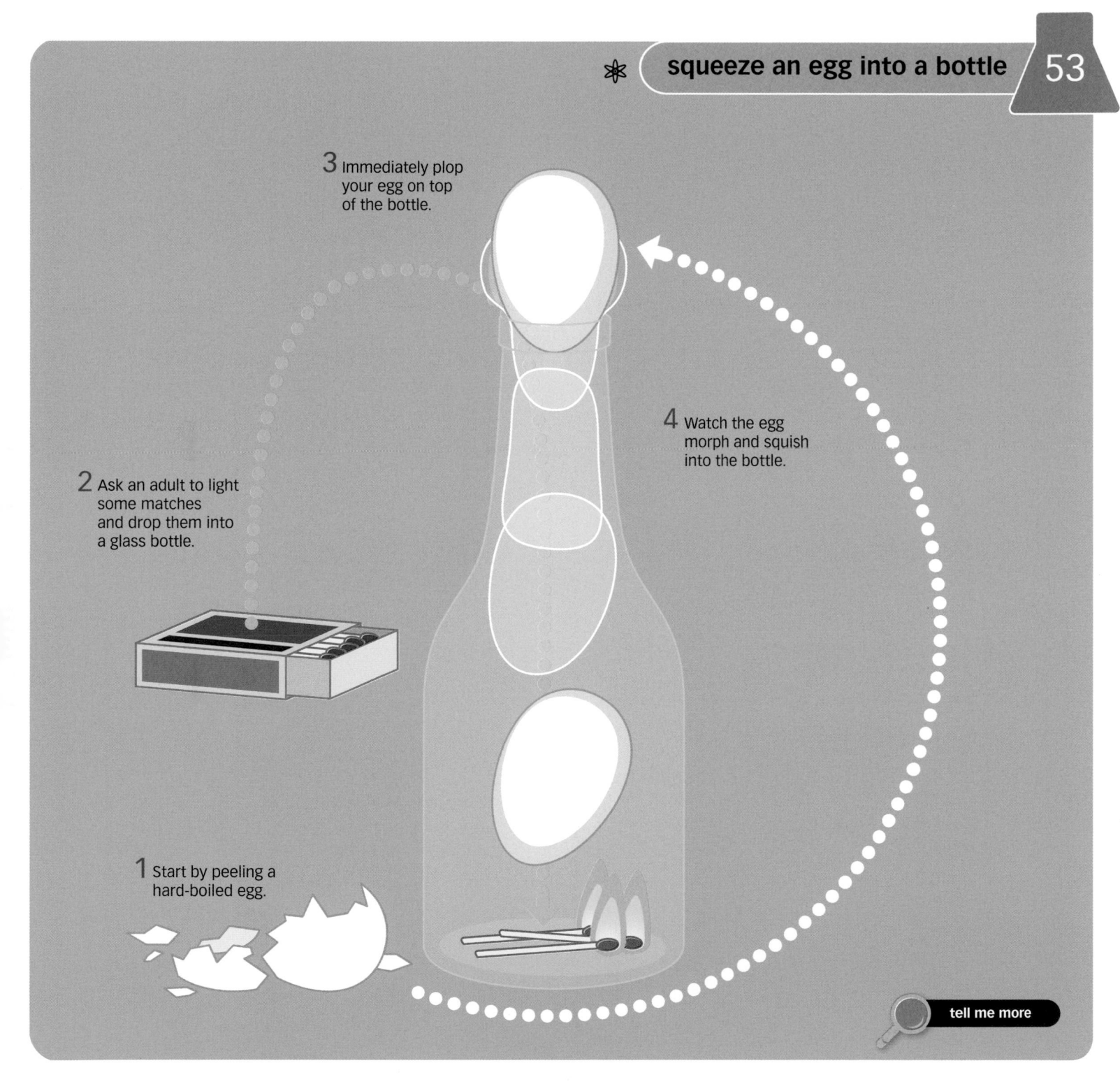

3 Immediately plop your egg on top of the bottle.

2 Ask an adult to light some matches and drop them into a glass bottle.

4 Watch the egg morph and squish into the bottle.

1 Start by peeling a hard-boiled egg.

tell me more

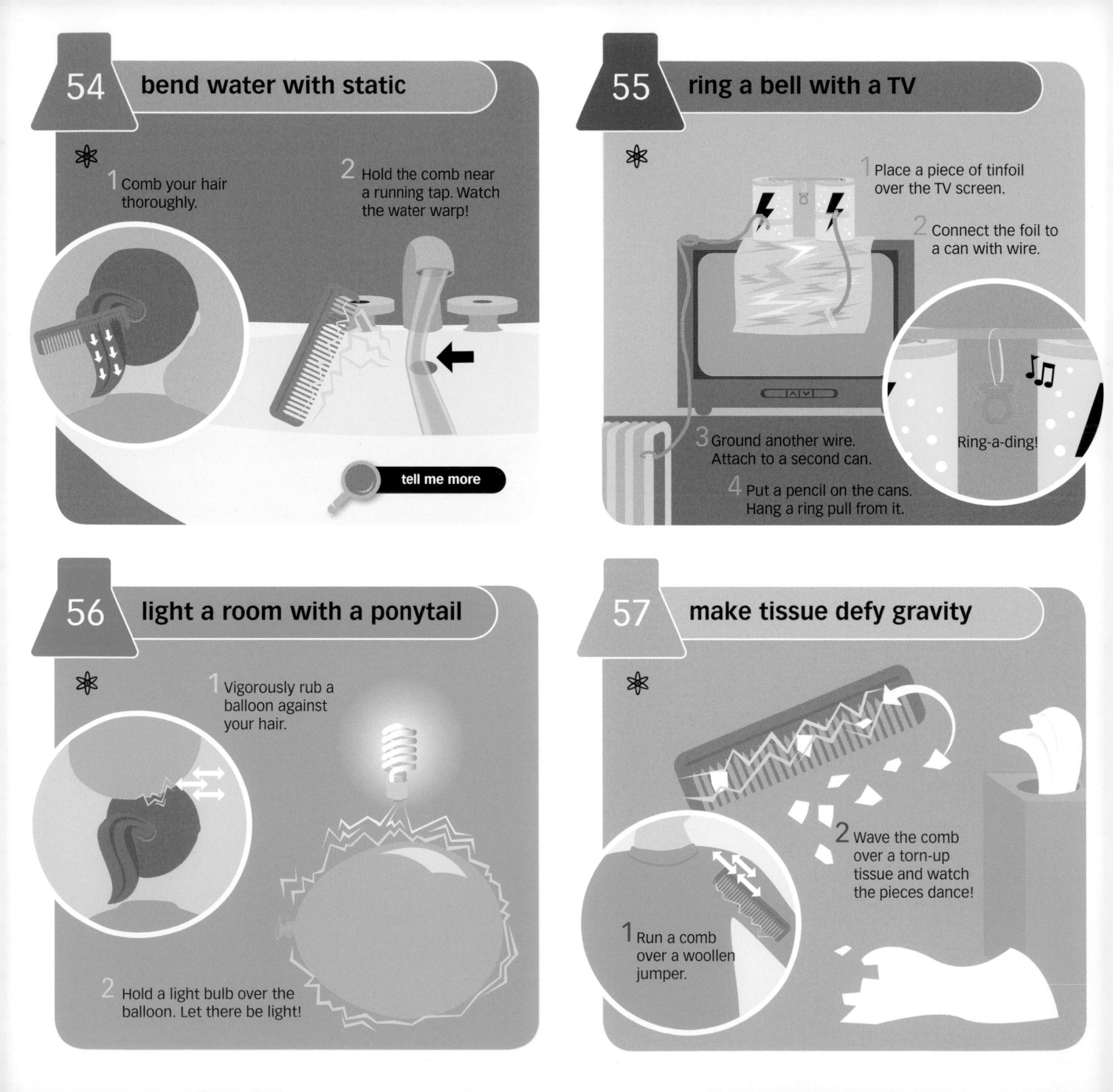

54 bend water with static

1 Comb your hair thoroughly.

2 Hold the comb near a running tap. Watch the water warp!

tell me more

55 ring a bell with a TV

1 Place a piece of tinfoil over the TV screen.

2 Connect the foil to a can with wire.

3 Ground another wire. Attach to a second can.

4 Put a pencil on the cans. Hang a ring pull from it.

Ring-a-ding!

56 light a room with a ponytail

1 Vigorously rub a balloon against your hair.

2 Hold a light bulb over the balloon. Let there be light!

57 make tissue defy gravity

1 Run a comb over a woollen jumper.

2 Wave the comb over a torn-up tissue and watch the pieces dance!

galvanised nails + copper wire + + + + wires with crocodile clips

Label your potatoes.

Press a galvanised nail into each potato.

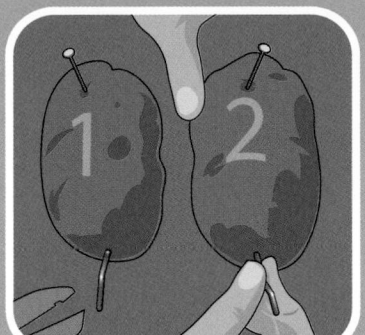

Stick a copper wire into the other end of each one.

Remove the digital clock's battery and battery cover.

Connect potato 1's wire to the positive side.

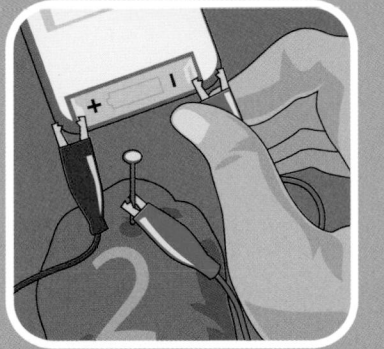

Link 2's nail to the negative side.

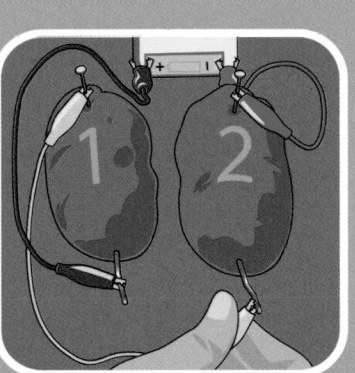

Connect 1's nail to 2's copper wire.

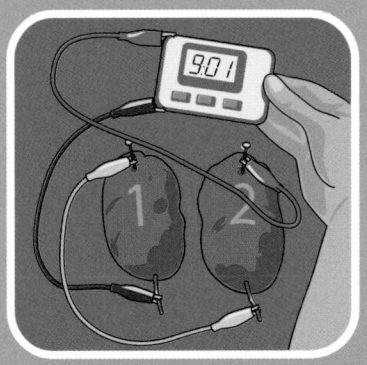

Set your clock to potato time!

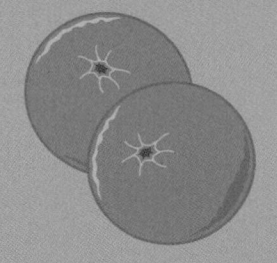

* Potatoes aren't the only powerful food in your kitchen – you can make a food clock out of these ingredients, too.

tell me more

borax   cornflour

½ tsp borax

2 tbsp warm water

Stir to dissolve the borax.

1 tbsp white glue

Pour glue into a jar.

1 tbsp cornflour

Add cornflour
to the glue.

½ tbsp borax
solution

Measure and add the
borax solution.

Add a few drops of
food colouring. Wait.

15 sec.

Stir.

Knead on a clean tabletop.

199   set up a bocce match

Roll into a ball.

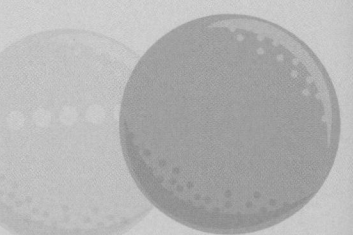

What *is* this magical borax stuff, anyway? It's a mineral
used in make-up and soap. It's also used in insect
killer, so store the ball in a plastic bag when you've
finished and then wash your hands. Never eat it!

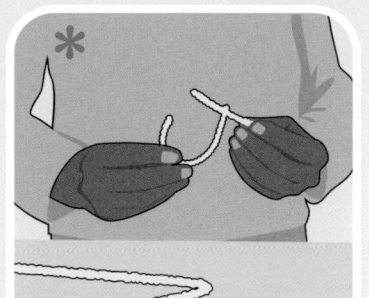

1

Bend a pipe cleaner into a letter. It must fit in a jar.

3 tbsp borax

240 ml
(8 fl oz)
very hot
water

2

Carefully add the borax to hot water.

3

4 drops food colouring

Add colouring. Stir until the borax dissolves.

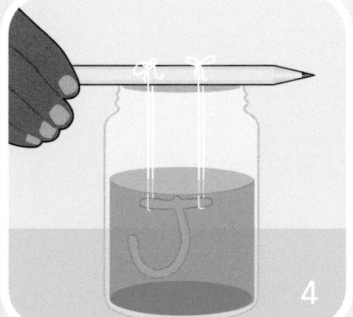

4

The pipe cleaner shouldn't touch the bottom.

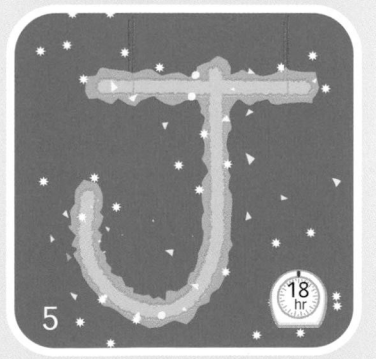

5

18 hr

Watch your crystals grow.

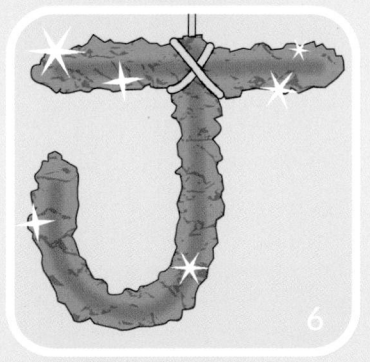

6

To display, hang your new bling with string.

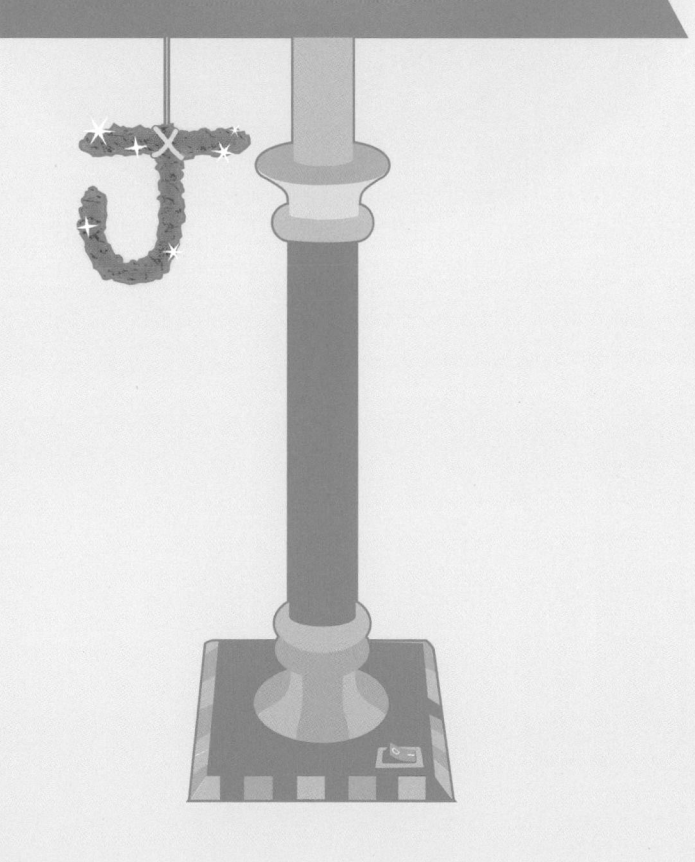

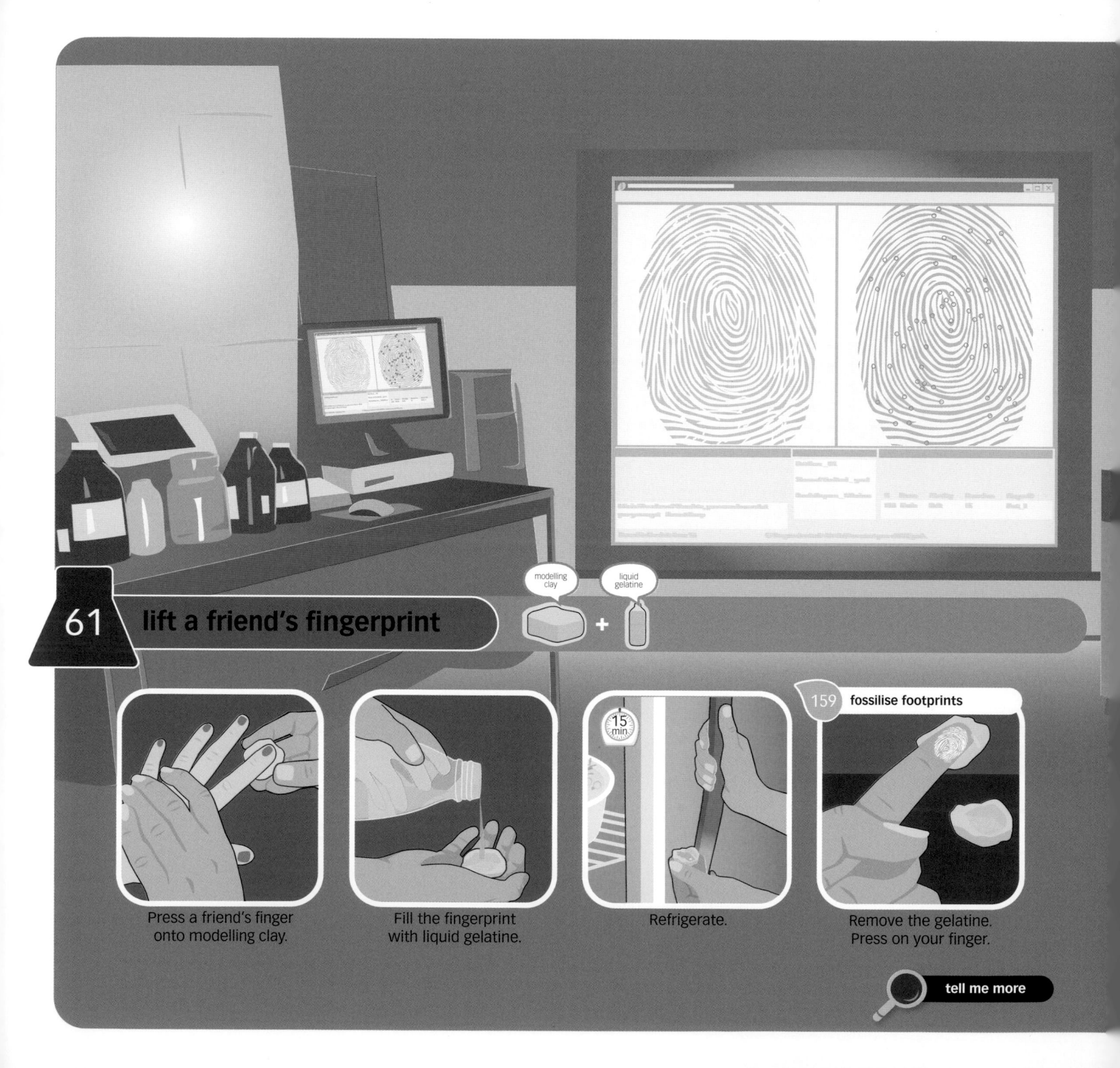

61 lift a friend's fingerprint

modelling clay + liquid gelatine

Press a friend's finger onto modelling clay.

Fill the fingerprint with liquid gelatine.

15 min. Refrigerate.

159 fossilise footprints

Remove the gelatine. Press on your finger.

tell me more

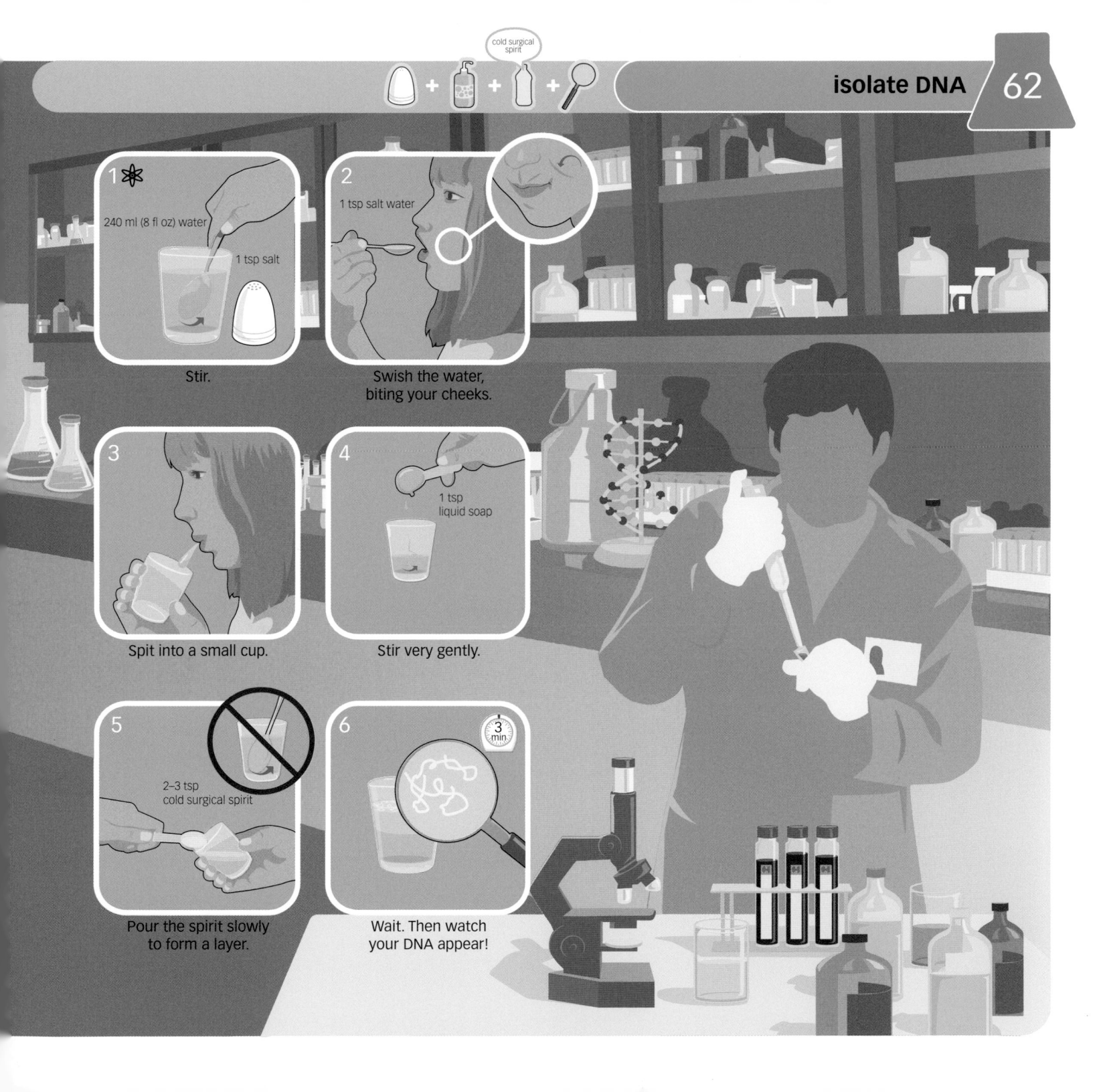

cold surgical spirit

1 ☀
240 ml (8 fl oz) water
1 tsp salt
Stir.

2
1 tsp salt water
Swish the water, biting your cheeks.

3
Spit into a small cup.

4
1 tsp liquid soap
Stir very gently.

5
2–3 tsp cold surgical spirit
Pour the spirit slowly to form a layer.

6
3 min
Wait. Then watch your DNA appear!

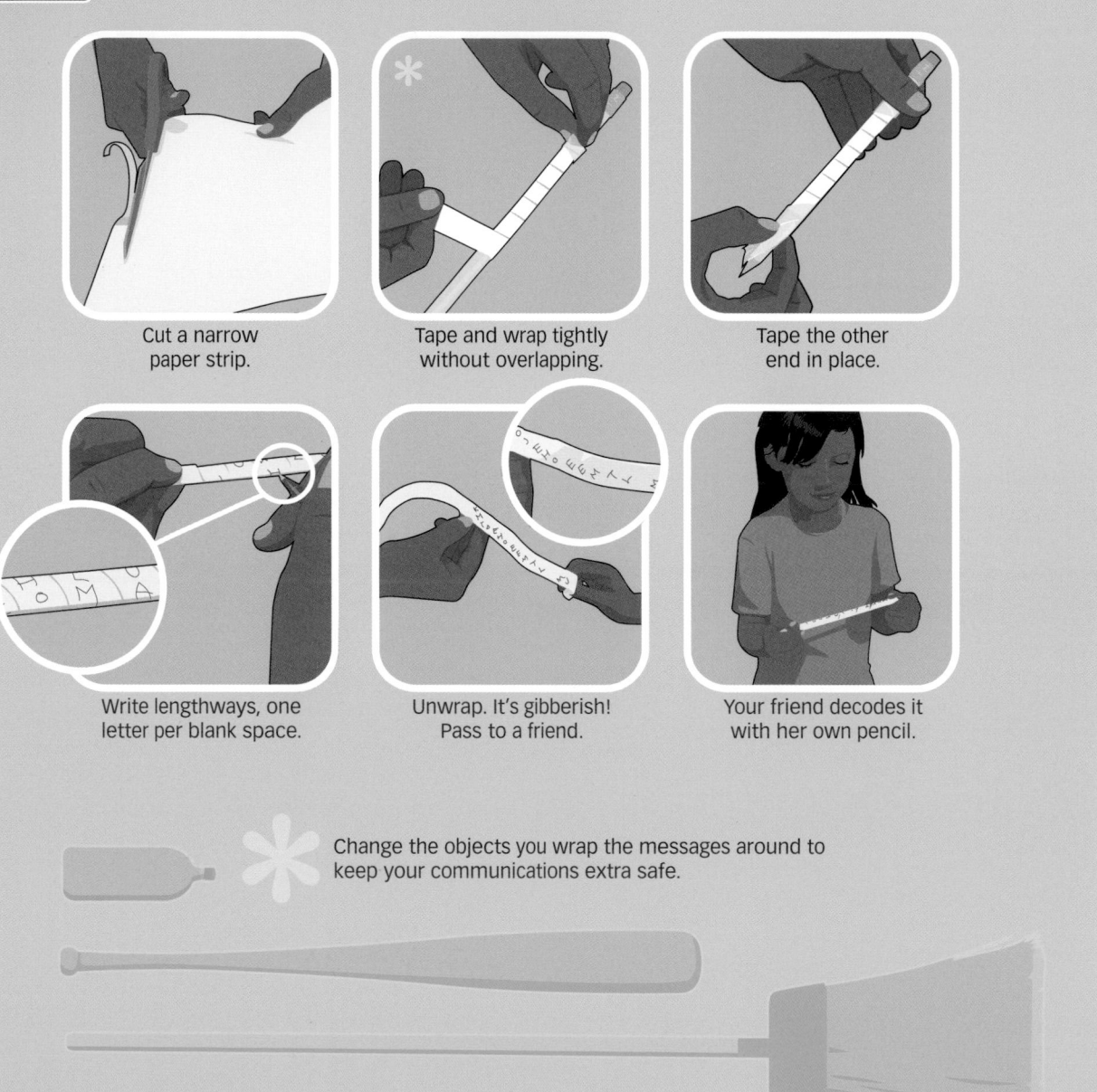

Cut a narrow paper strip.

Tape and wrap tightly without overlapping.

Tape the other end in place.

Write lengthways, one letter per blank space.

Unwrap. It's gibberish! Pass to a friend.

Your friend decodes it with her own pencil.

Change the objects you wrap the messages around to keep your communications extra safe.

tell me more

★ = quick flash
— = long flash

a ★—	n ★ —	1 ★————
b —★★★	o ———	2 ★★———
c —★—★	p ★——★	3 ★★★——
d —★★	q ——★—	4 ★★★★—
e ★	r ★—★	5 ★★★★★
f ★★—★	s ★★★	6 —★★★★
g ——★	t —	7 ——★★★
h ★★★★	u ★★—	8 ———★★
i ★★	v ★★★—	9 ————★
j ★———	w ★——	0 —————
k —★—	x —★★—	
l ★—★★	y —★——	
m ——	z ——★★	

If you want to send a secret message across the street, all you need is Morse code and a torch. Using the guide on the left, write out your message letter by letter. You can send it when darkness falls.

Your partner will understand you better if you count to three with your torch off between each letter and count to seven with the torch off between each word.

tell me more

Are there words or phrases you and your friends say a lot? Make up a shortcut instead of spelling it out. Here are some examples.

★★—★★	'My brother is a geek.'
—★—★—	'Must go – Mum's coming!'
——★——	'Whatever!'
—★★★—	'You're my best mate.'

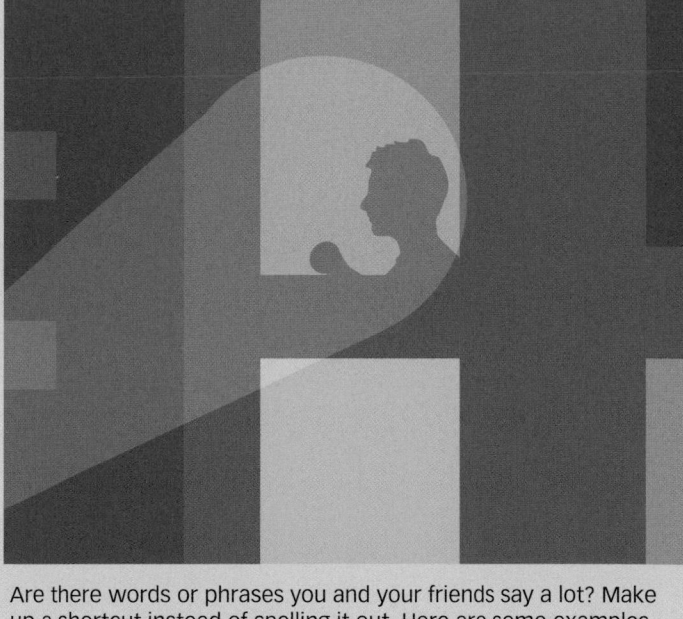

spy with a periscope

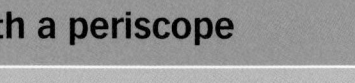 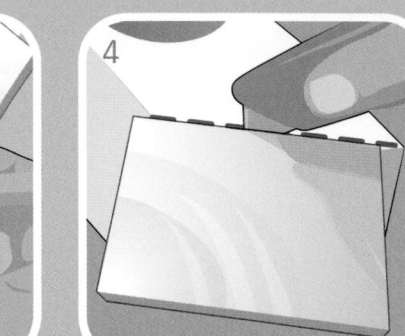

1
Cut the tops off two cartons.

2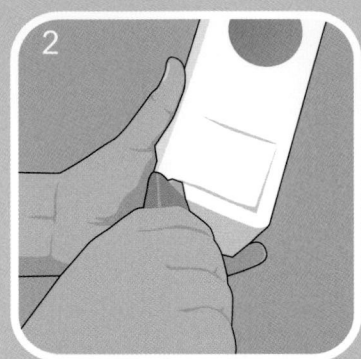
Cut a window near the bottom of one carton.

3
Mark a diagonal line the height of your mirror.
45°
45°

4
Cut on the line; repeat on the carton's opposite side.

5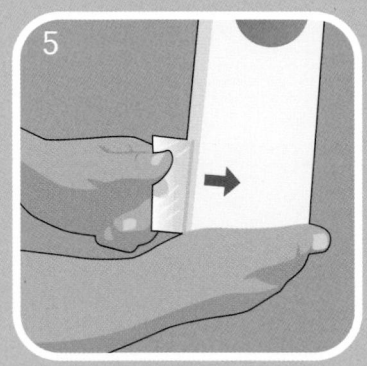
Slide a mirror into the slot. Secure with tape.

6
Look in the window – you should see the ceiling.

7
Repeat the process with the second carton.

8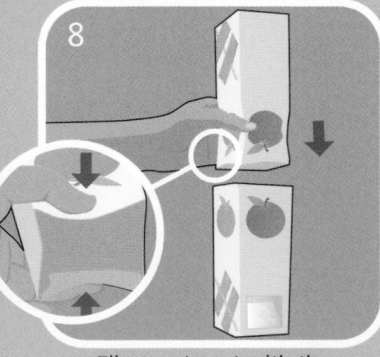
Flip one. Insert with the window facing backwards.

9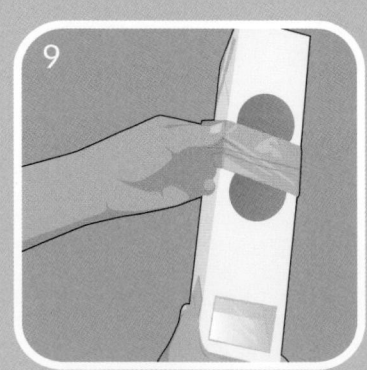
Tape securely.

10
Decorate your periscope.

11
Get spying!

small mirrors

1. Squeeze half a lemon.

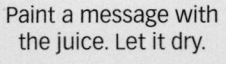

2. Paint a message with the juice. Let it dry.

3. Hand the 'blank' paper to a friend.

4. Heat reveals your juicy secret!

* If you want to be extra stealthy, wait for the lemon juice to dry, then write a decoy message in ordinary ink on top. When you heat the paper, the secret message will rise to the top!

tell me more

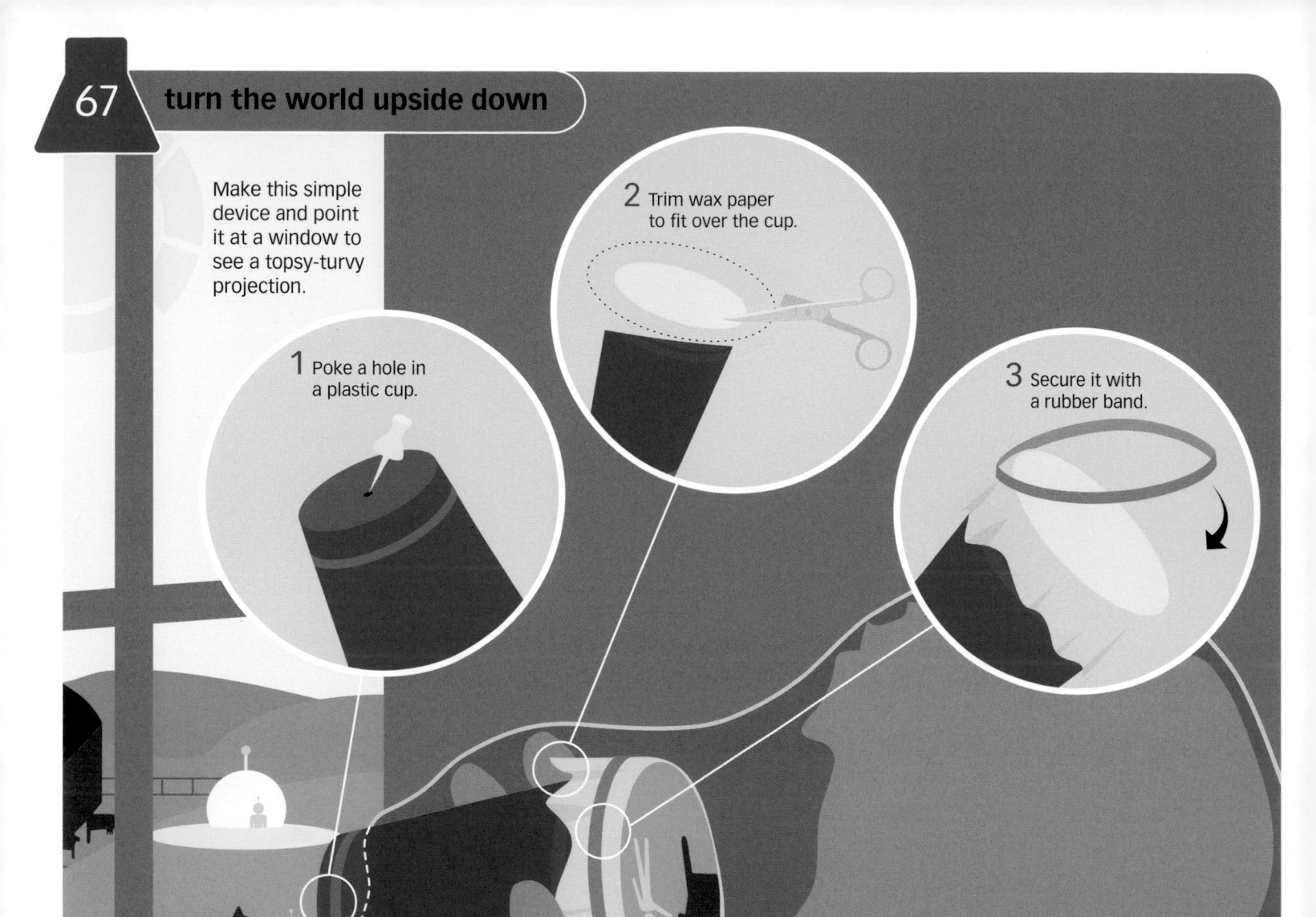

Make this simple device and point it at a window to see a topsy-turvy projection.

1 Poke a hole in a plastic cup.

2 Trim wax paper to fit over the cup.

3 Secure it with a rubber band.

4 Turn out the lights and hide under a blanket to see the world flip out!

tell me more

empty pill bottle + clear plastic lid + old CD + superglue

1. Saw off a bottle's bottom and its cap's top.

2. Trace the cap onto a lid three times and cut.

3. Glue circles to the cap top and the bottle top.

4. Make a stencil the same length as the bottle. Cut out.

5. Trace three times onto the CD. Cut out.

6. Slide in the CD strips. Trim to fit.

7. Glue a window to the bottom of the bottle.

8. Draw a pattern on the cap window.

9. Decorate the bottle. Put beads in the cap and screw on.

Be careful! If you look straight at an eclipse, you'll injure your eyes. Instead, use a handy eclipse viewer for your own private sun show!

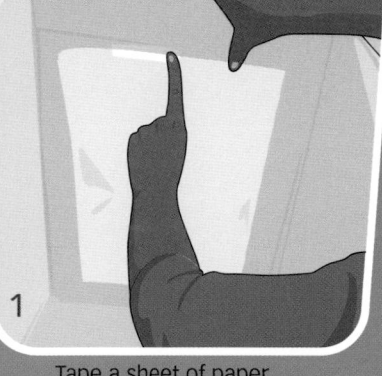

1 Tape a sheet of paper inside a box.

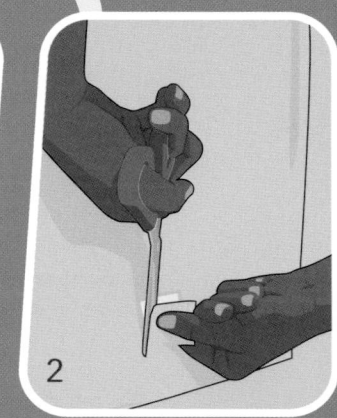

2 Cut an opening opposite the paper.

3 Tape tinfoil over the opening. Prick a hole.

124 spot pictures in the moon

4 Cut a space for your head.

Use the longest box you can find to get an extra-large projection.

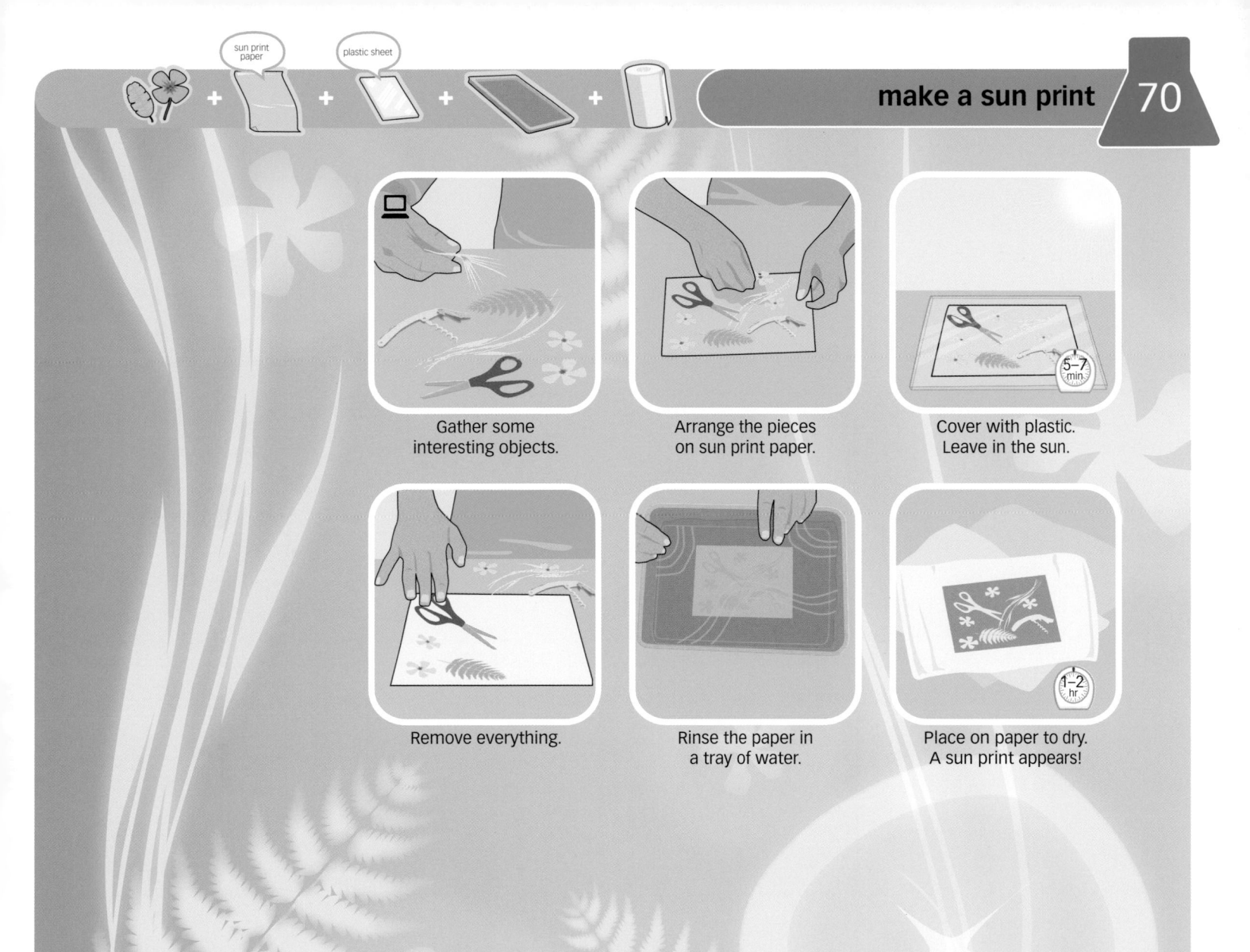

Gather some interesting objects.

Arrange the pieces on sun print paper.

Cover with plastic. Leave in the sun.

Remove everything.

Rinse the paper in a tray of water.

Place on paper to dry. A sun print appears!

tell me more

71 get cooking in a solar oven

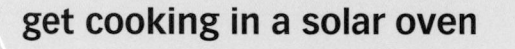

black construction paper · plastic sheet

Draw a square on a pizza box lid near the edges.

Cut along three of the lines to make a flap.

Open the flap and fold it back.

Wrap and tape tinfoil inside the flap.

72 make a light bulb

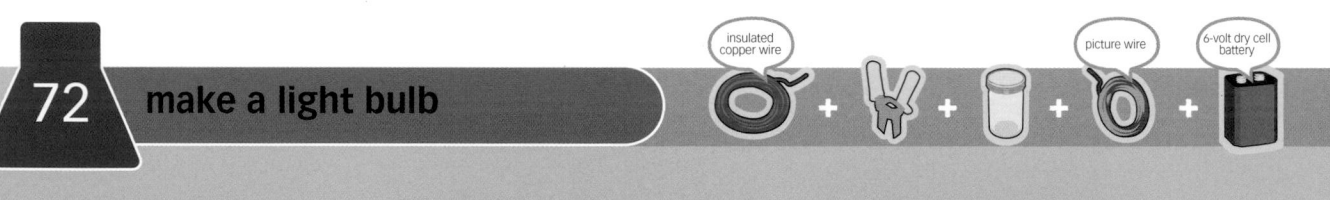

insulated copper wire · picture wire · 6-volt dry cell battery

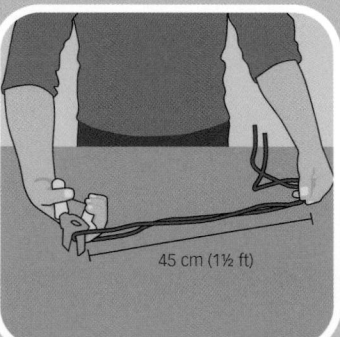

45 cm (1½ ft)

Cut a copper wire in half.

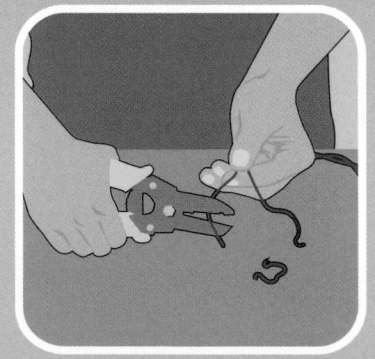

Strip the insulation from the ends.

Poke holes in the lid of a glass jar.

Bend the wires through and shape into hooks.

Line the inside of the
box with tinfoil.

Cover the base with
heavy black paper.

Prop the top open so it
gets lots of sunlight.

Add marshmallows or other treats
and cover with clear plastic.

Once the light stops burning, give the wires
plenty of time to cool off before touching!

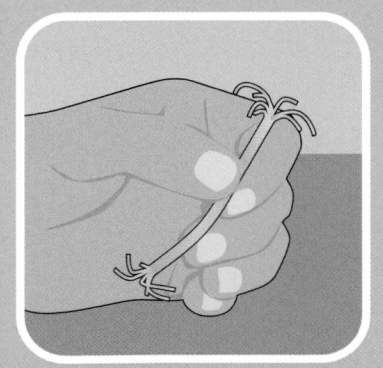

Unravel the ends of
a bit of picture wire.

Twist the wire ends
around the hooks.

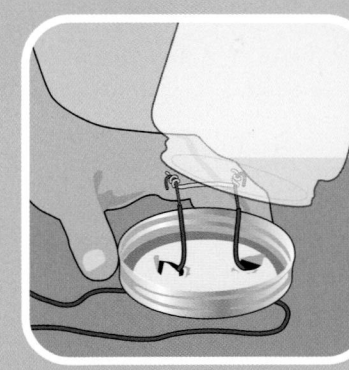

Cover with the jar.

Touch the wires to the
battery terminals.

trap shadows

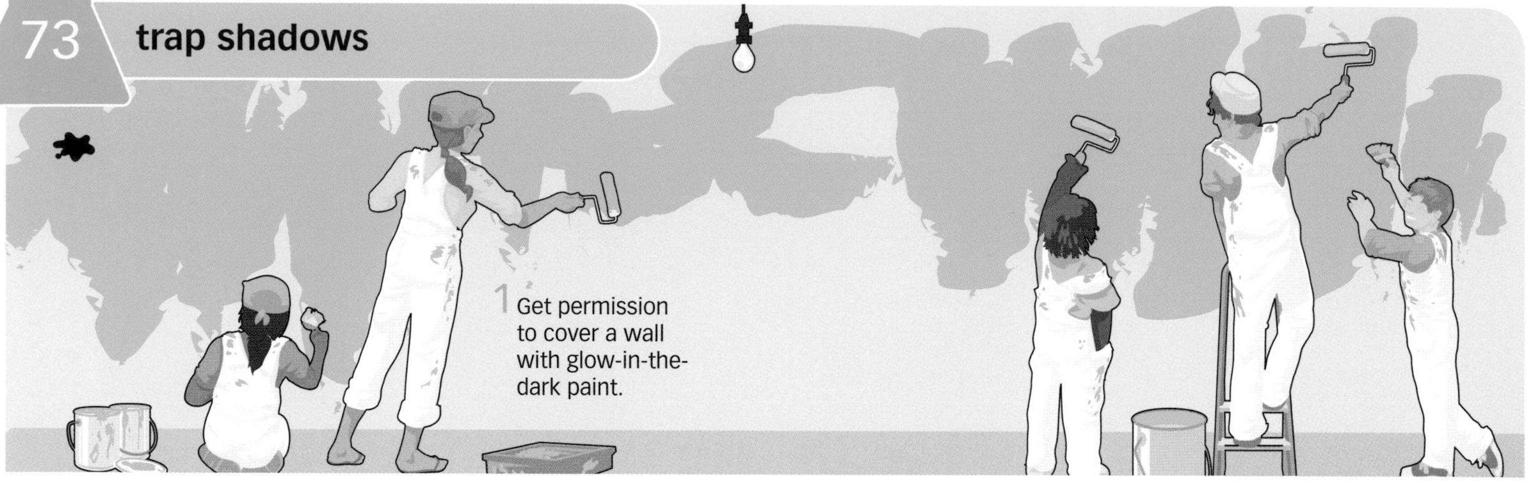

1 Get permission to cover a wall with glow-in-the-dark paint.

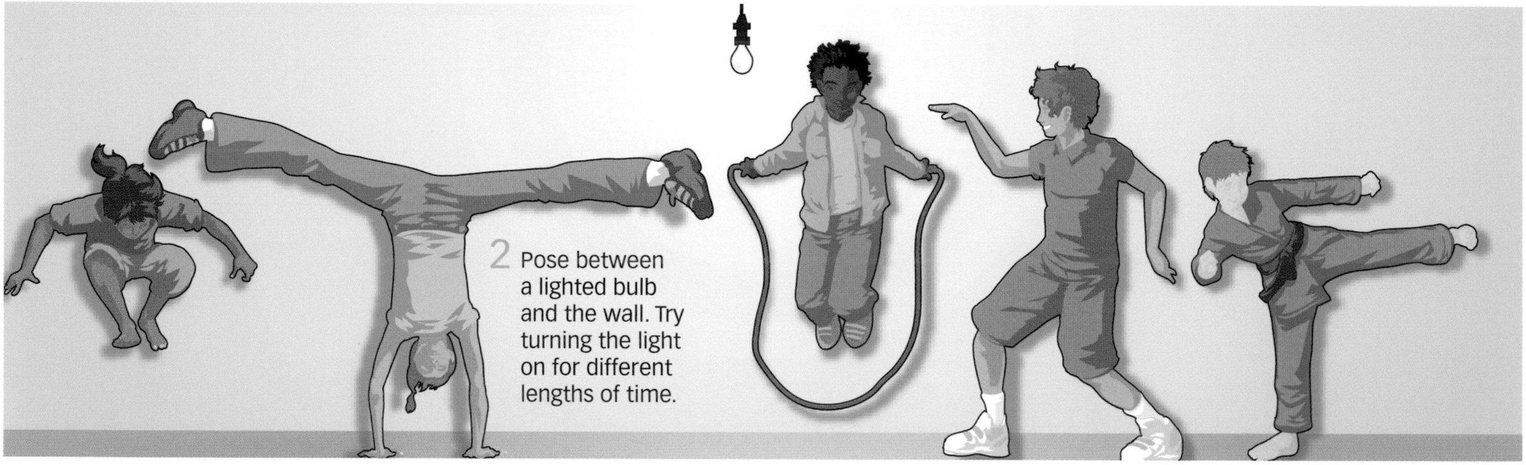

2 Pose between a lighted bulb and the wall. Try turning the light on for different lengths of time.

3 Turn out the light and meet your shadow!

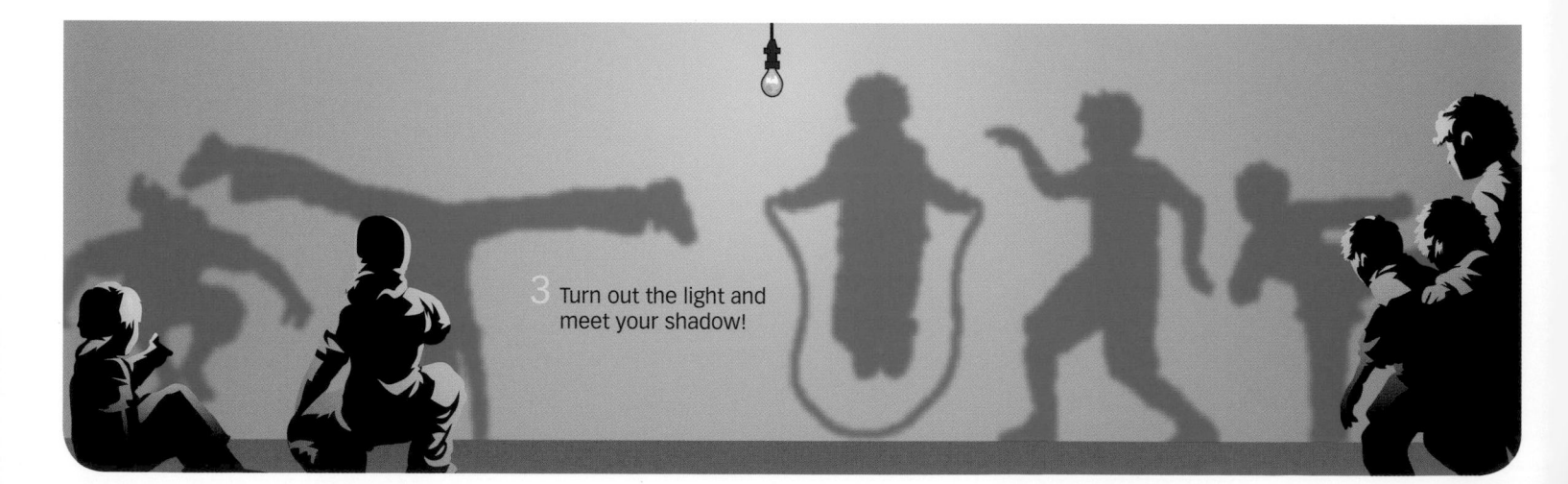

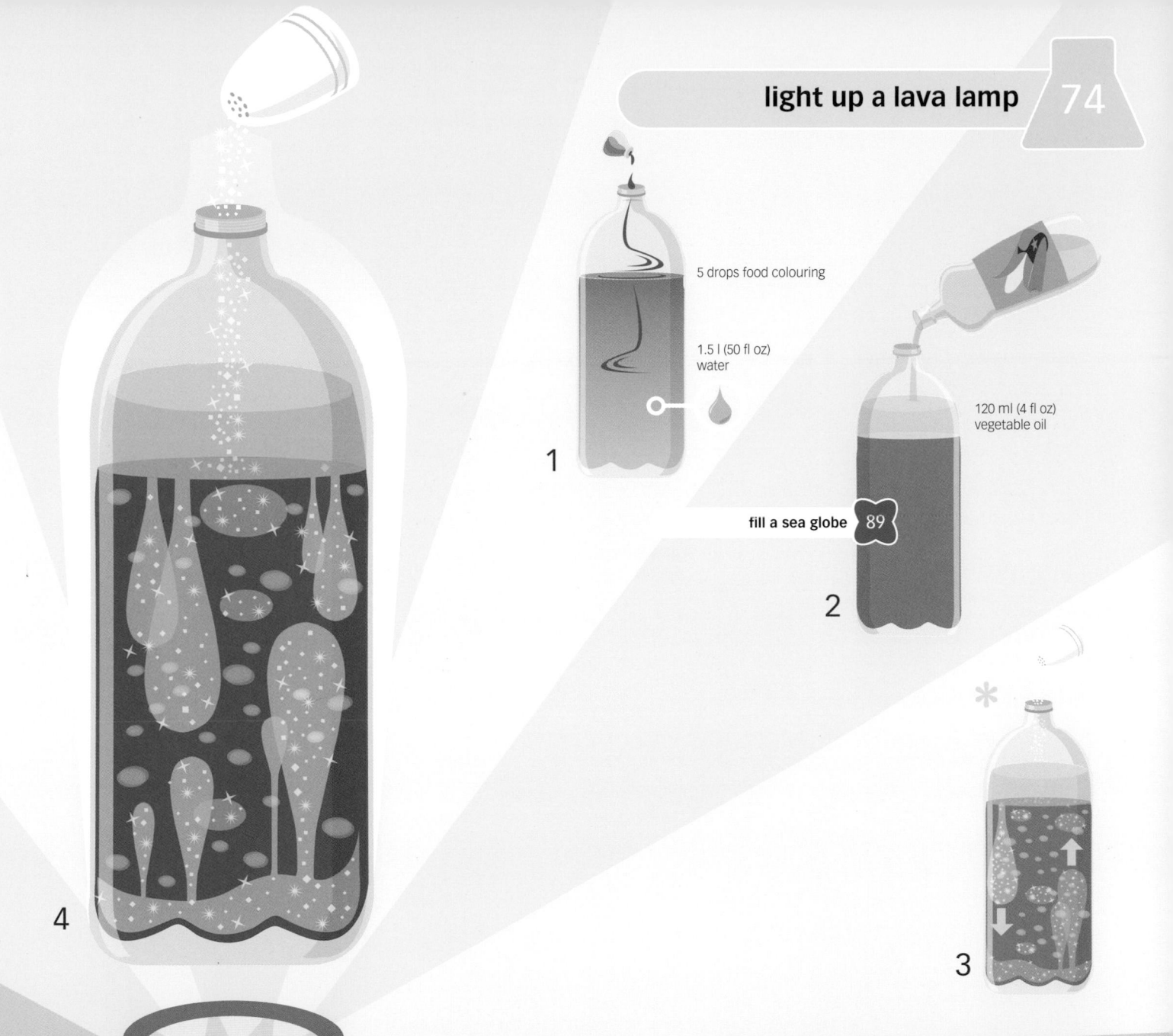

5 drops food colouring

1.5 l (50 fl oz) water

1

120 ml (4 fl oz) vegetable oil

fill a sea globe 89

2

3

4

Salt is the magic ingredient – your 'lava' will keep flowing as long as you continue adding salt. Turn out the lights and hold the bottle over a torch to make a lamp that's supergroovy.

2 LED bulbs   watch battery

Remove the matches.

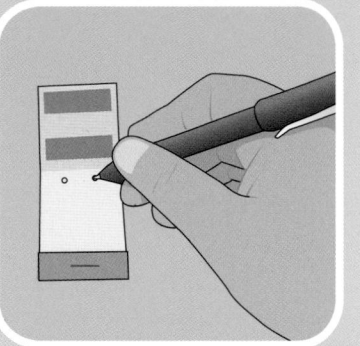

Mark two dots where
the lights will go.

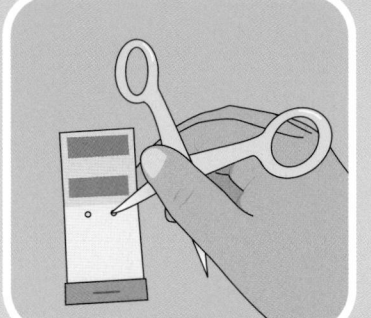

Poke two holes – one
for each bulb.

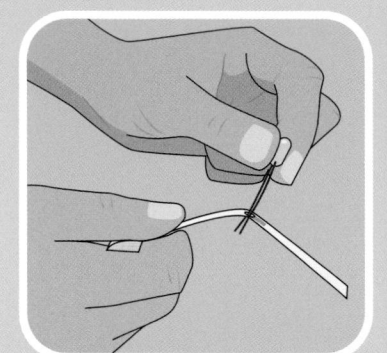

Insert the LED wires
from the outside.

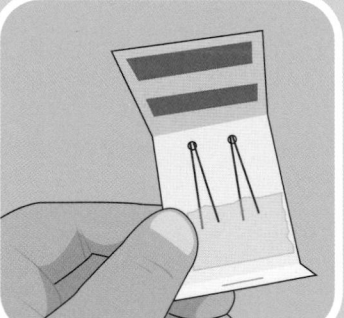

Tape both left-hand wires
to the matchbook.

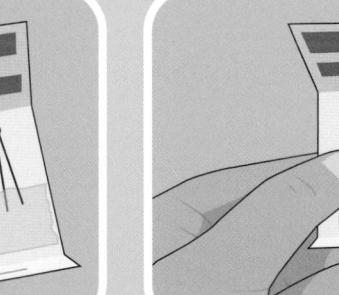

Slide the battery under the
loose right-hand wires.

Press to test your light.

Tape the edges of the
battery to the matchbook.

Shine on!

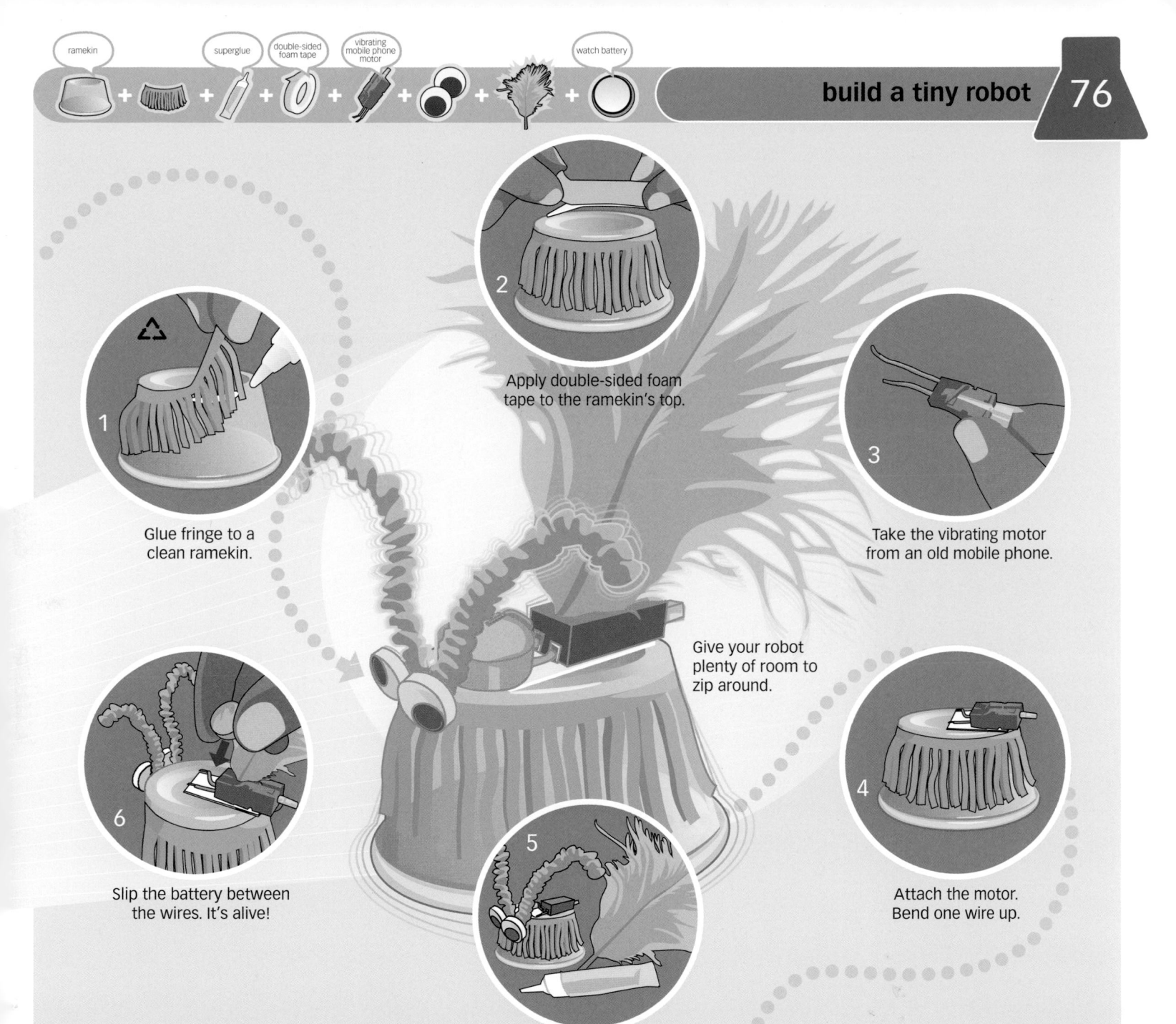

ramekin + superglue + double-sided foam tape + vibrating mobile phone motor + + + watch battery

1 Glue fringe to a clean ramekin.

2 Apply double-sided foam tape to the ramekin's top.

3 Take the vibrating motor from an old mobile phone.

4 Attach the motor. Bend one wire up.

5 Decorate your robot.

6 Slip the battery between the wires. It's alive!

Give your robot plenty of room to zip around.

set off an exploding volcano

clear vinegar

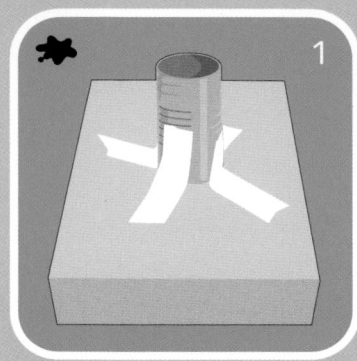

1 Tape a tin can to a cardboard box lid.

2 Scrunch up newspaper and tape around the can.

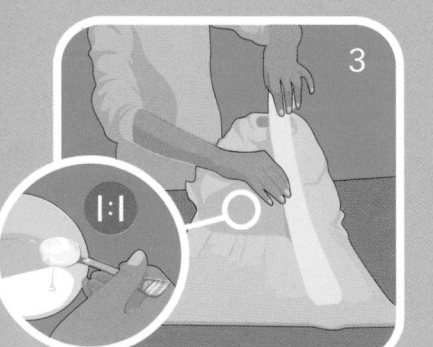

3 Form a volcano with paper dipped in flour and water.

1:1

4 Let dry. Decorate with paint and action figures.

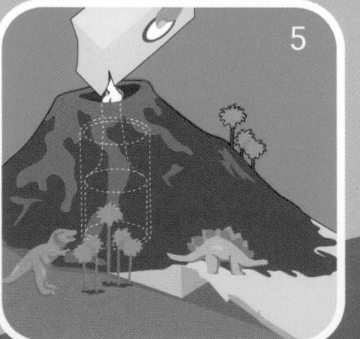

5 Fill the can halfway with baking soda.

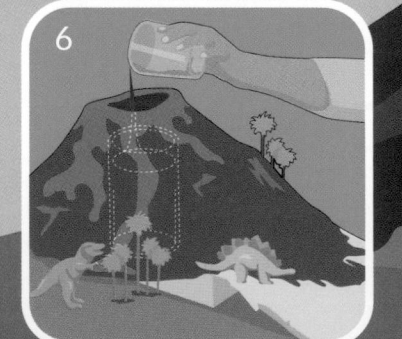

6 Fill with vinegar dyed with food colouring.

tell me more

78 launch a rocket

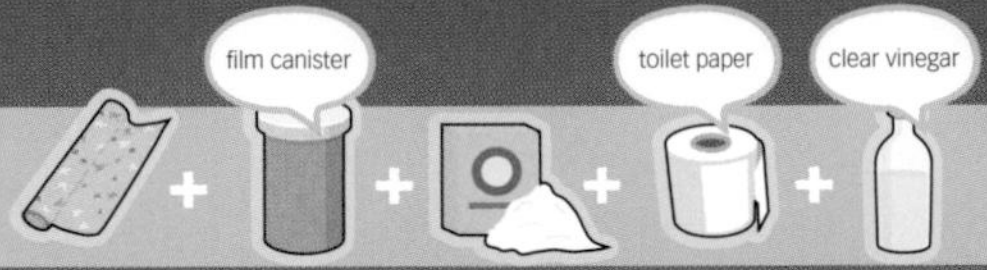

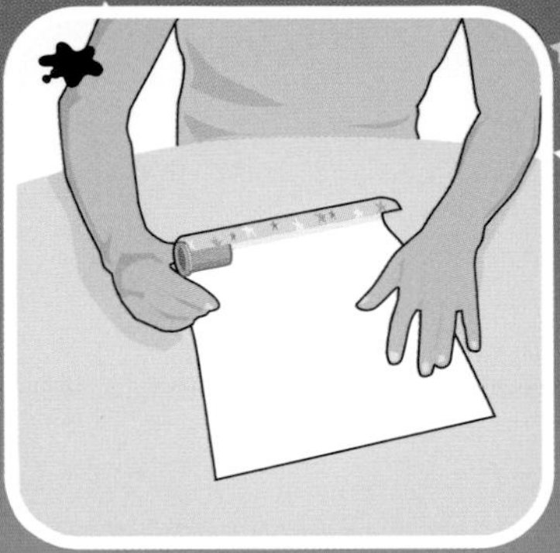

Roll an open film canister or plastic jar in paper.

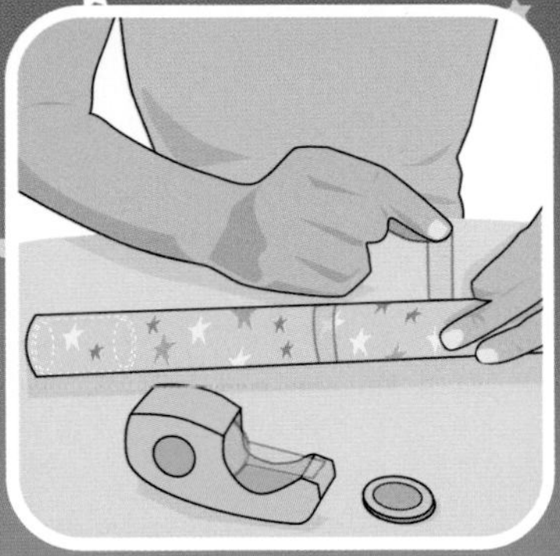

Tape the tube around the canister.

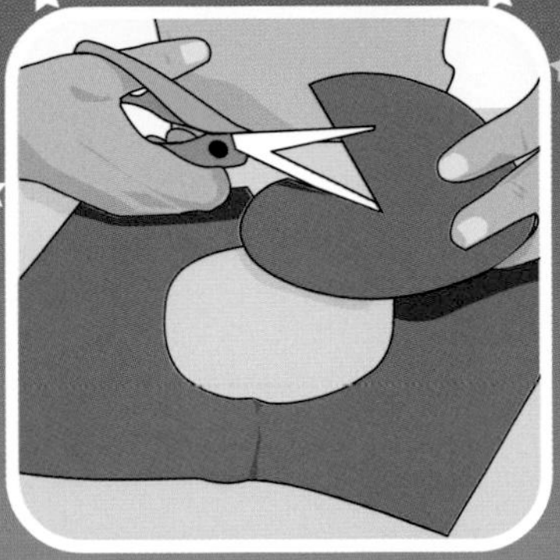

Cut out a paper circle and make a slit to the centre.

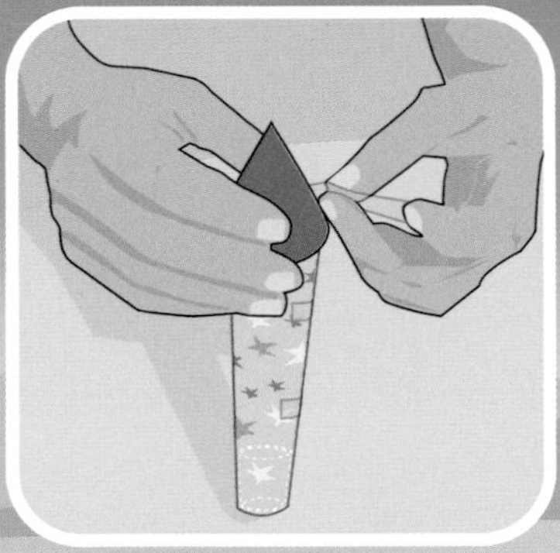

Fold it into a cone and tape it on top.

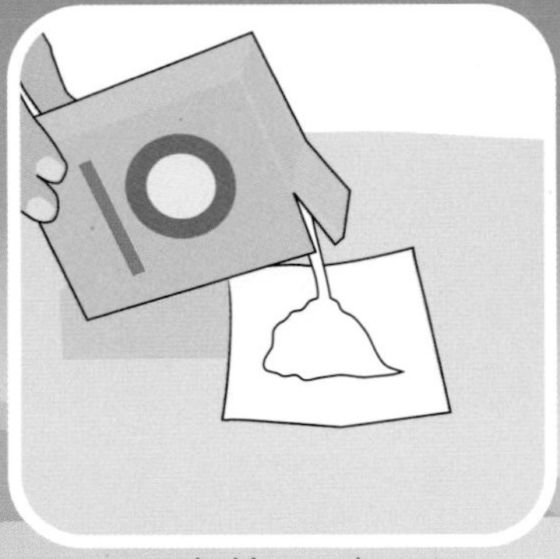

Pour baking soda onto a square of toilet paper.

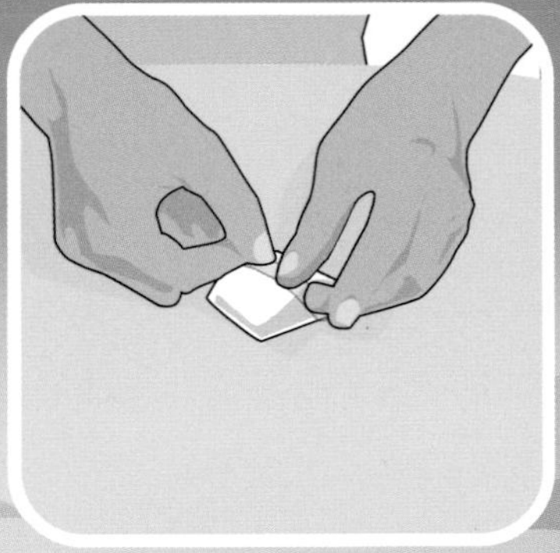

Tape it to make a packet. Take everything outdoors.

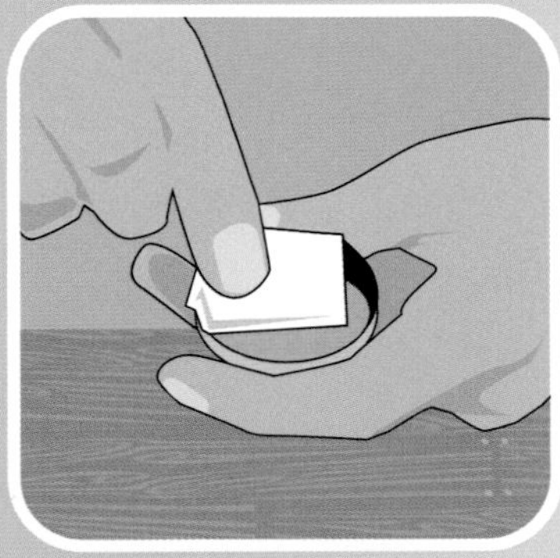

Put the packet in the canister lid.

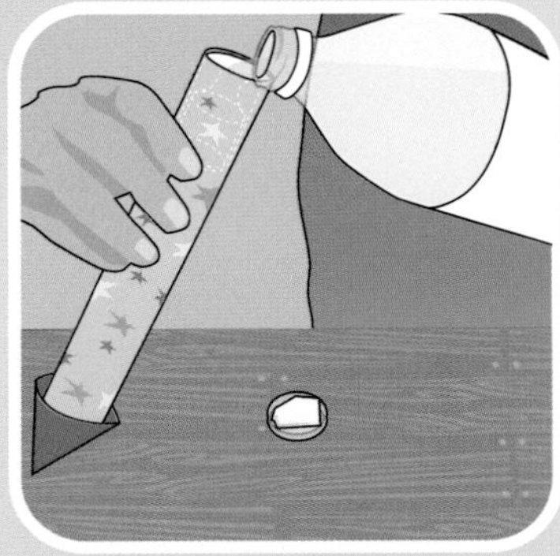

Fill half the canister with vinegar. Put on the lid.

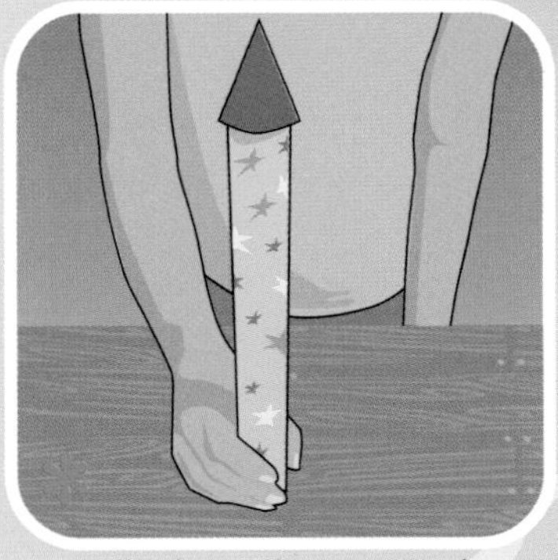

Flip the rocket over and stand back for blast-off!

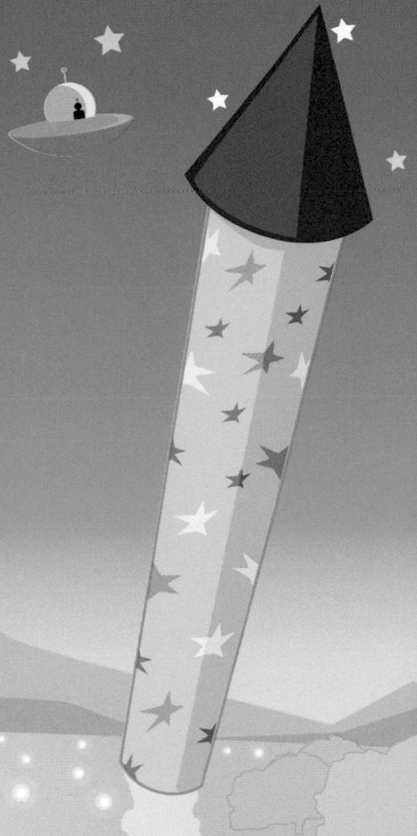

* You're building a pretty powerful rocket here. Always point it away from people and windows!

create

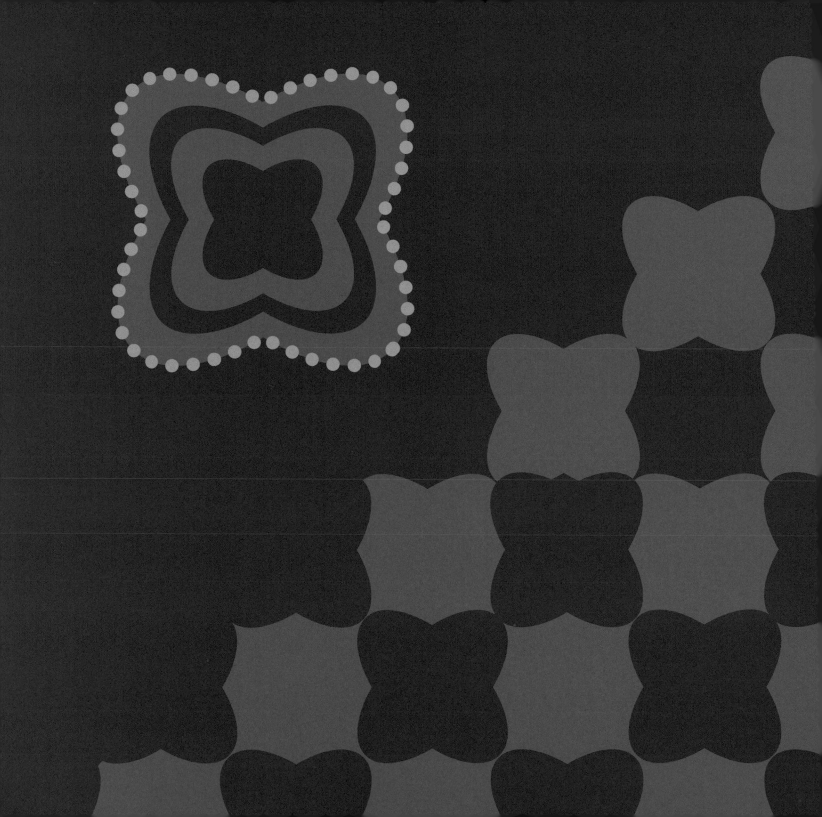

32 lolly sticks

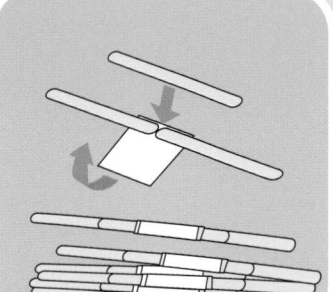

Tape together nine sets
of three lolly sticks.

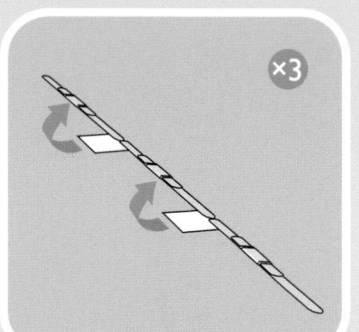

×3

Tape three sets
end to end.

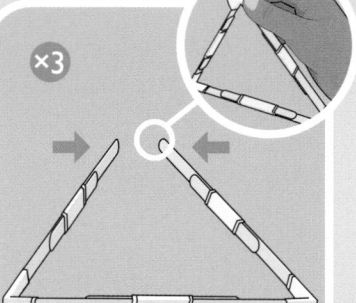

×3

Fold into a triangle and
tape the ends together.

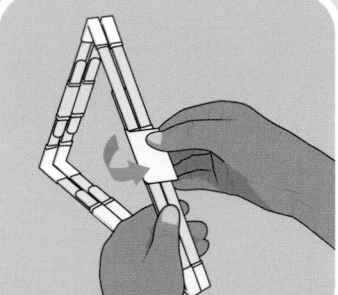

Tape a hinge between
two triangles.

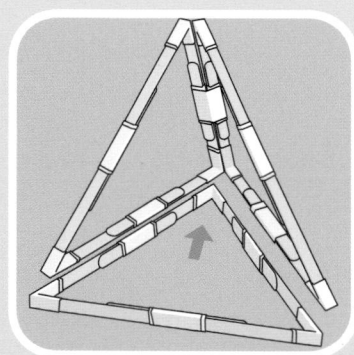

Open the hinge and tape
in the third triangle.

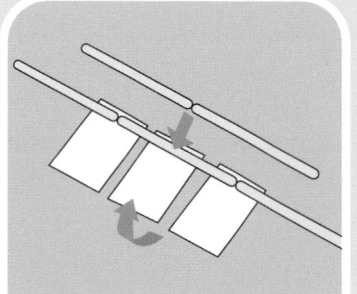

Tape five sticks together
to make the catapult arm.

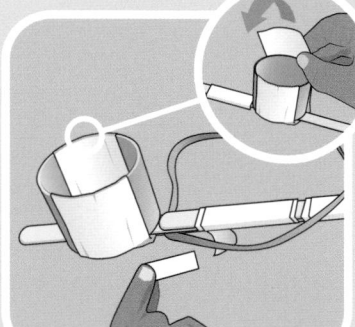

Attach the cup. Tape a
rubber band below it.

Tape a paper clip to the
end of the arm.

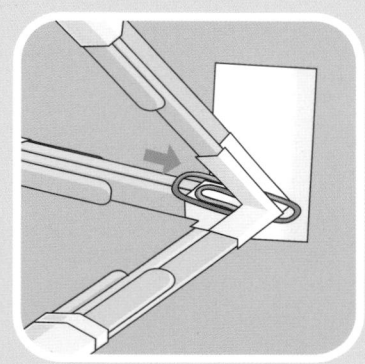

Tape another paper clip to
one corner of the base.

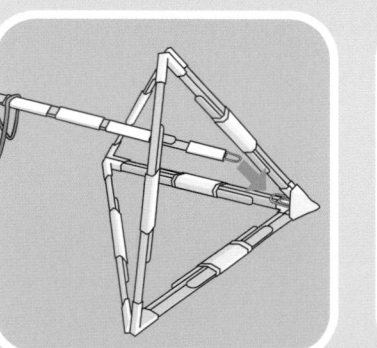

Hook the arm clip
into the base clip.

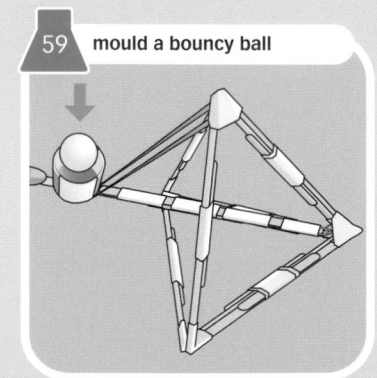

Tape the rubber band to
the top of the base.

59 mould a bouncy ball

Add your projectile. Pull
the arm down to fire.

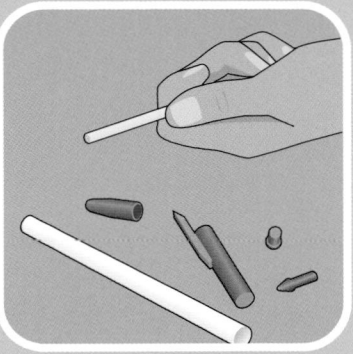

Take apart a ballpoint pen that has run out of ink.

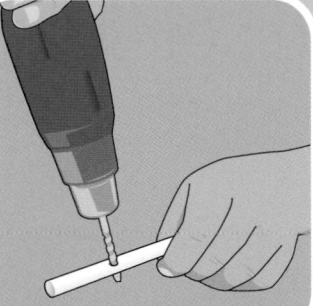

Ask an adult to drill a hole through the tube's centre.

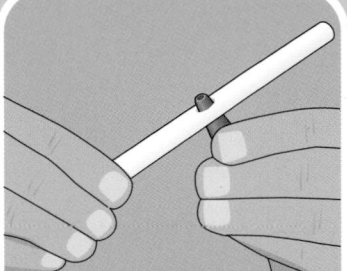

Push the hollow tip through the hole.

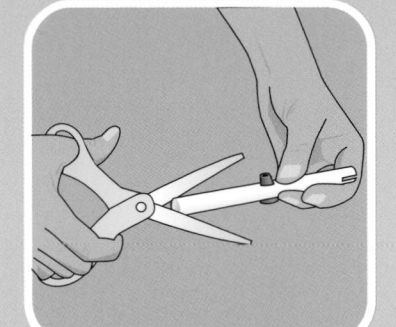

Cut two notches in each end.

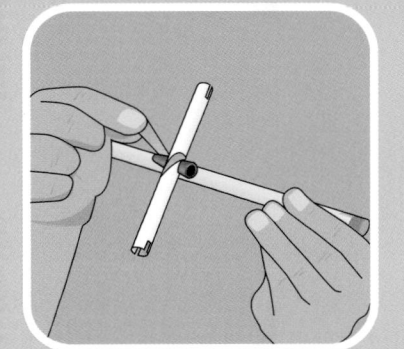

Secure the pen at right angles to a pencil.

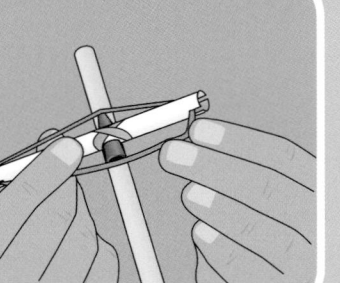

Place a rubber band in the notches.

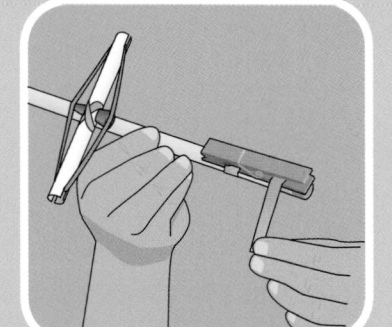

Tape the clothes peg on so it can still open.

Load the ink tube through the hollow tip.

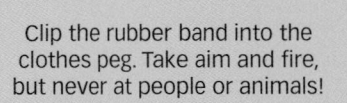

Clip the rubber band into the clothes peg. Take aim and fire, but never at people or animals!

design a kite

You can make a kite with lots of things you find around your house. Decorate a rubbish bag or old umbrella fabric for the sail, for instance, and use fabric strips for the tail.

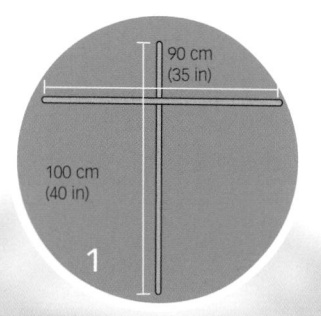

90 cm
(35 in)

100 cm
(40 in)

1

Make a cross shape
with the dowels.

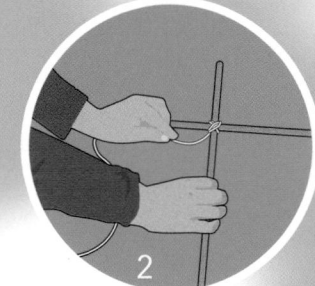

2

Wrap string tightly
at the joint. Tie.

3

Notch the ends of
the shorter stick.

4

Wrap with string.
Make loops at the top
and bottom. Tie.

2.5 cm (1 in)

5

Trace an outline
on the paper.

big sheet of
paper

kite spool

Tie a kite spool to the
string, near the joint.

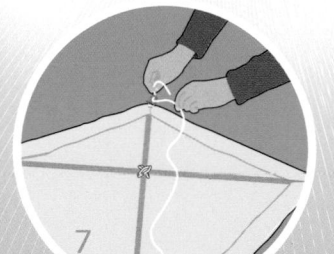

Tie a string between
the loops.

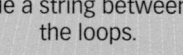

Leaving loops free,
fold over and glue.

1

With the wind behind
you, hand over the kite.

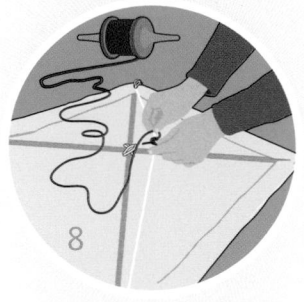

2

Unravel string as your
friend backs away.

3

Your friend holds
the kite high.

4

Get your friend
to toss the kite.

5

Walk into the wind
with your arms up.

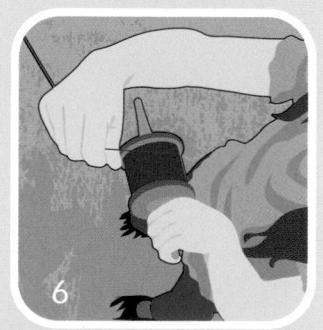

6

Adjust string to raise
or lower the kite.

83 fold a paper aeroplane

1

2

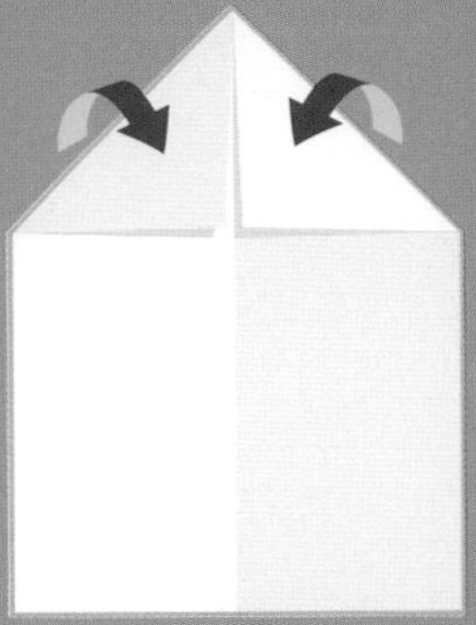

3

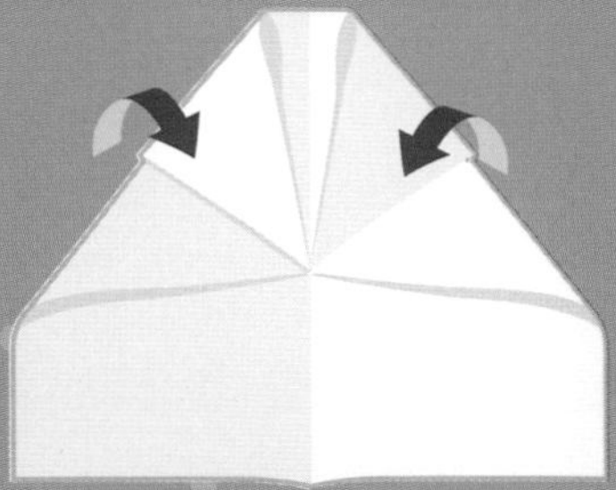

4 Turn the paper over, then fold down the corners.

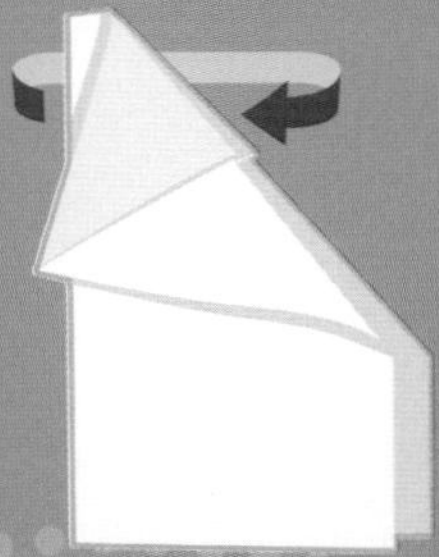

5 Fold in half.

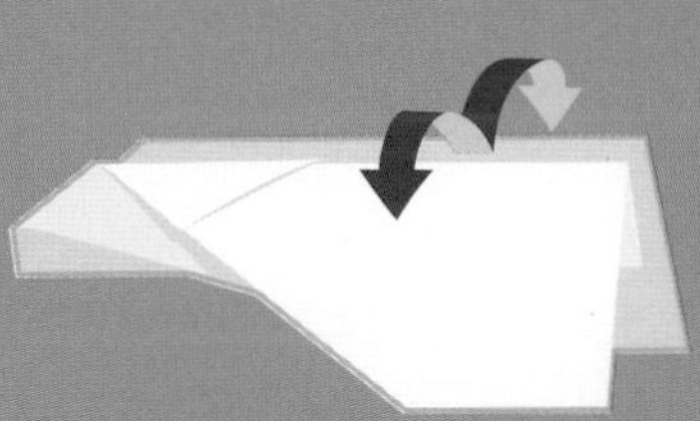

6 Turn the paper to the side, then fold down the wings.

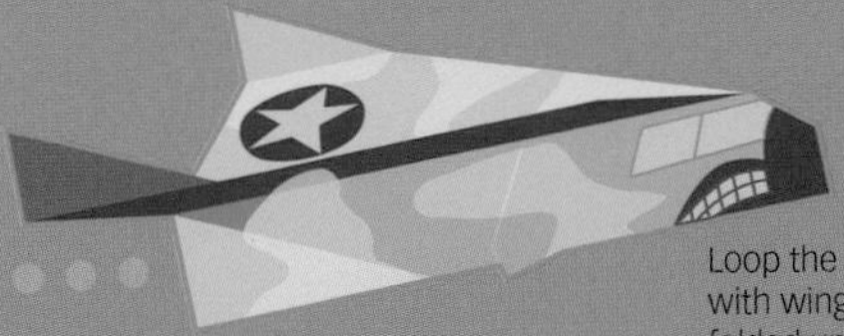

Loop the loop with wing points folded up.

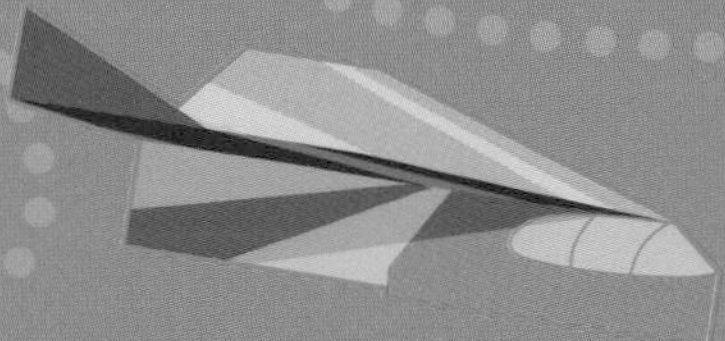

Fold one tip up and one tip down to corkscrew.

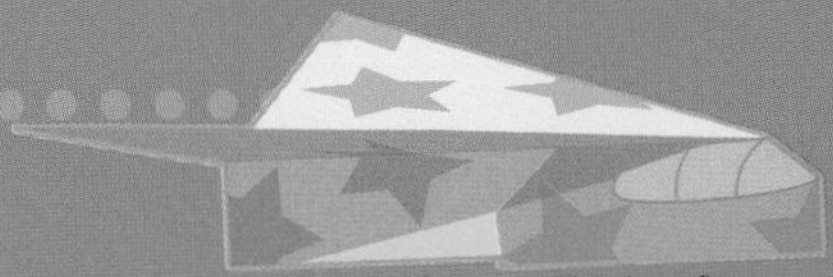

Fly straight with wings flat.

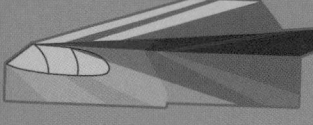

Point one tip down to boomerang.

Try folding the wing tips up or down to get the perfect trajectory. Scare your enemies by giving your fighter jet a fearsome paint job.

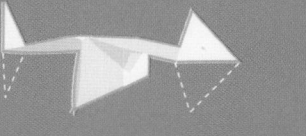

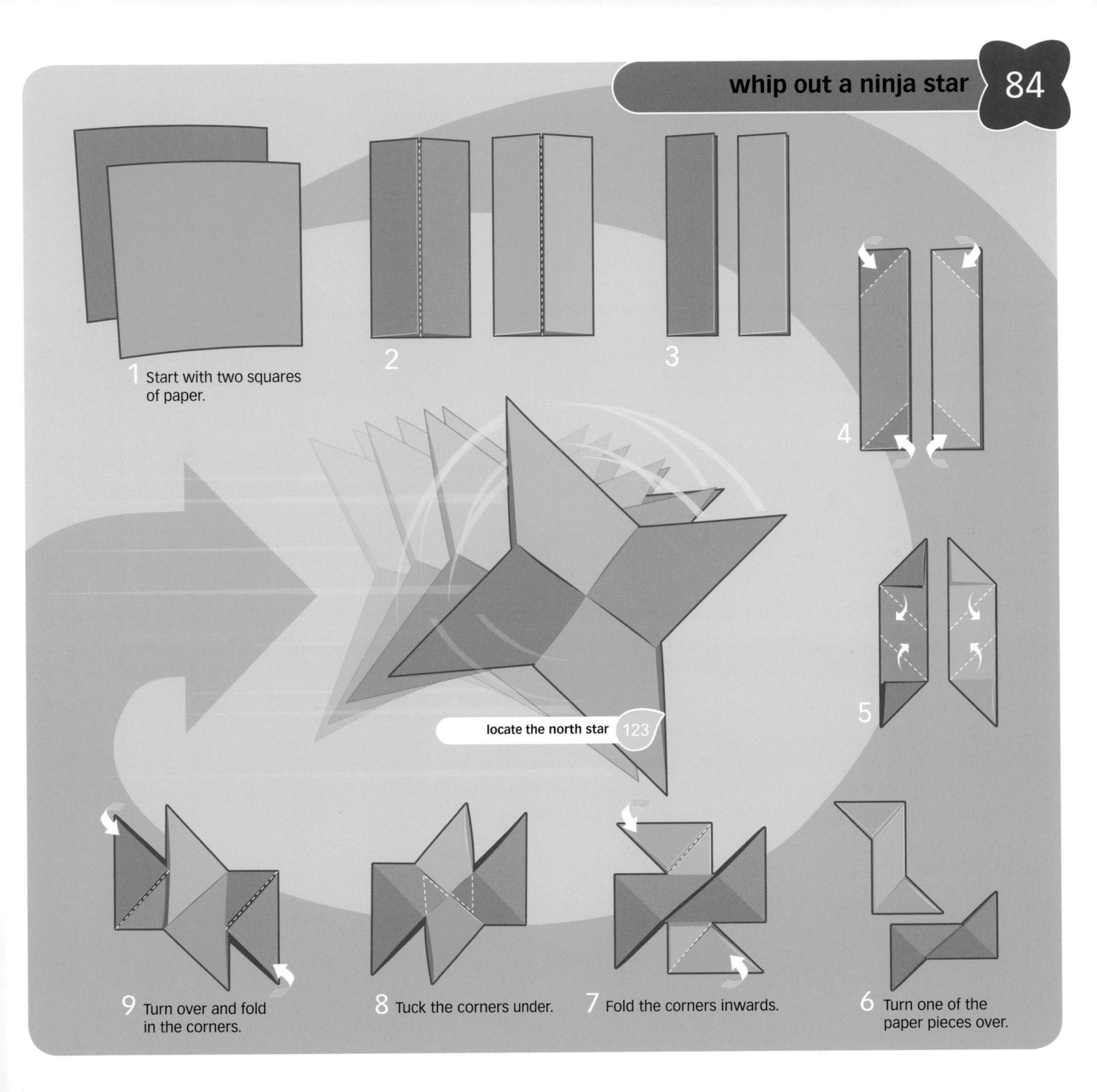

1 Start with two squares of paper.

2

3

4

5

6 Turn one of the paper pieces over.

7 Fold the corners inwards.

8 Tuck the corners under.

9 Turn over and fold in the corners.

locate the north star 123

liquid starch

ALUM

oil paint

½ tsp alum

500 ml
(18 fl oz)
liquid starch

1
Mix well.

2
Thin paint with water so it
drips quickly off a spoon.

3
Make squiggles and
splotches of paint.

9
Once the paper's dry,
flatten it with a warm iron.

157 mix up seed paper

4
Swirl a stick through
the paint.

8
12 hr
Hang the paper to dry.

5
Lay a sheet of paper
on the surface.

7
Rinse gently under
cold water.

6
Remove the paper and let
the starchy water drip off.

tell me more

tissue paper

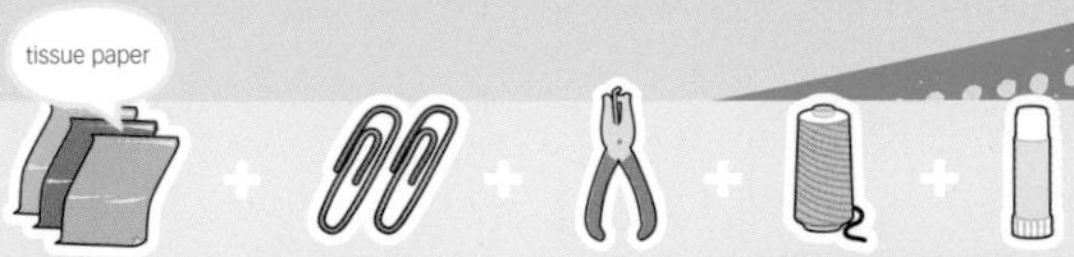

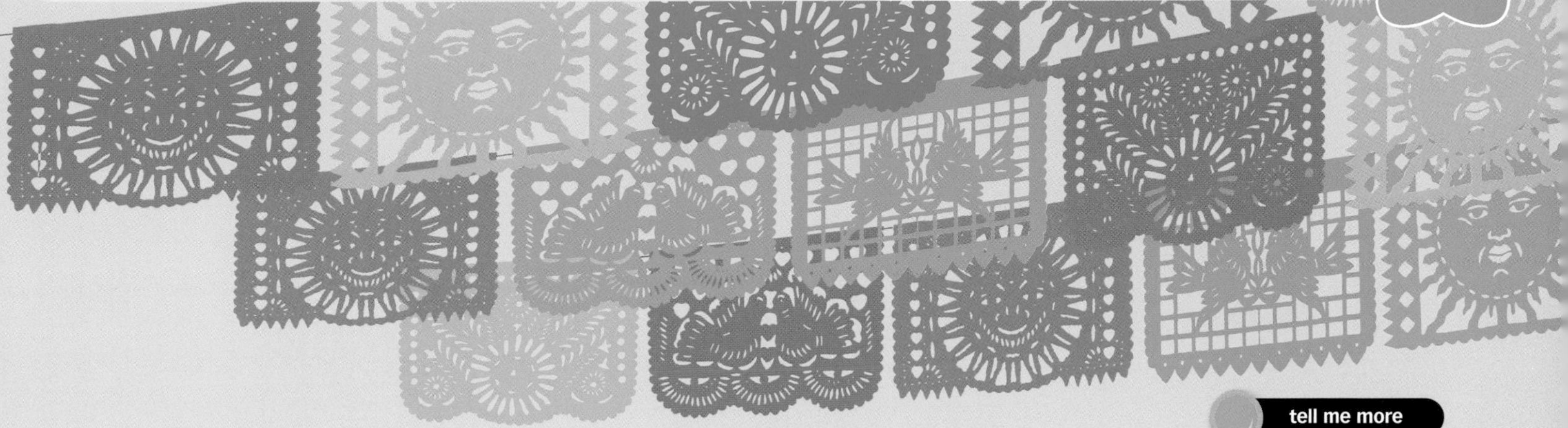

tell me more

Fold tissue papers in half, then fold in half again.

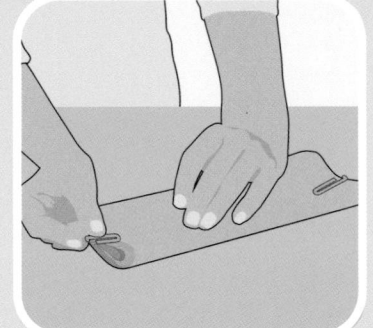

Clip at each end.

Draw a pattern.

Cut along the fold.

Use a hole punch.

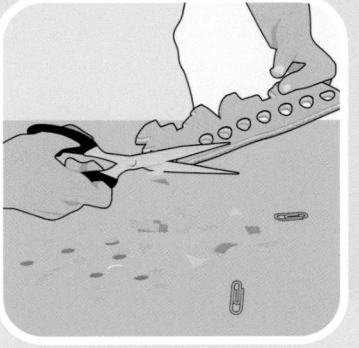

Cut a pattern along the bottom edges.

Unfold and separate.

Glue a string along the top edge. Fold the edge over.

87 paste up a piñata

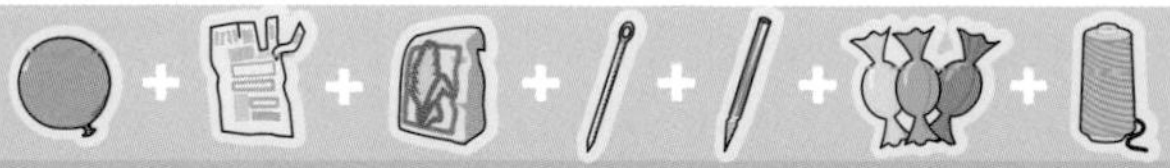

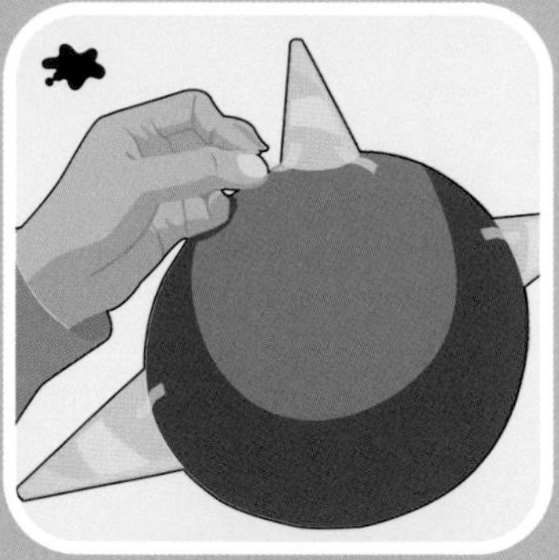

Tape newspaper cones
to a balloon.

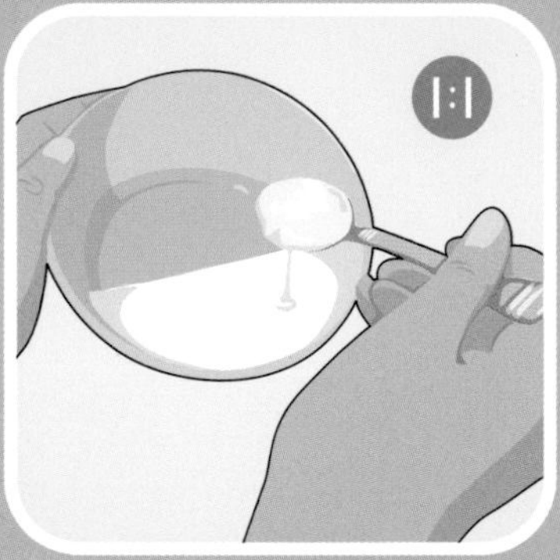

1:1
Mix one part water
with one part flour.

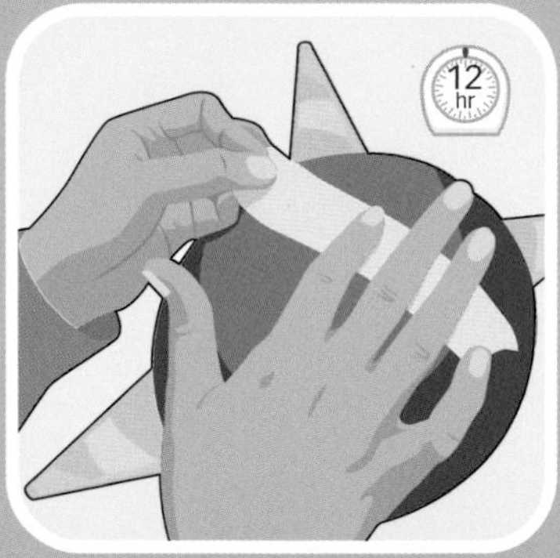

12 hr
Dip newspaper in the mix.
Cover the balloon. Let dry.

36 stick a pin in a balloon 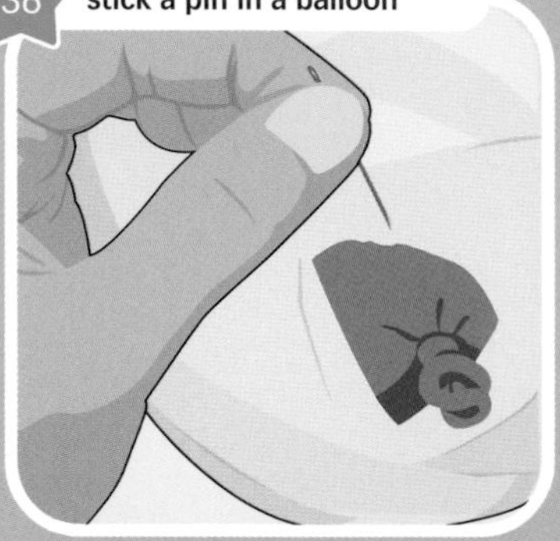
Pop the balloon.

tell me more

88 light paper-bag luminarias

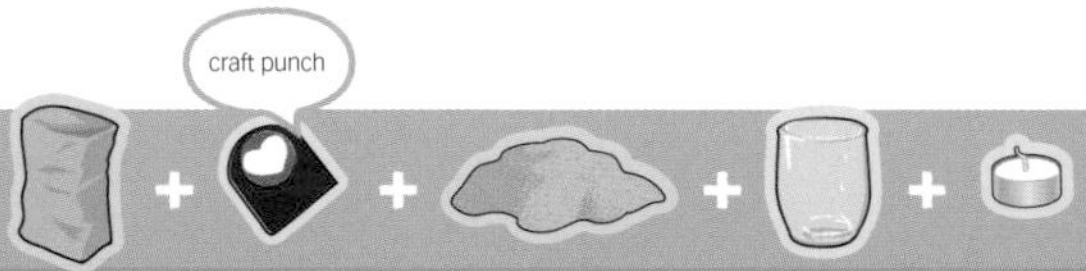

craft punch

Fold down the bag's top.

*
Make patterns with a
decorative hole punch.

Cover the bottom
with sand.

Put a candle in a small jar.

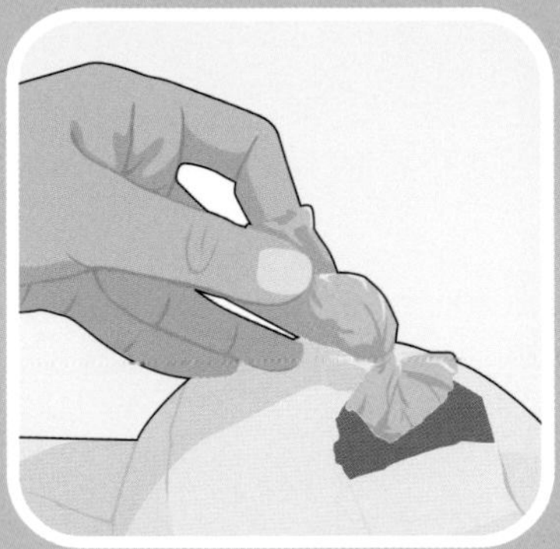

Remove the balloon, then fill the piñata with sweets.

Poke a hole near the large opening.

Thread a string through the two holes. Seal.

Decorate and hang up your piñata. Crack it open with a good whack!

Nestle the jar in the sand.

Ask an adult to light the candle.

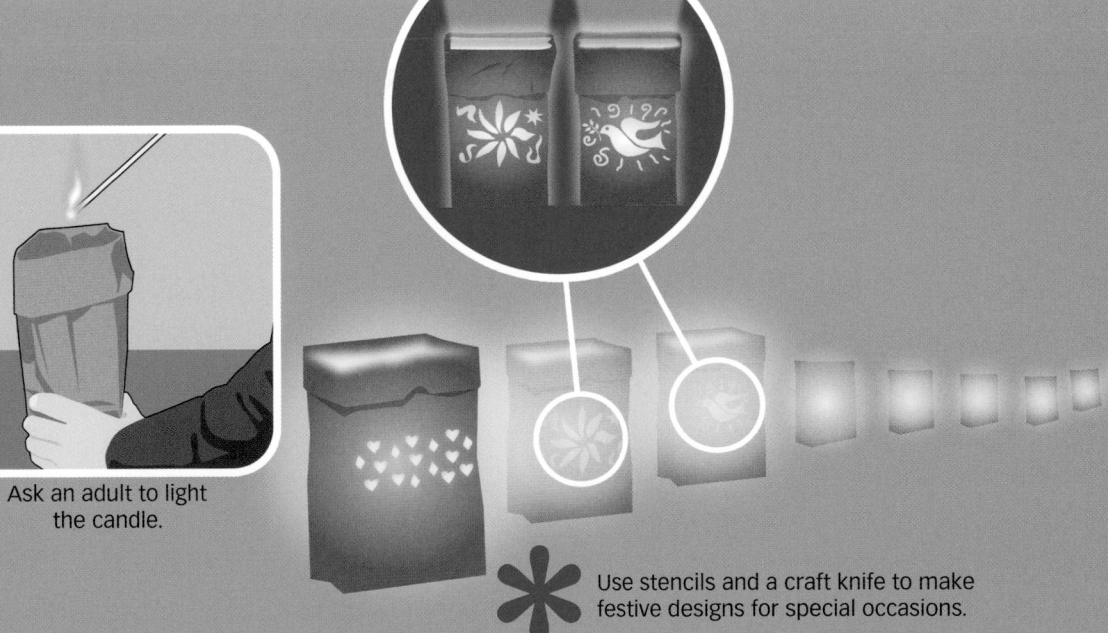

Use stencils and a craft knife to make festive designs for special occasions.

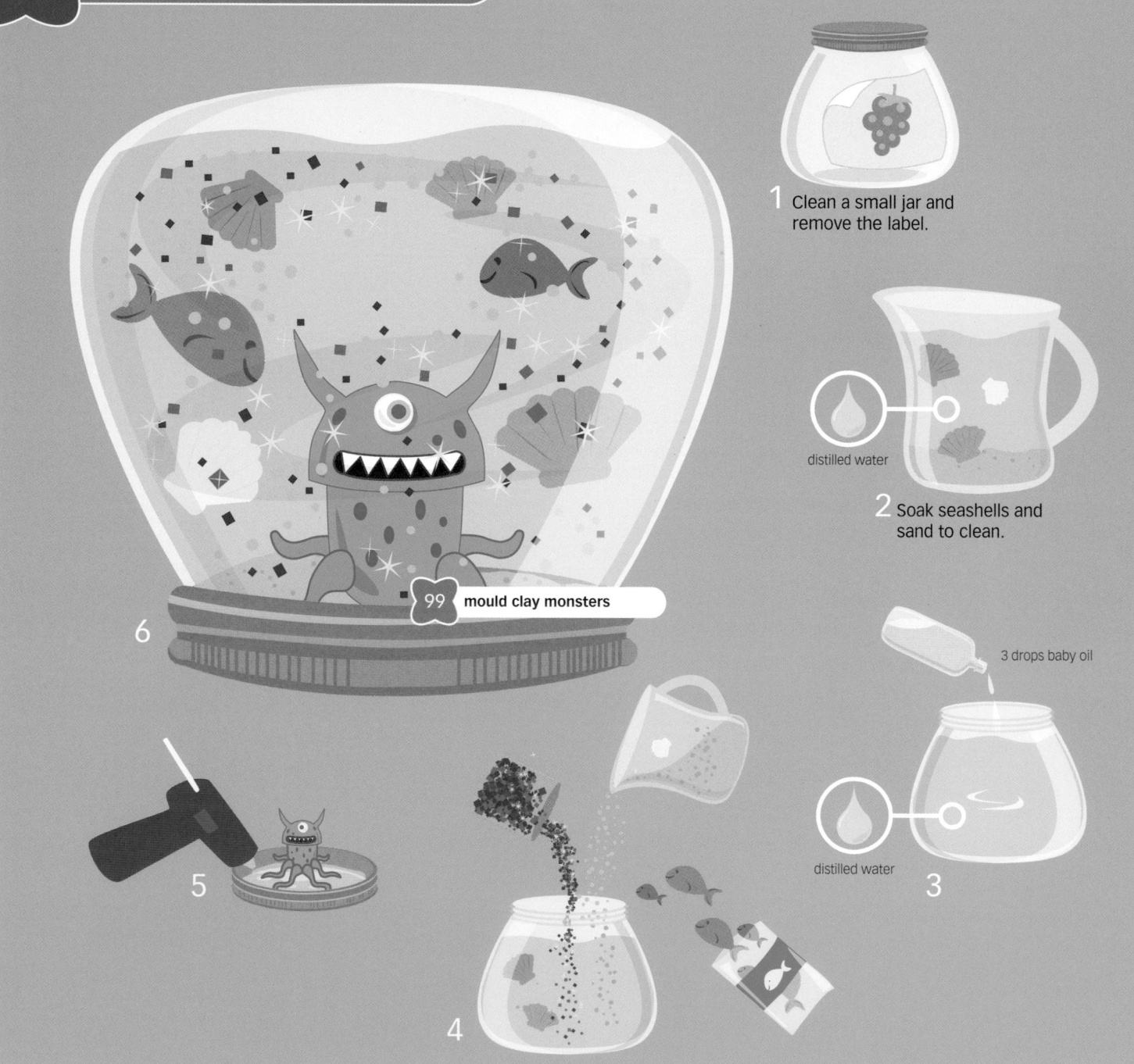

1 Clean a small jar and remove the label.

distilled water

2 Soak seashells and sand to clean.

3 drops baby oil

distilled water

3

6

99 mould clay monsters

5

4

Fill a pot with damp sand.

Press a mould into the sand.

Carefully remove the mould.

Press shells into the sides so you see their backs.

Melt candles in a can inside a pan of water.

90°C (190°F)

Dip a string into the wax. Turn down the heat.

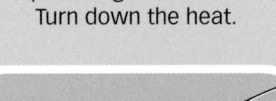

Bury the end of the string in the sand.

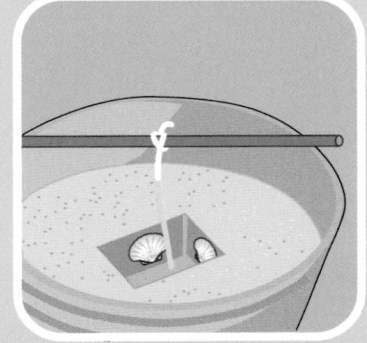

Lay a stick across the pot and tie on the string.

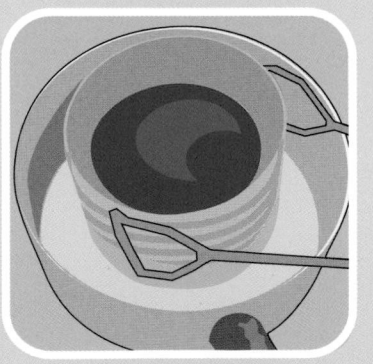

Remove the can.

Carefully fill the hole with hot wax.

2 hr

Leave the wax to cool, then remove your candle.

Ask an adult to light the candle.

old candle ends

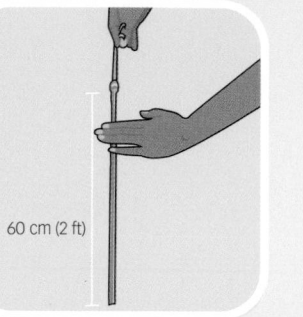

Tie four threads
together. Flatten.

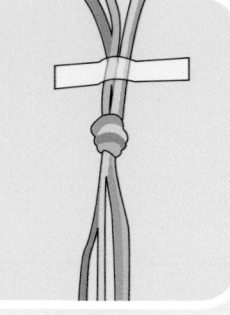

Tape down.

Knot the first thread
around the second.

Pull tight and
knot it again.

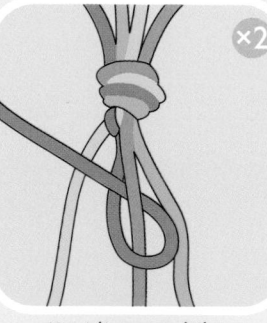

Knot it around the
third thread.

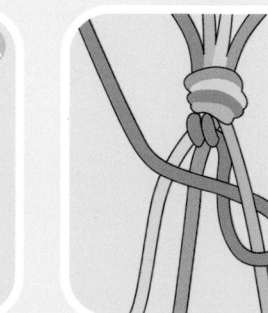

Knot it around the
fourth thread.

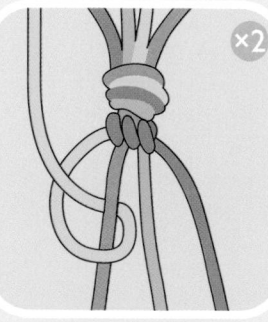

Start again with the
new first thread.

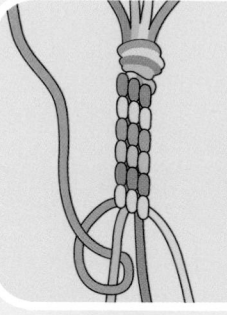

Continue until it fits
your wrist. Tie off.

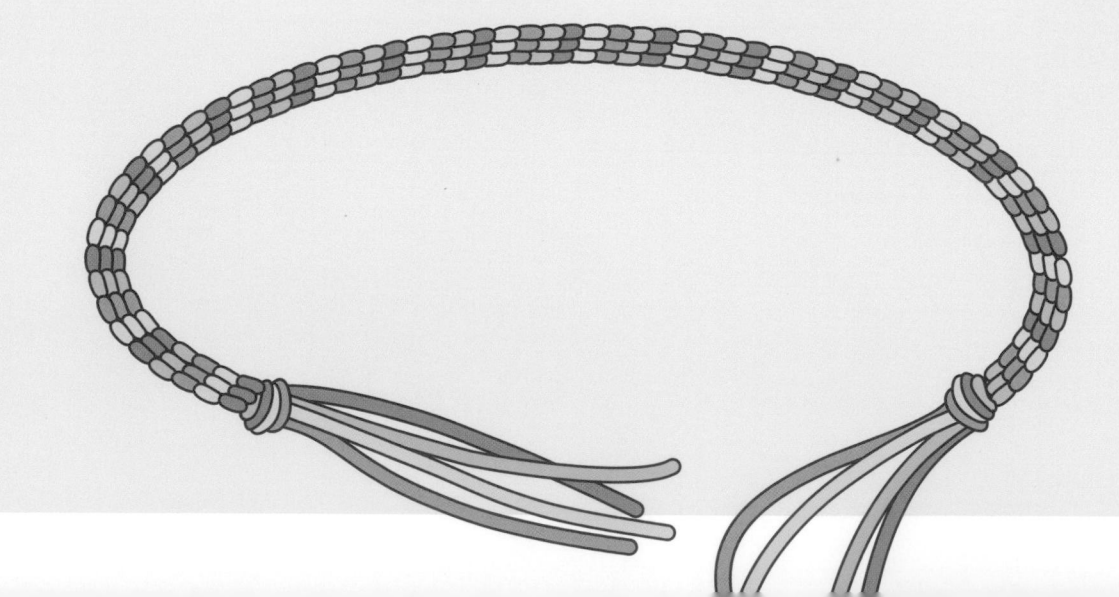

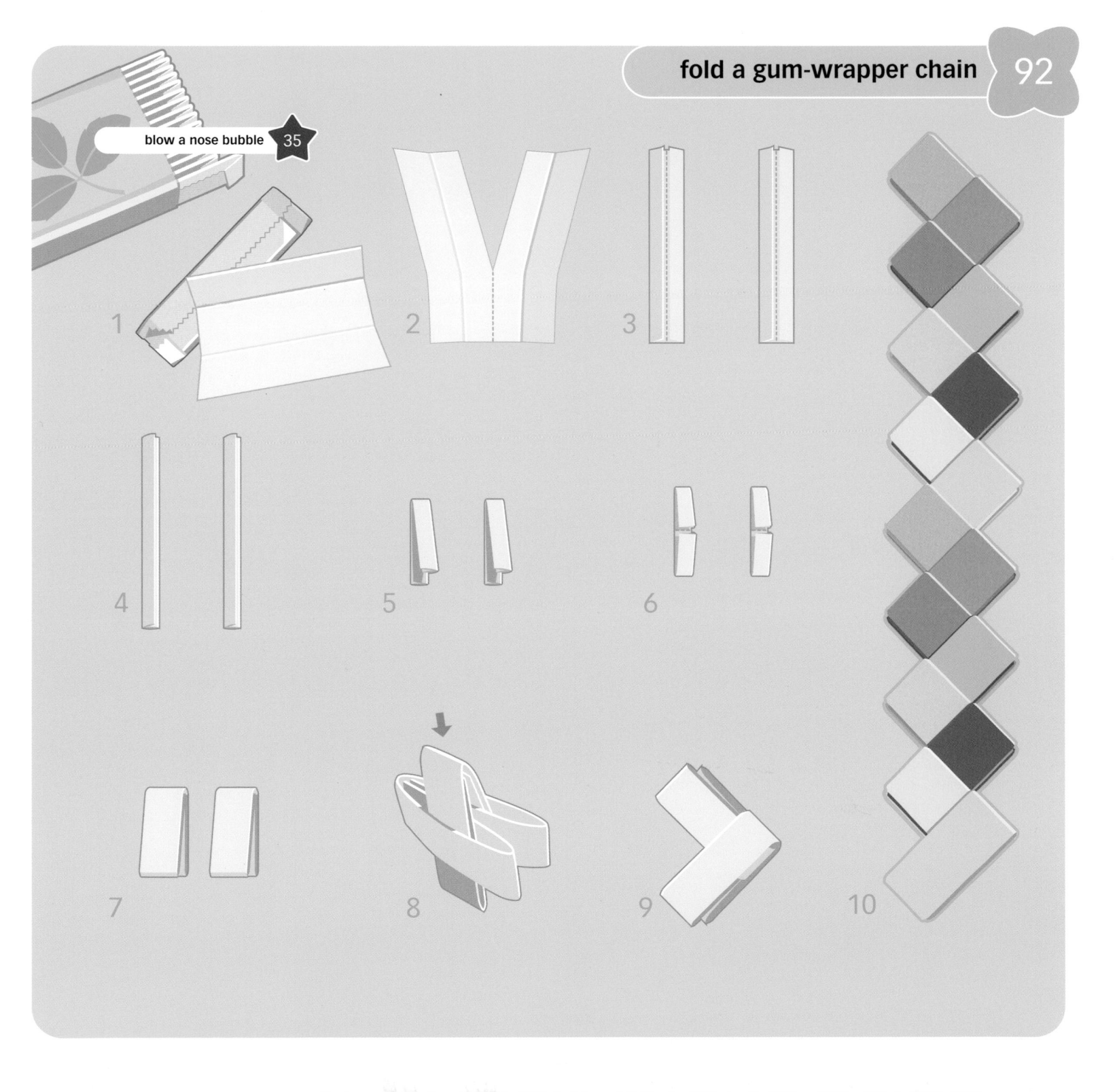

blow a nose bubble 35

1

2

3

4

5

6

7

8

9

10

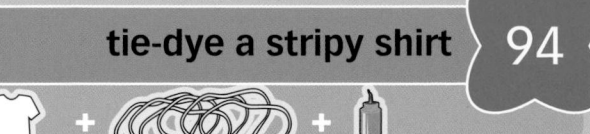

1

Pinch the centre.

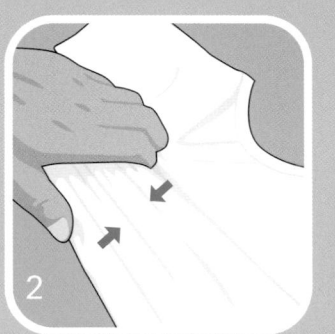

2

Scrunch the top and bottom together.

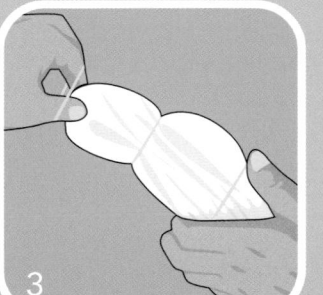

3

Twist on two sets of rubber bands.

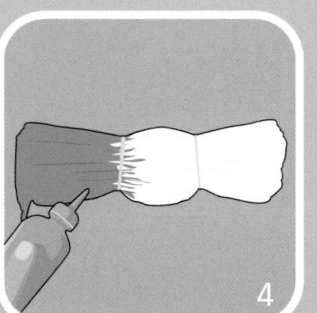

4

Soak with dye. Wash before wearing.

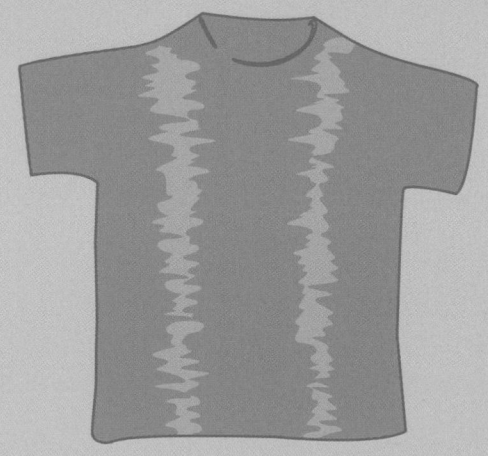

1

Pinch the centre.

2

Twist around the centre point.

3

Add rubber bands to look like a sliced cake.

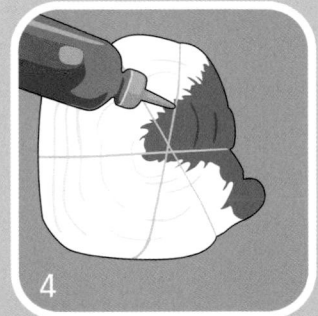

4

Soak with dye. Wash before wearing.

cover an MP3 player   clear tape

Trace the MP3 player.

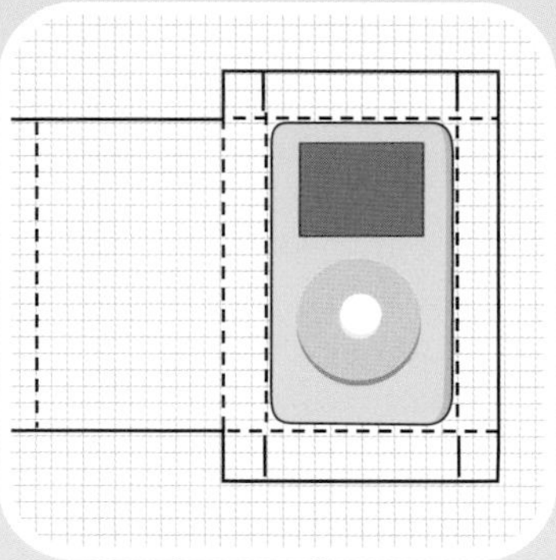

Measure and draw the sides, back and tabs.

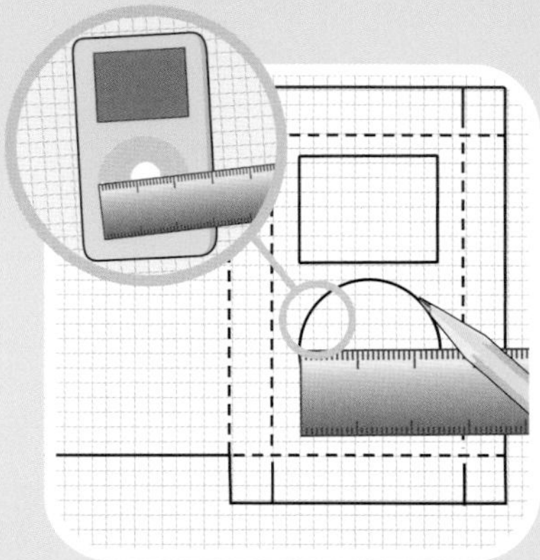

Draw the click wheel, screen, holes and buttons.

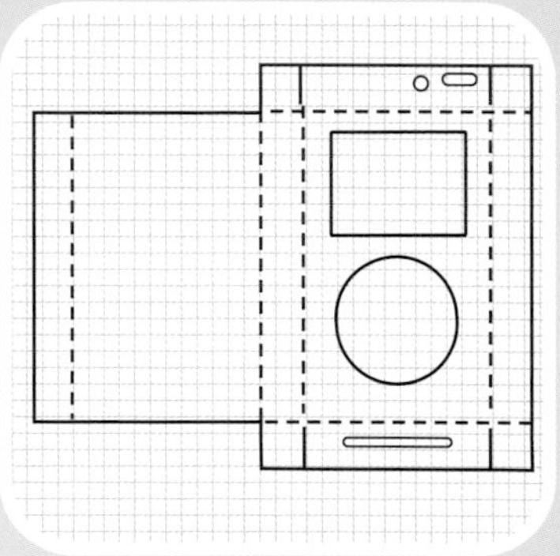

Check that you've drawn all the tabs and parts.

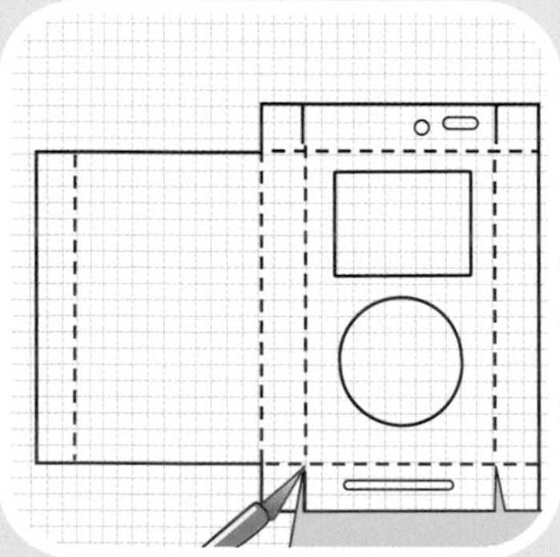

Cut out the template. Make notches in the tabs.

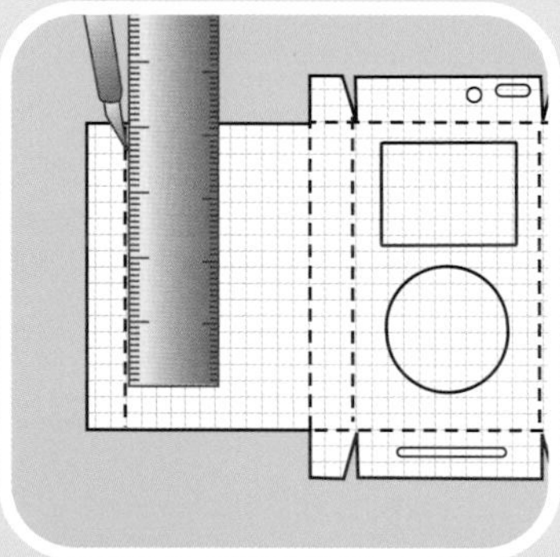

Using the back of a craft knife, score the fold lines.

Test out your template. Adjust if needed.

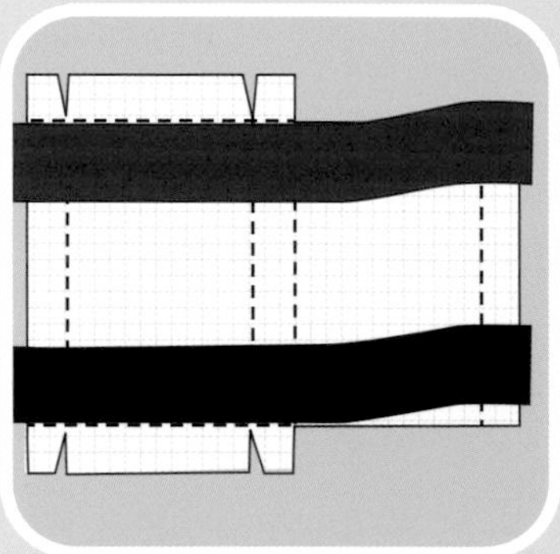

Turn it over and cover one side in duct tape.

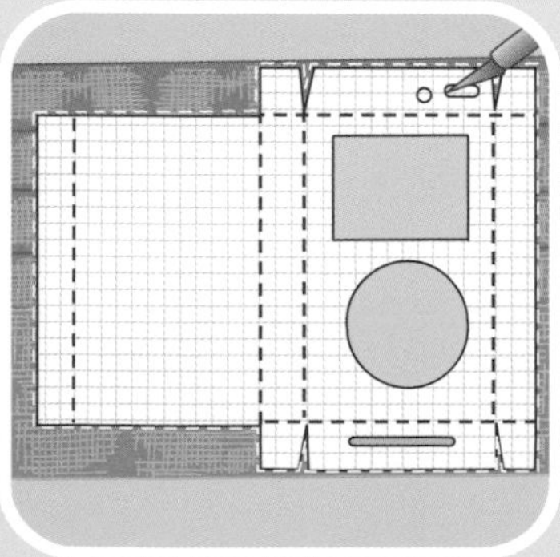

Trim off the excess tape. Cut away all holes.

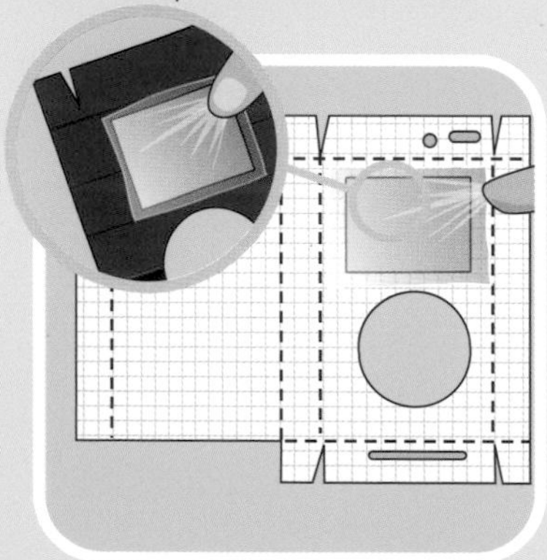

Protect the screen with clear tape on both sides.

A tiny piece of tape closes the top for easy access.

Rock on!

1 💻

2

3

4

5

6

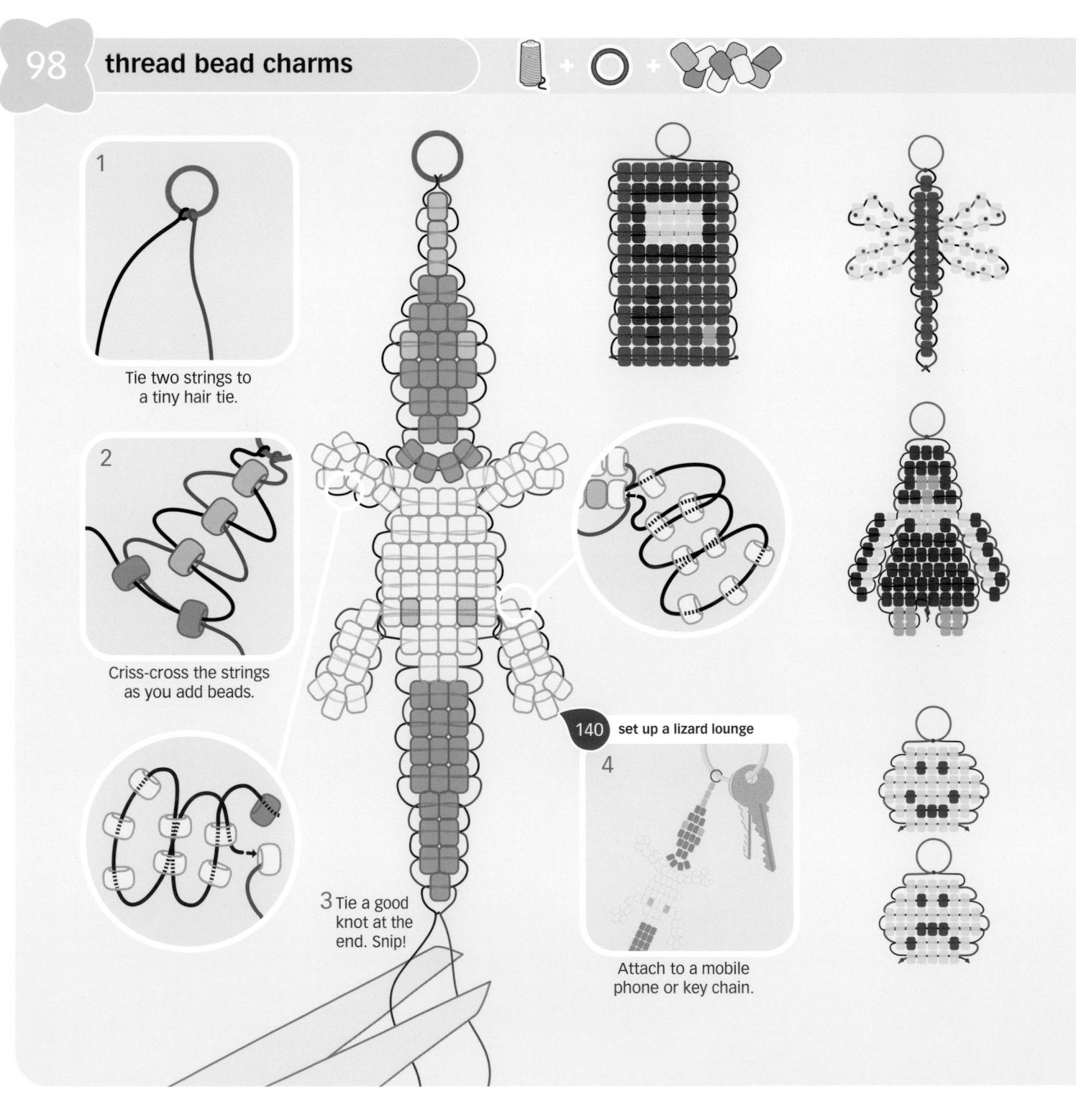

1 Tie two strings to a tiny hair tie.

2 Criss-cross the strings as you add beads.

3 Tie a good knot at the end. Snip!

140 set up a lizard lounge

4 Attach to a mobile phone or key chain.

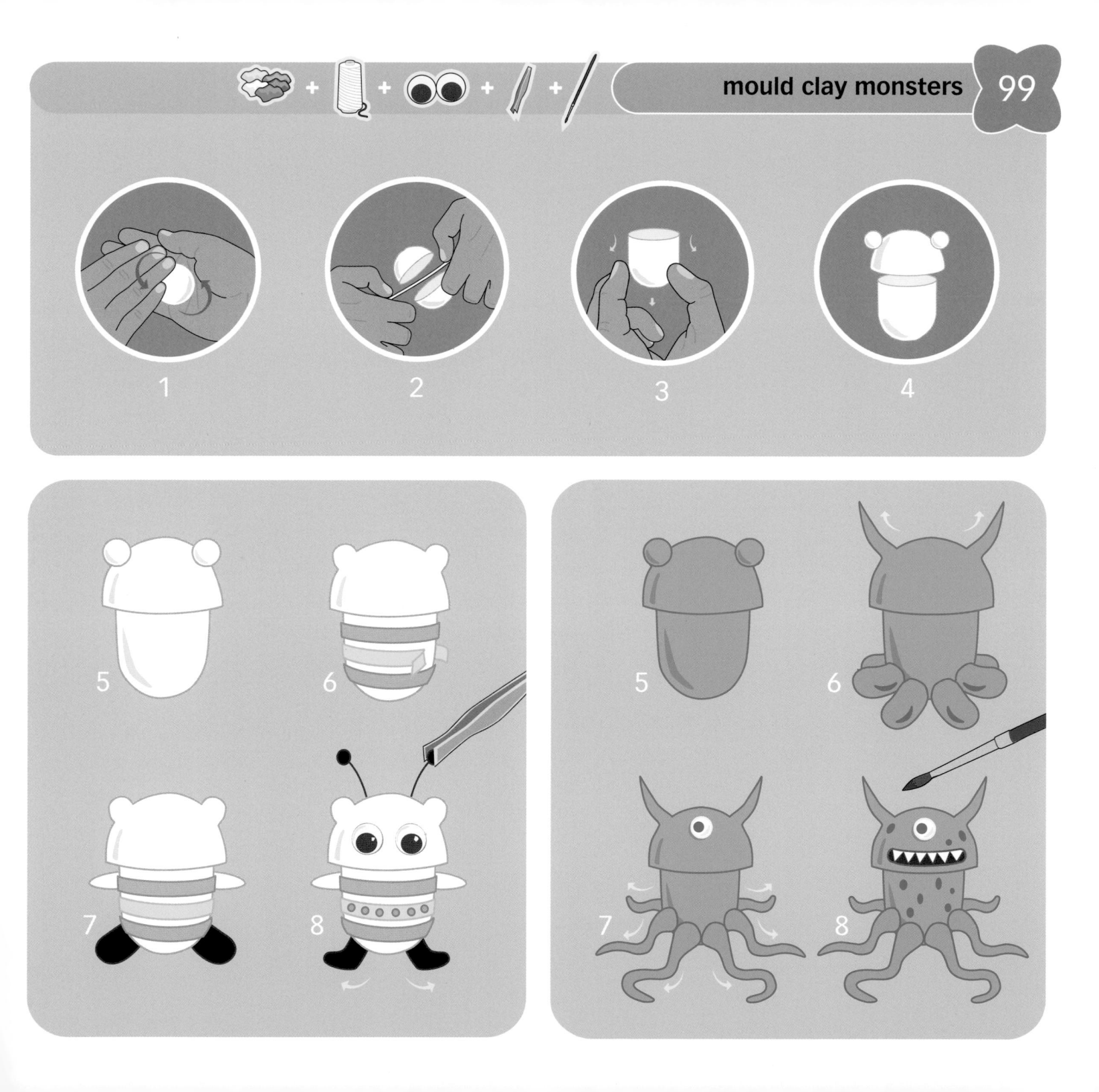

72 make a light bulb

draw a cat 101

sketch a dog 102

greet a new dog 136

draft a horse 103

tell me more

105   **flip out with a flip book**

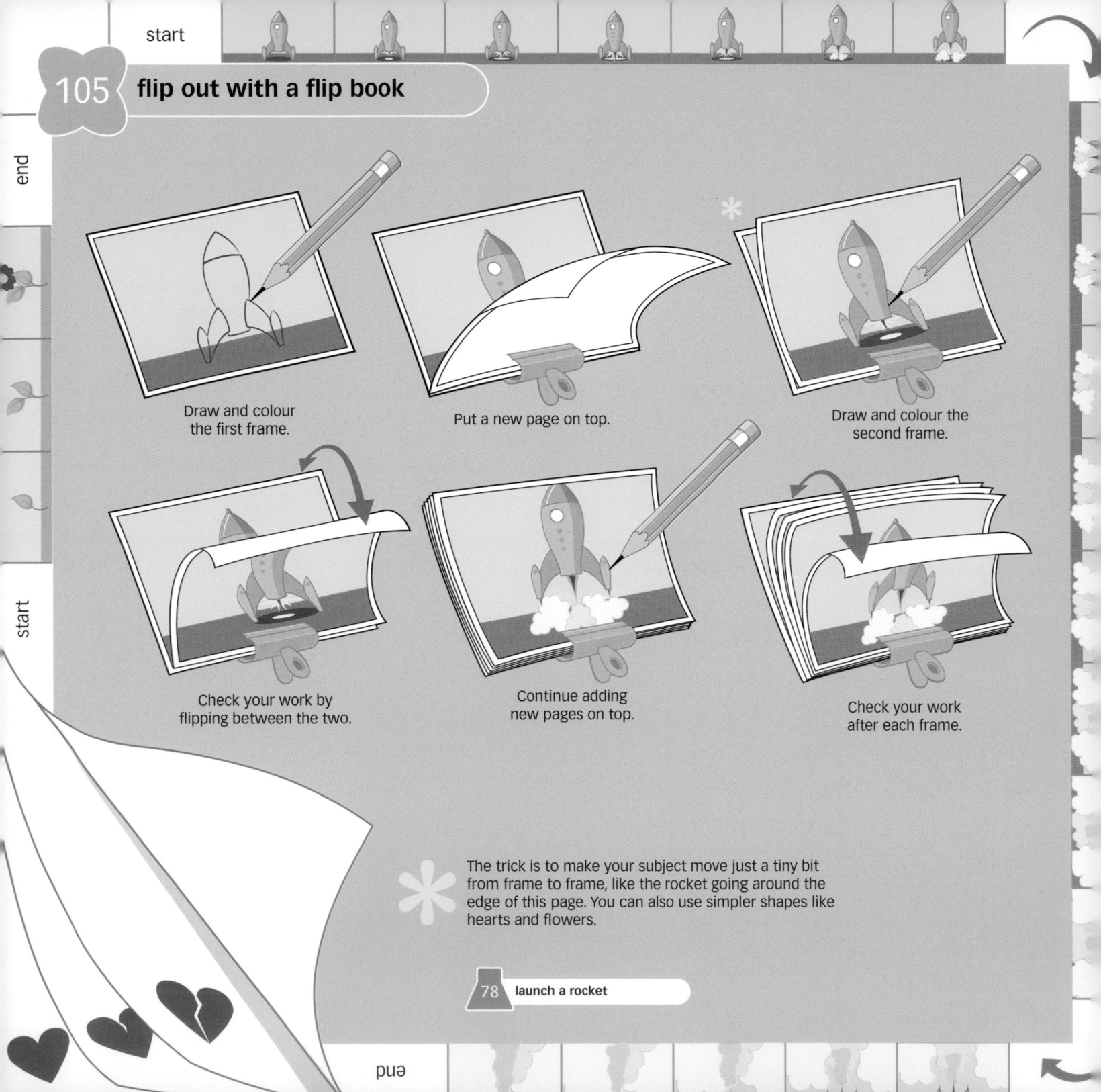

Draw and colour
the first frame.

Put a new page on top.

Draw and colour the
second frame.

Check your work by
flipping between the two.

Continue adding
new pages on top.

Check your work
after each frame.

*The trick is to make your subject move just a tiny bit
from frame to frame, like the rocket going around the
edge of this page. You can also use simpler shapes like
hearts and flowers.

78   **launch a rocket**

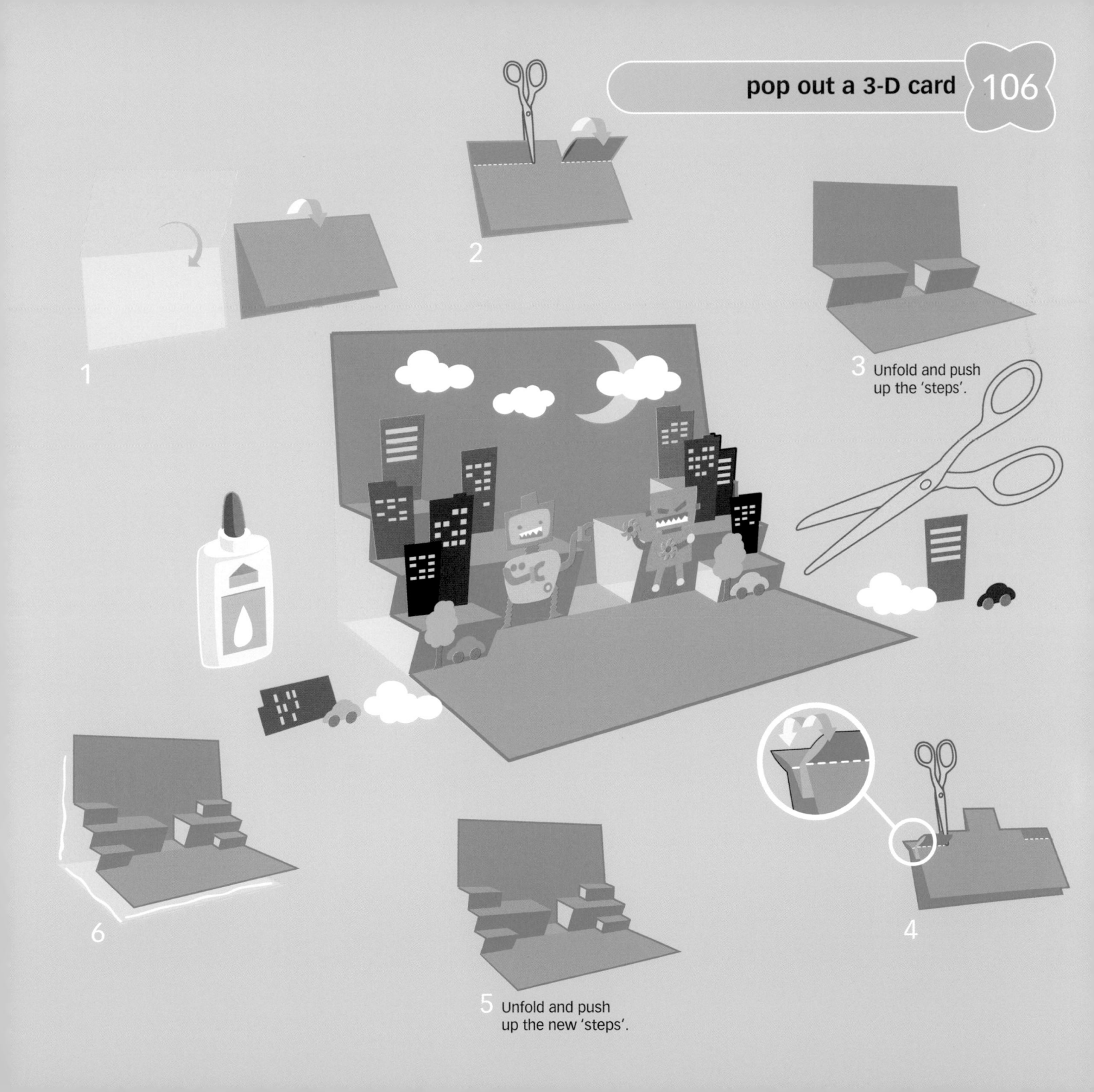

1

2

3 Unfold and push
up the 'steps'.

4

5 Unfold and push
up the new 'steps'.

6

carry a comic-book bag

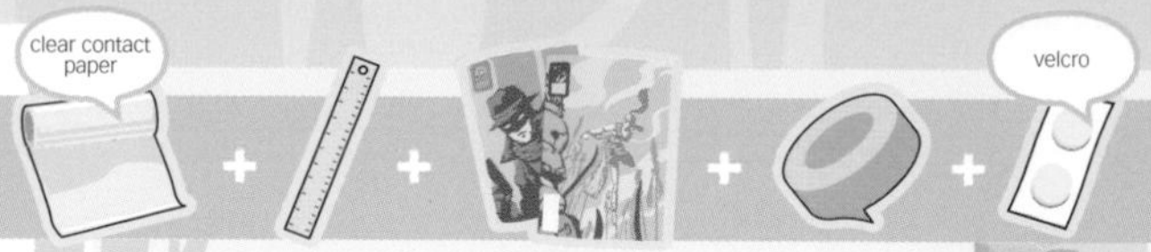

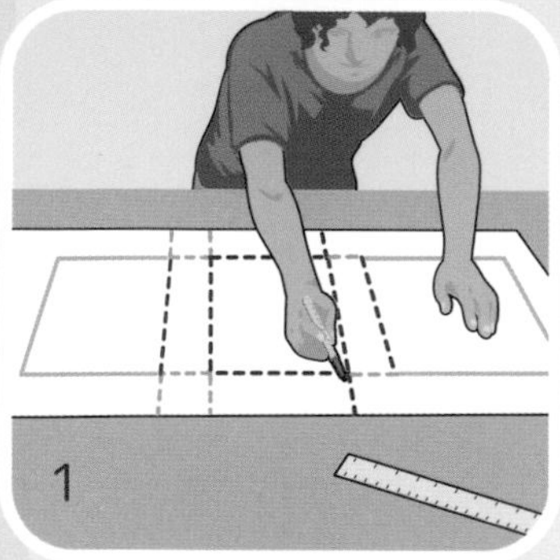

clear contact paper + 📏 + 📖 + 📼 + velcro

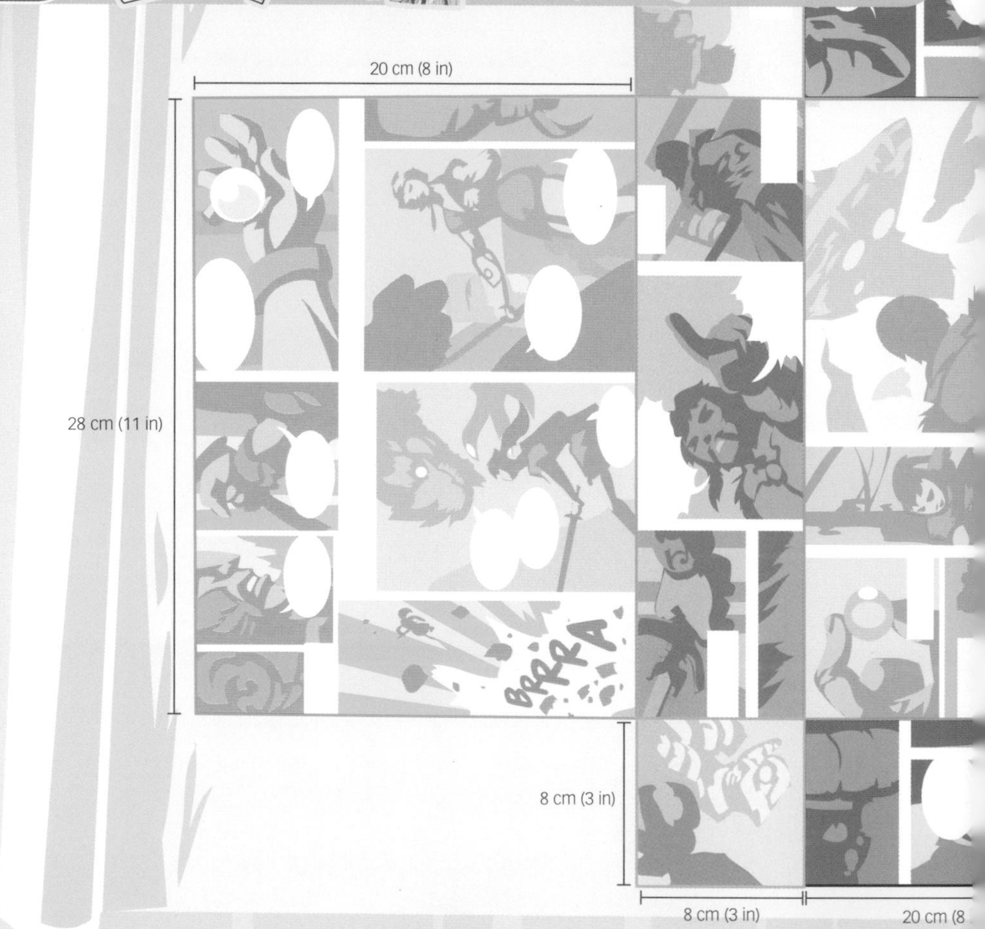

1 Draw the template on clear contact paper.

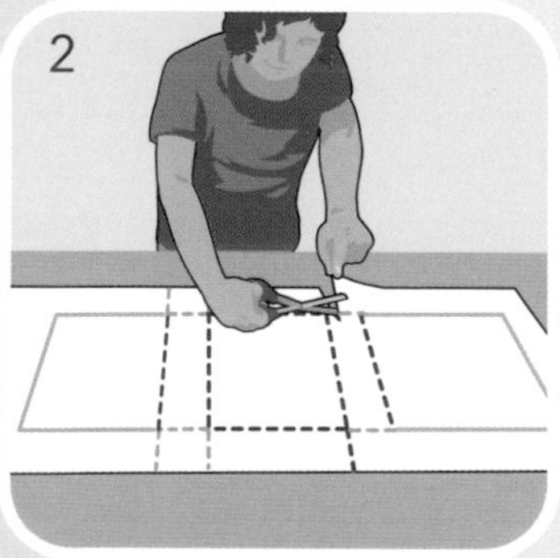

2 Cut out the template.

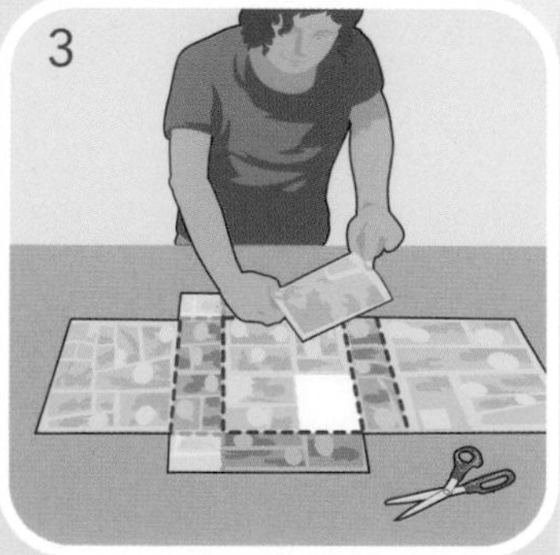

20 cm (8 in)

28 cm (11 in)

8 cm (3 in)

8 cm (3 in)   20 cm (8

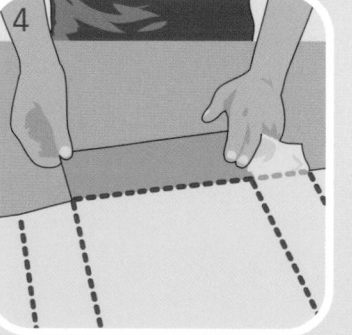
3 Put the comic pages on the template. Trim them.

4 Expose the sticky side and place comics face down.

5 Cover the other side with contact paper. Trim.

6 Fold tabs up and tape.

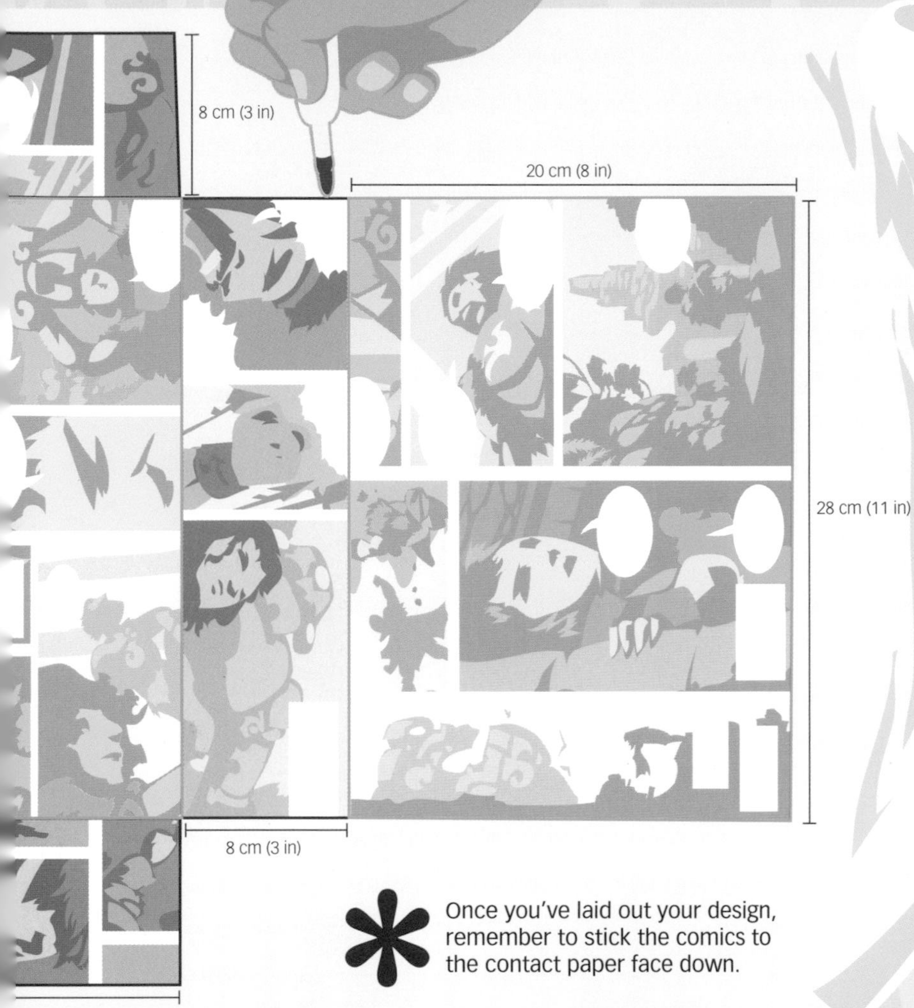

8 cm (3 in)

20 cm (8 in)

28 cm (11 in)

8 cm (3 in)

✳ Once you've laid out your design, remember to stick the comics to the contact paper face down.

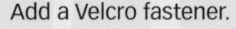

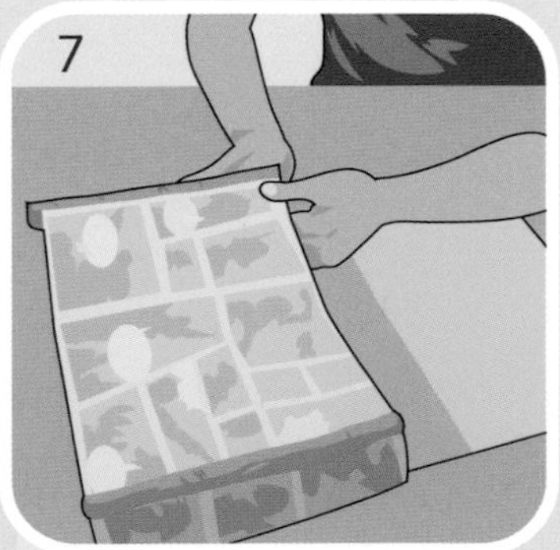

12

Marvel at your new bag!

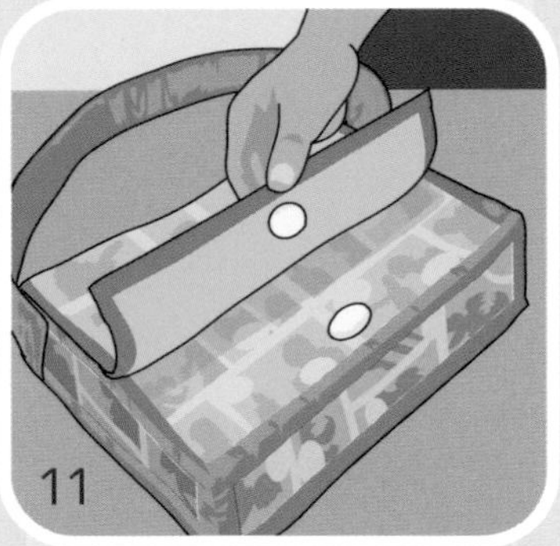

11

Add a Velcro fastener.

7

Reinforce all seams, folds and corners with tape.

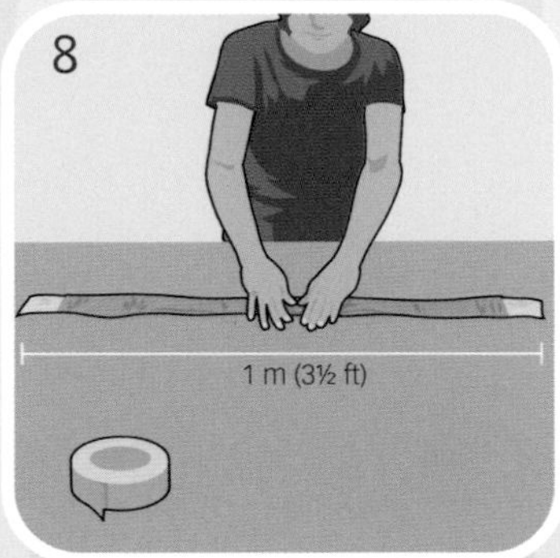

8

1 m (3½ ft)

Make a strap by taping duct-tape strips together.

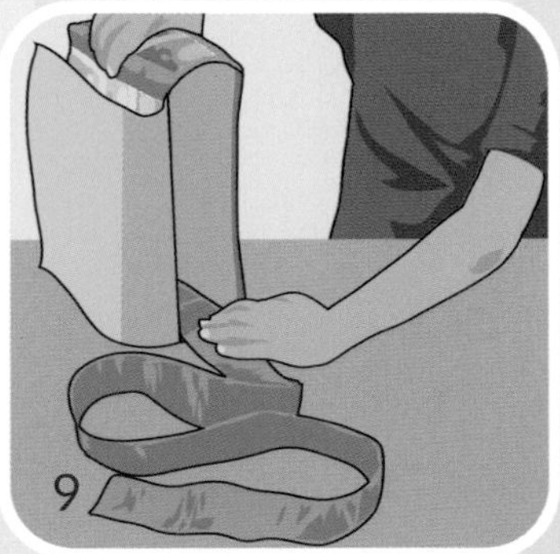

9

Fix the strap inside the bag with tape.

10

Tape the strap to the outside, too.

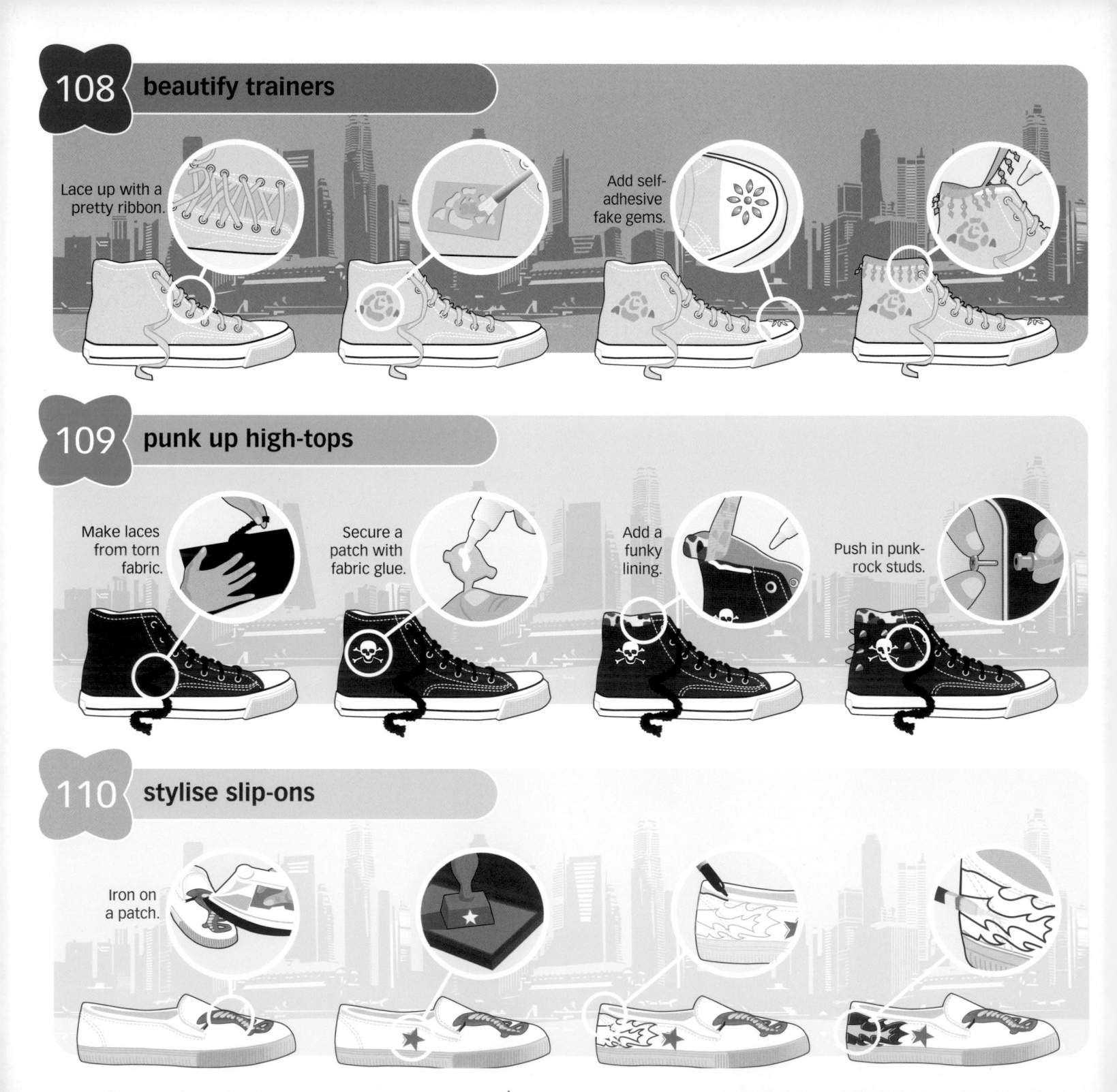

108 beautify trainers

Lace up with a pretty ribbon.

Add self-adhesive fake gems.

109 punk up high-tops

Make laces from torn fabric.

Secure a patch with fabric glue.

Add a funky lining.

Push in punk-rock studs.

110 stylise slip-ons

Iron on a patch.

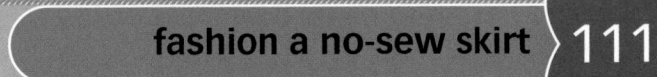

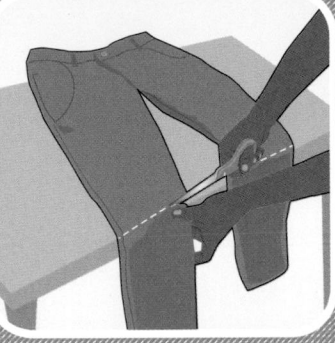

Cut off the legs.

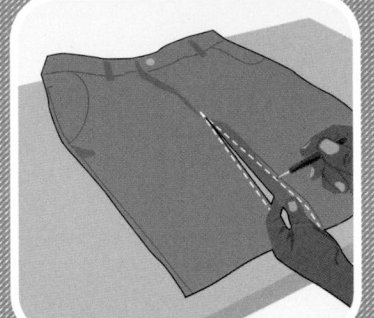

Open up the leg and crotch seams.

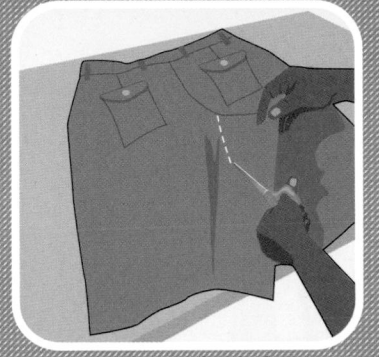

Trim excess fabric from jeans' front and back.

Glue down the back flap.

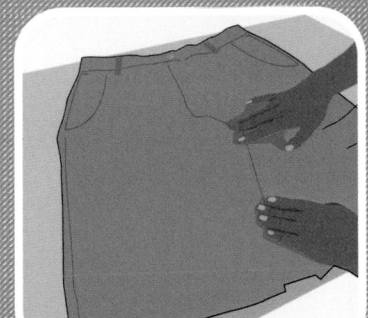

Turn the skirt over and glue down the front flap.

Let the glue dry. Decorate with fabric paint.

1

2

Add glitter to
wet polish.

1

Allow
to dry.

2

1

2

@

3

@

Press onto polish.
Allow to dry.

4

@

@

1

Allow to dry.

2

3

1

Allow
to dry.

2

3

Loop lots of wool
around your forearm.

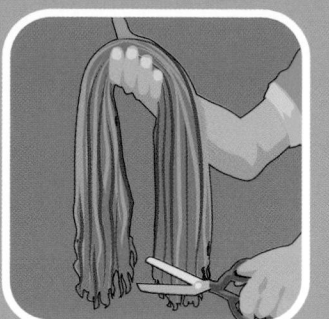

Snip.

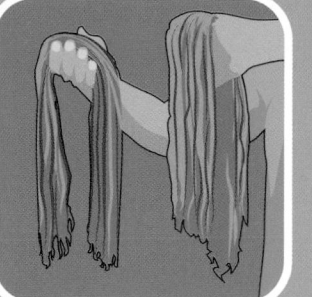

Separate ten to
fifteen strands.

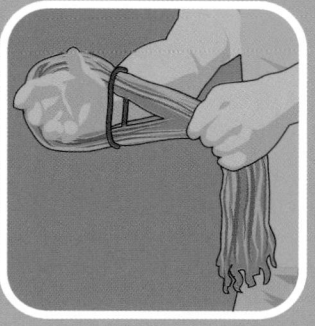

Loop over your wrist.
Slide on a hairband.

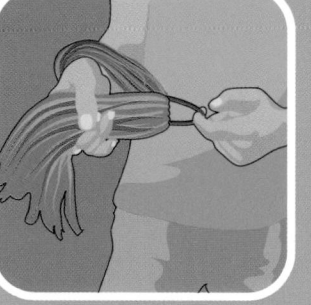

Hold the hairband.
Grab the wool.

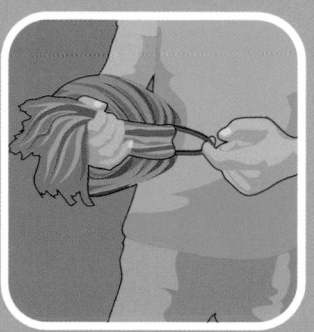

Pull wool through the
loop on your arm.

Ta-da!

Add more wool
as desired.

Use as a funky
hairband.

tracing paper

surgical spirit

Apply clear deodorant.

Place the drawing face down.

Rub with water.

Trace an image.

tell me more

Colour in with permanent ink.

Using surgical spirit, blend for a shaded effect.

115 annoy with a balloon horn

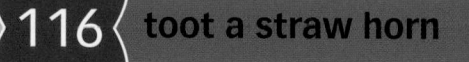
film canister

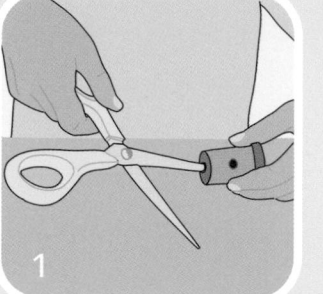

1

Poke a hole in the side and the bottom.

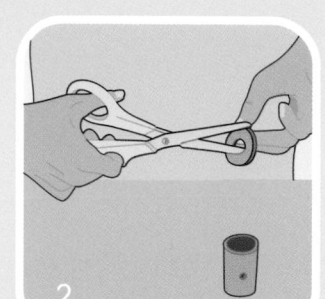

2

Poke a hole in the cap.

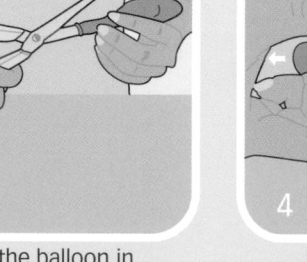

3

Slit the balloon in half along its fold.

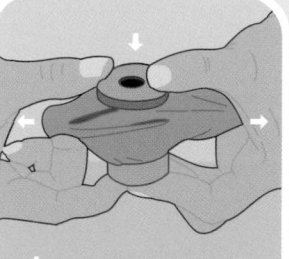

4

Stretch over the canister. Add the cap.

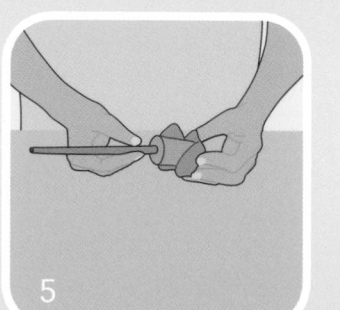

5

Stick the straw into the bottom hole.

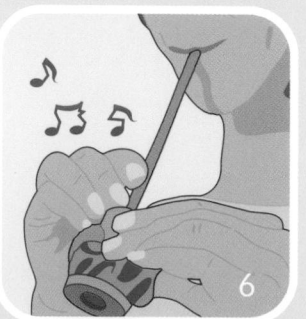

6

Cover part of the side hole and blow.

116 toot a straw horn

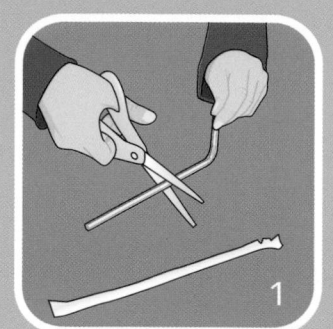

1

Cut a straw in half. Discard the bent end.

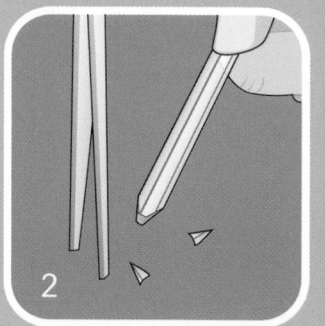

2

Trim the end as shown.

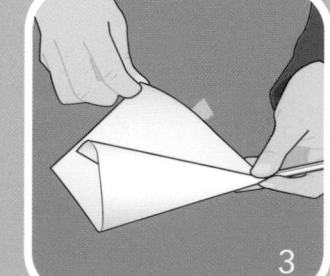

3

Make a paper cone around the straw.

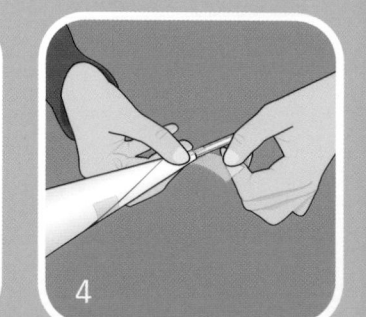

4

Tape the cone and straw together.

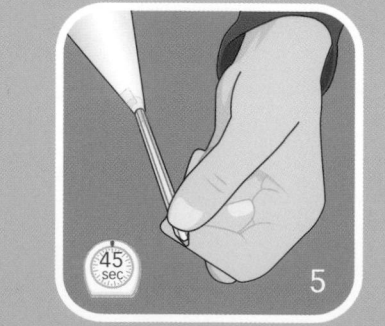

5

Pinch the end of the straw tightly and hold.

6

Place between your lips. Toot away!

 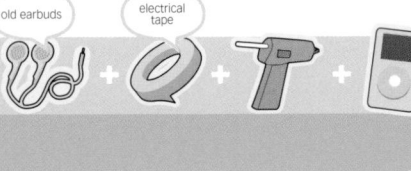
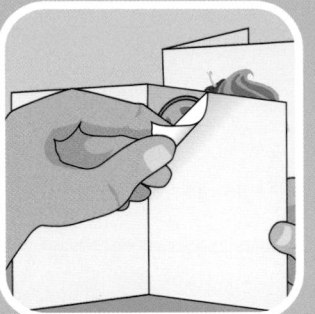

Unfold and flatten the boxes.

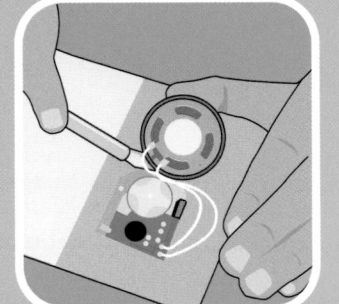

Peel open the greeting cards.

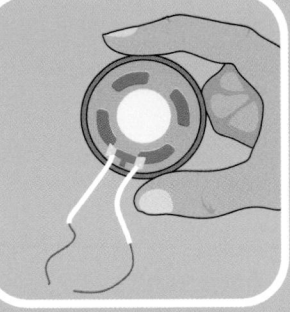

Remove the speaker from each card.

Cut the wires at the circuit board. Strip.

Cut the earbuds off old headphones.

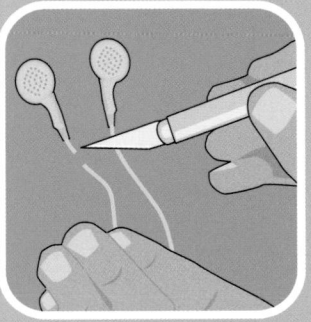

Strip the wires. Cut any fibres from wires.

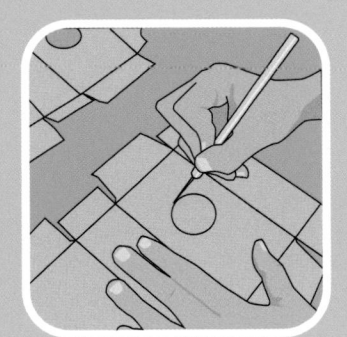

Twist the wires together and tape.

Trace the speaker on the box and cut out.

Cut a hole at the bottom for the wires.

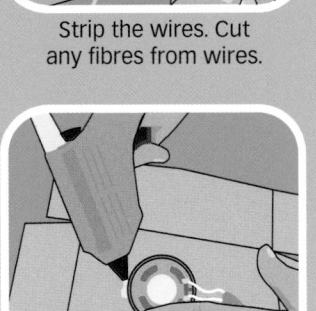

Glue each speaker into its window.

Run the wires out of the holes. Glue shut.

moonwalk in style 213

Plug in and rock out!

transparent film + photo emulsion + framed mesh screen + squeegee + glass + + + + screen-printing ink

Design a graphic.

Copy it onto transparent film.

Turn out the lights. Squeegee emulsion.

Repeat on the other side. Let it dry.

Tape down the transparent film.

Add the glass.

Expose under a 250-watt bulb.

Remove the glass and rinse thoroughly.

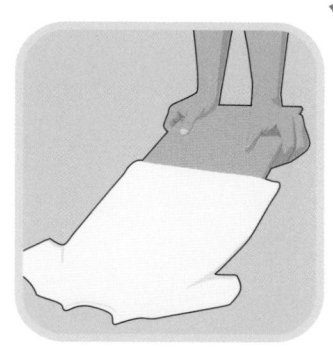
Slide a cardboard 'spacer' into the shirt.

152 dye clothes naturally
Squeegee ink over the design.

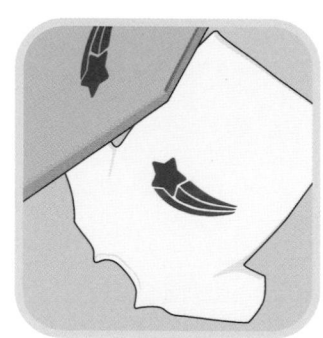
Lift the screen without smudging.

Hang your shirt to dry, you rock star!

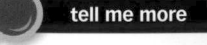
tell me more

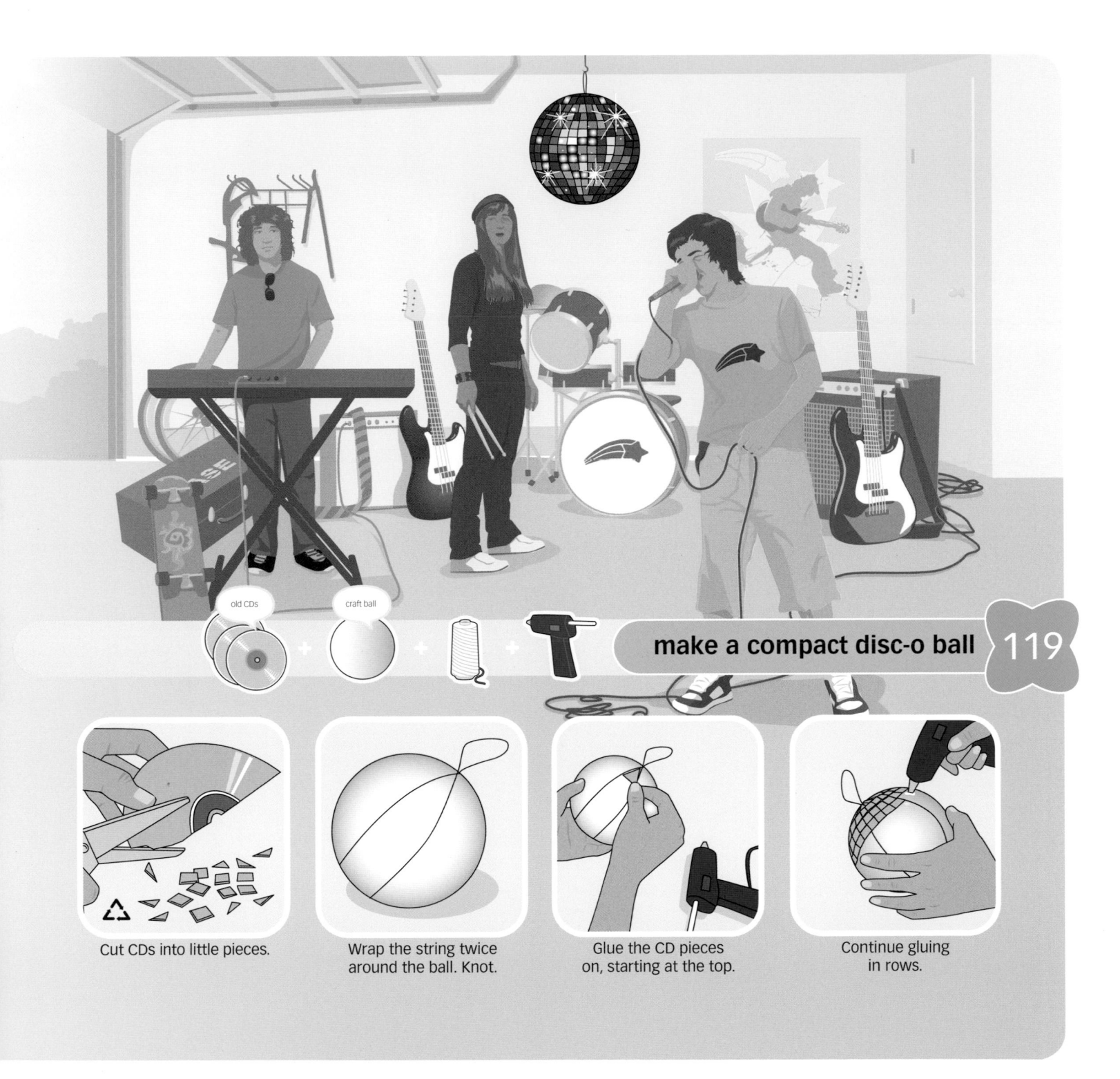

old CDs + craft ball + +

make a compact disc-o ball 119

Cut CDs into little pieces.

Wrap the string twice around the ball. Knot.

Glue the CD pieces on, starting at the top.

Continue gluing in rows.

explore

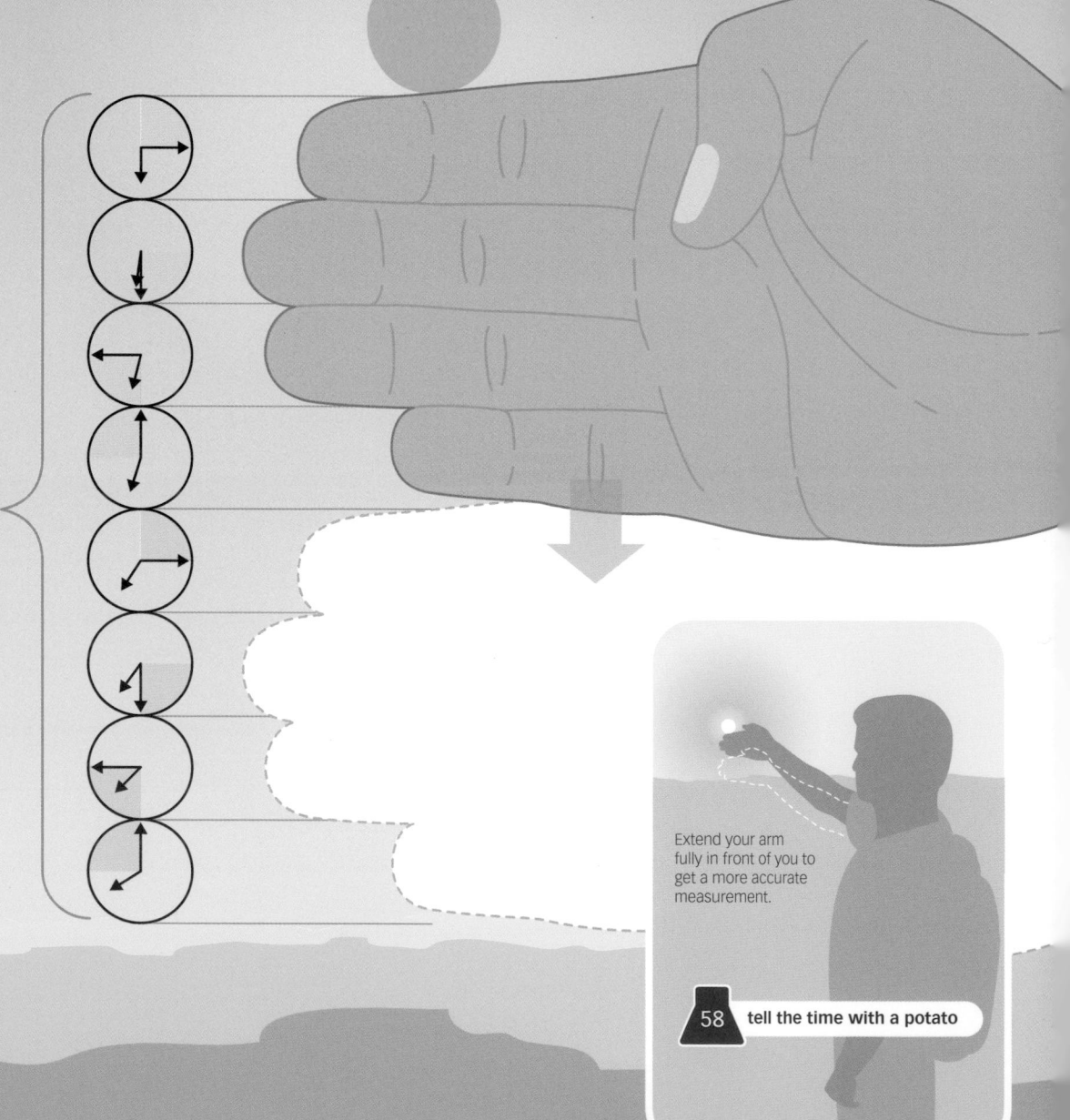

Straighten your arm away from your body and hold your hand just below the sun (don't look right at the sun!). Now count the fingers between the sun and the horizon. Each finger stands for about fifteen minutes (so each hand represents one hour). The closer you are to the Earth's poles, the less accurate this trick will be.

Extend your arm fully in front of you to get a more accurate measurement.

58 tell the time with a potato

121 set up a solar compass

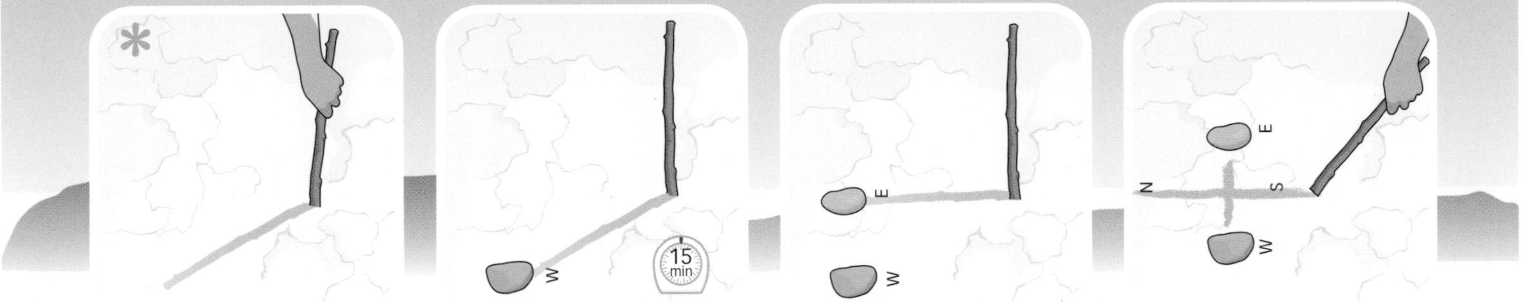

Place a tall, straight stick in the ground.

Mark the end of the shadow. Wait.

Mark the new end of the shadow.

Connect the marks, then make a cross.

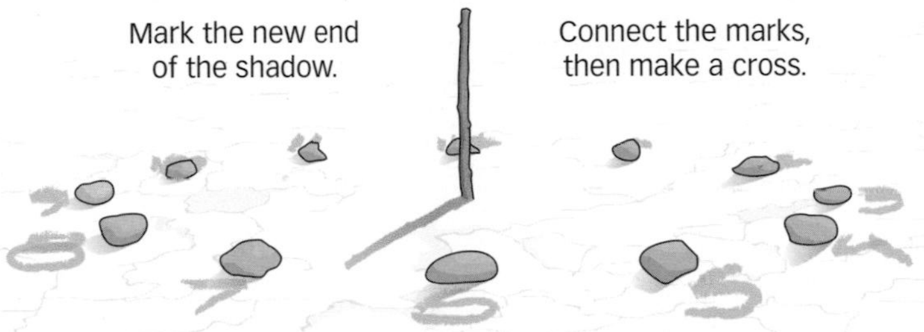

This compass is more accurate the closer you are to the equator and the equinoxes. Once you've set it up, you can mark the end of the stick's shadow every hour to make a sundial.

122 make a magnetic compass

The needle will align along the north-south axis. You'll have to use other clues, like the sun's position in the sky, to tell which end of the needle points north.

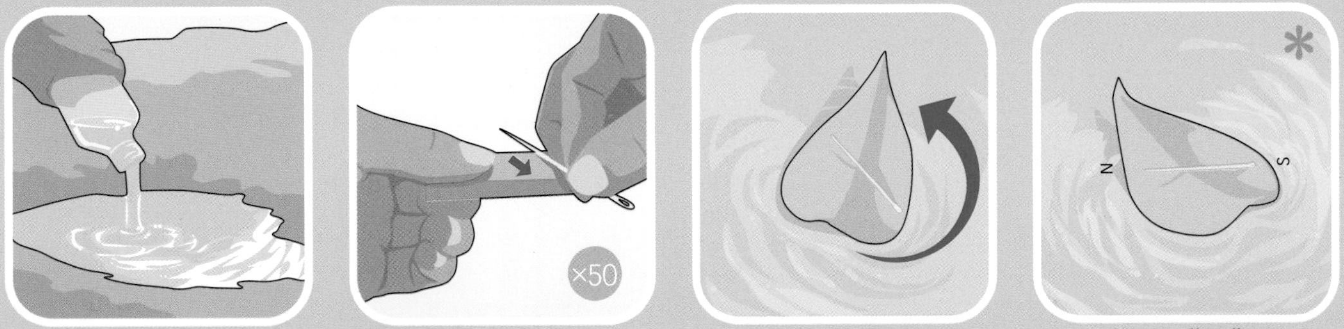

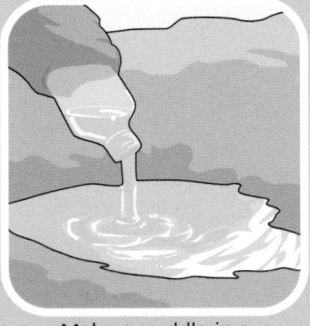

Make a puddle in a sheltered place.

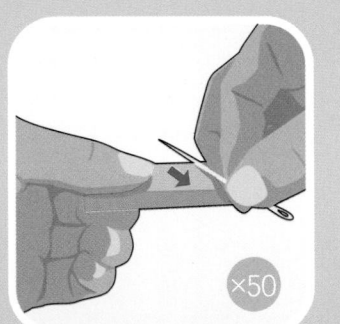

Rub a needle against a magnet.

Put the needle on a leaf in the puddle.

The needle aligns with the poles.

tell me more

locate the north star

First, locate the Plough (also known as the Big Dipper). Imagine a line between the two stars on the right-hand side of the Plough. Extend that line five times, and you'll hit Polaris, the North Star.

polaris
(north star)

ursa major

ursa minor

plough
(big dipper)

When you're in the Northern Hemisphere, finding the North Star is the handiest way to orient yourself at night.

spot pictures in the moon

The dark patches you see on the moon are ancient basins filled with hardened lava, or basalt. It's easy for us to see shapes in these basins which led to the moon myths and stories many cultures have told for thousands of years.

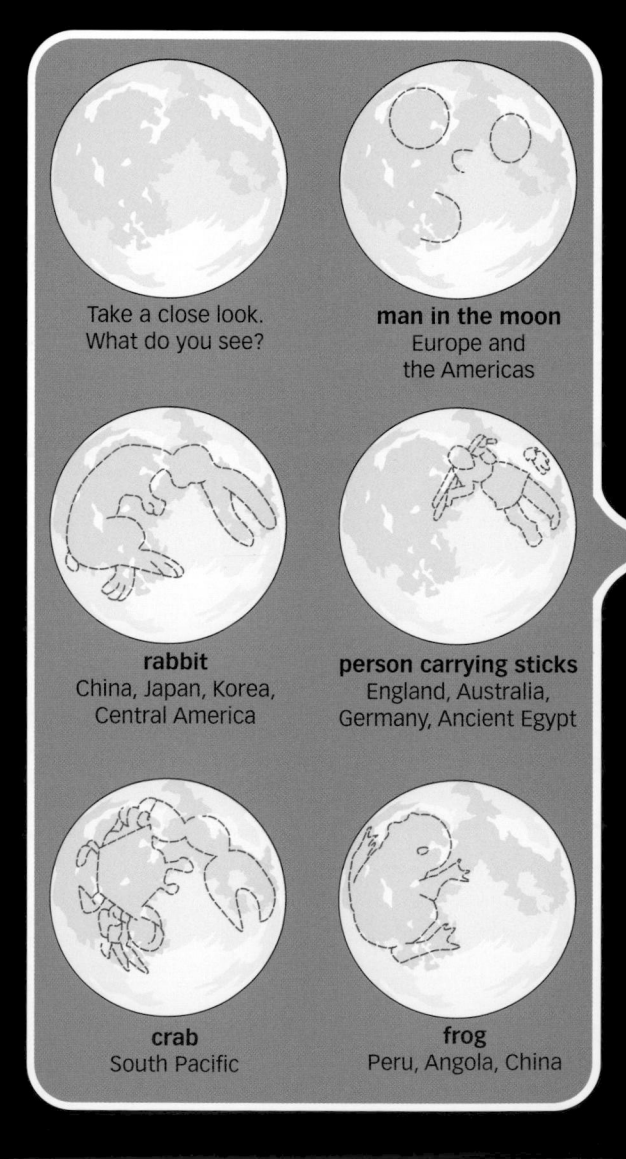

Take a close look. What do you see?

man in the moon
Europe and the Americas

rabbit
China, Japan, Korea, Central America

person carrying sticks
England, Australia, Germany, Ancient Egypt

crab
South Pacific

frog
Peru, Angola, China

The moon doesn't rotate as it circles the Earth, and the same part of the moon is always facing the sun. But we see different moon phases because we see the moon's bright face from a different angle each night.

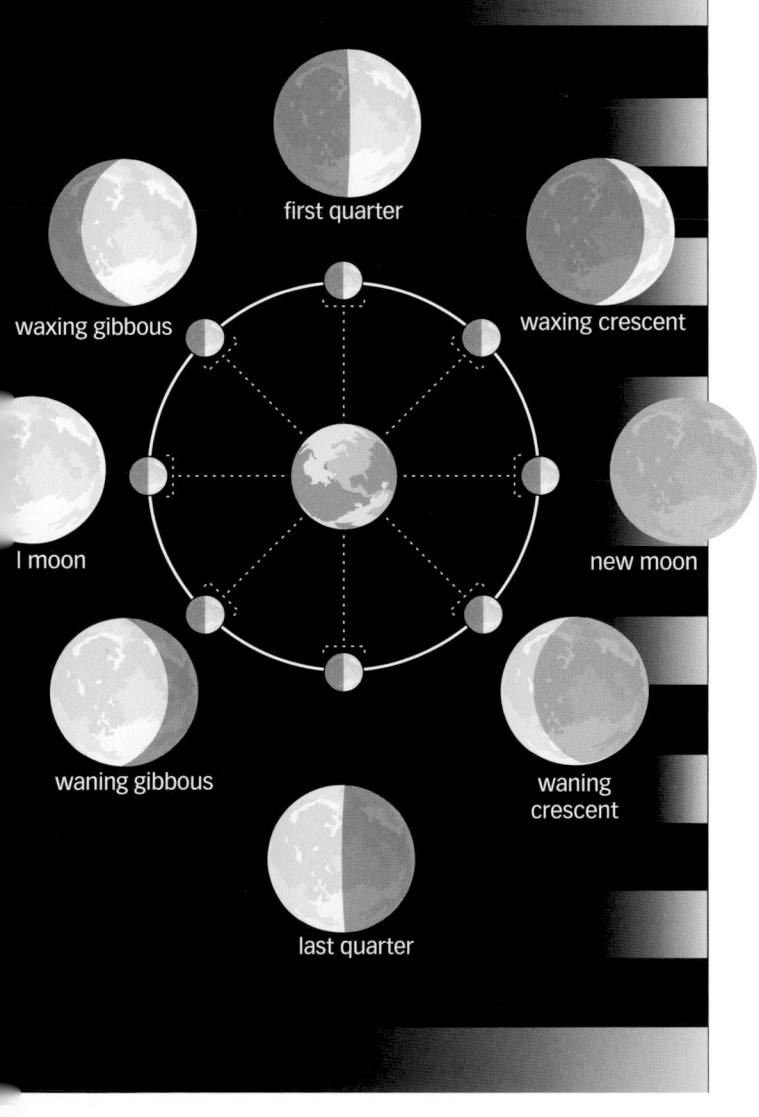

first quarter

waxing crescent

waxing gibbous

l moon

new moon

waning gibbous

waning crescent

last quarter

Want to find your way to the South Pole when you're in the Southern Hemisphere? Here's how!

rigil kent

hadar

southern cross (crux)

south pole

First, find the Southern Cross. Imagine a line down the long part of the cross, and lengthen that line four and a half times. Then find the bright stars Rigil Kent and Hadar just to the left of the Cross. Locate the point halfway between these two, and imagine a line from there to the end of the Southern Cross line. Bingo!

construct a lean-to shelter

1 Find a tree with a low branch.

2 Use a sturdy branch as a roof beam.

3 Lean smaller branches on the beam.

4 Cover the branches with leaves.

5 Make a warm floor with grass, leaves or pine needles.

*If you'd like to drink your found water, be sure to boil it first – which will kill off all the nasty germs.

Tie a towel below your knee.

tell me more

Cut a small hole.

2 hr

Flip the cup as you remove it.

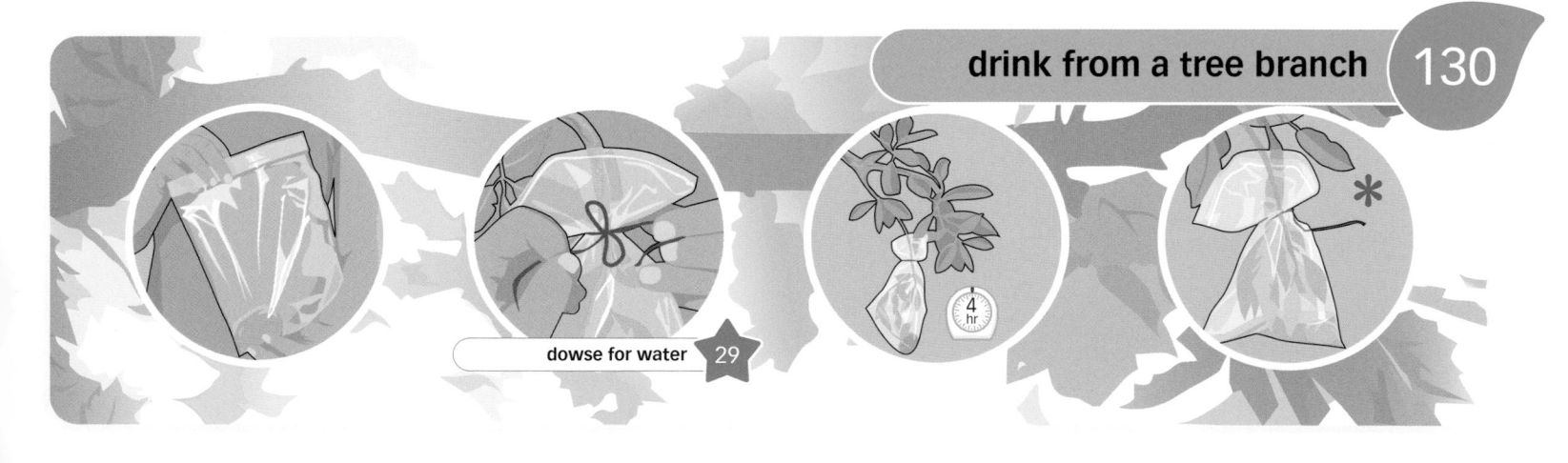

dowse for water 29

4 hr

tell me more

cumulonimbus

altocumulus

cirrostratus

cirrus

cirrocumulus

6 km
(4 mi)

10 km
(6 mi)

11 km
(7 mi)

Many cultures believe that nature gives clues that it's about to rain. Watch for these signs from around the world, and you may never get caught in a surprise shower again!

The weather vane spins around twice.

Spiders leave their webs.

nimbostratus

stratocumulus

stratus

cumulus

contrail

184 concoct chocolate anthills

Ants move their eggs to higher ground.

Cats wash behind their ears.

Doors and windows are hard to open.

Crows fly low to the ground.

Cows lie down.

Tree leaves turn over.

Grass is dry in the morning.

3 km (2 mi)

0 km (0 mi)

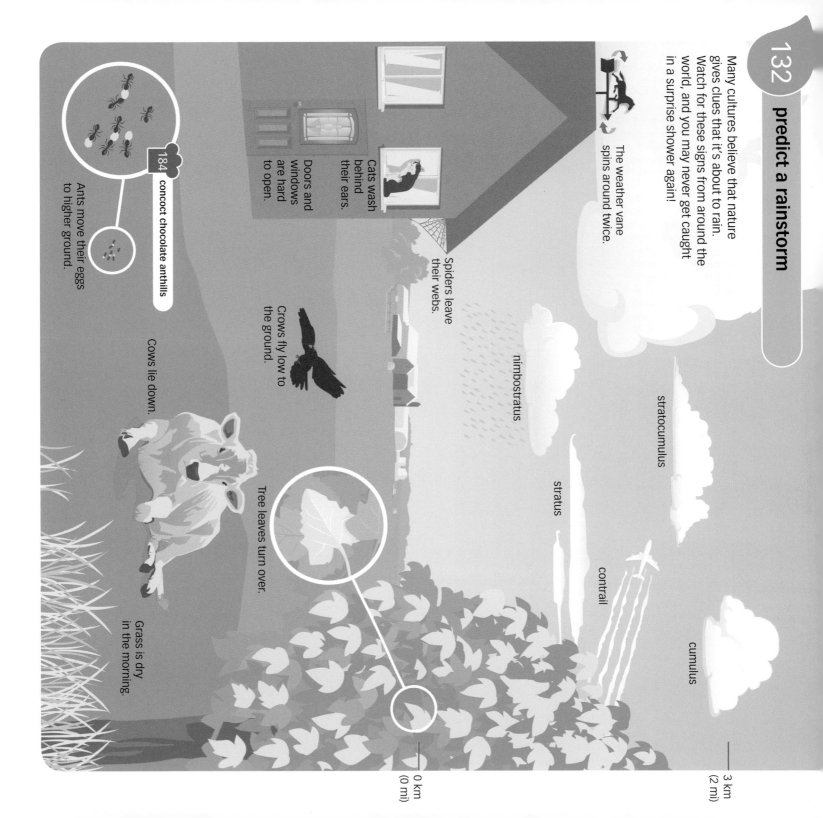

blaze a trail

Time to lay a trail! Make these simple symbols with straw, sticks or stones so that your friends can follow your path. Just remember: The last person down the path should take down the signs.

not the way

turn left

danger

tube-like with tapered ends

teardrop-shaped

pellets with bone and hair

birds of prey

cat family

tell me more

turn right

head this way

identify droppings and tracks 134

When you're out hiking, look for animal prints and droppings. Then use this guide to work out what animals have been in your neck of the woods.

oval with a
pointed end

small, circular
pellets

looks like
pencil lead

dog family

deer family

rabbit family

rodents

learn dog body language

raised fur

hunched posture

bared teeth

aggressive

tucked-in tail

scared

turned head

exposed belly

relaxed

licking and sniffing

greeting

lowered tail

open mouth

playful

lowered front end

greet a new dog

May I stroke your dog?

Check with the owner first.

Approach slowly from the front.

Let the dog sniff your fist.

Stroke the dog under the chin first.

raised tail

forward ears

flattened ears

alert

annoyed

twitching tail

exposed belly

narrowed pupils

bristling fur

swishing tail

happy

blinking eyes

attacking

scared

crouching

draw a cat 101

Put some baby food on your fingers.

Gently dab it on his nose.

Let him get a good taste.

He'll soon be all yours!

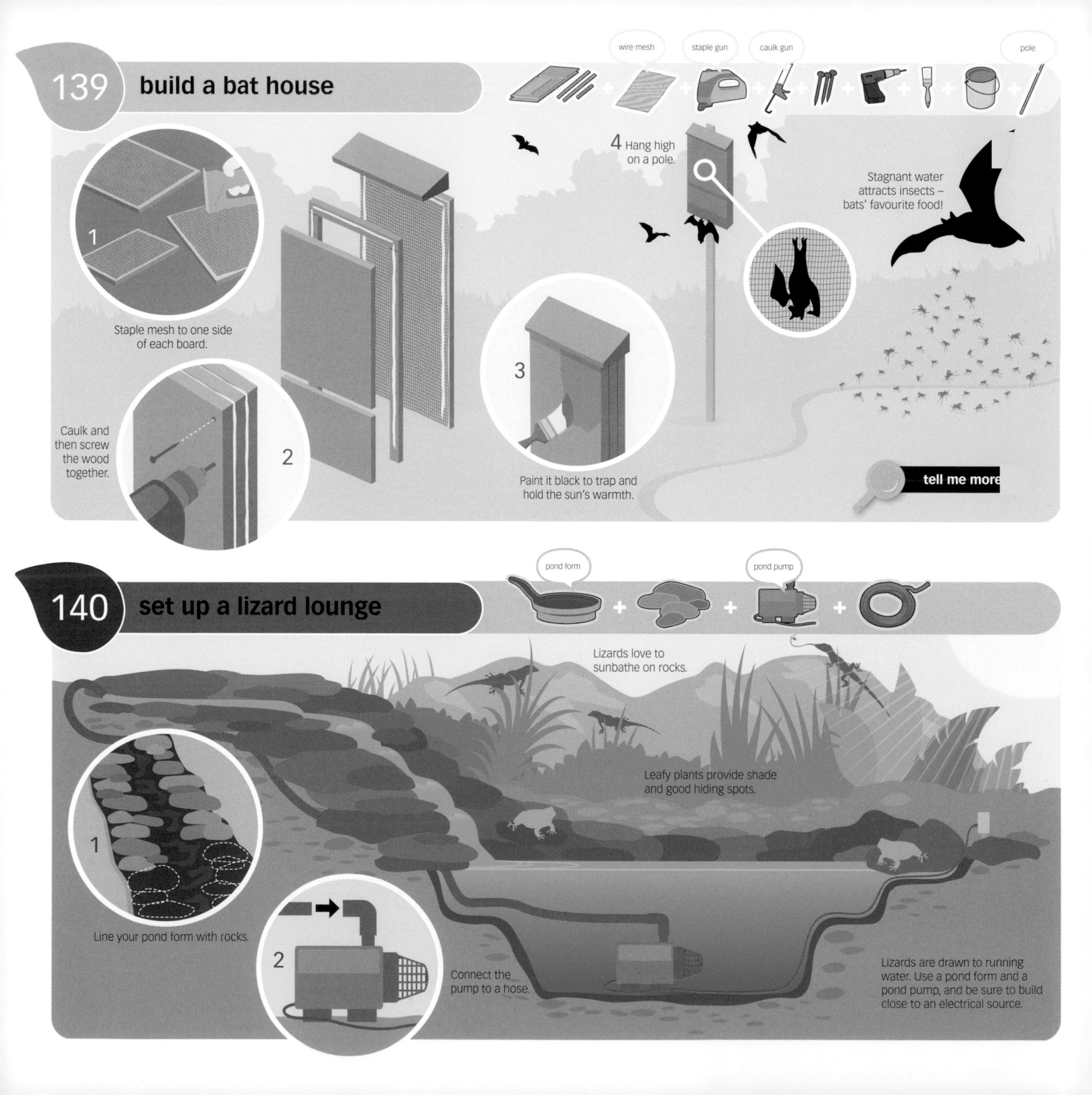

139 build a bat house

wire mesh + staple gun + caulk gun + pole

1 Staple mesh to one side of each board.

2 Caulk and then screw the wood together.

3 Paint it black to trap and hold the sun's warmth.

4 Hang high on a pole.

Stagnant water attracts insects – bats' favourite food!

tell me more

140 set up a lizard lounge

pond form + pond pump

Lizards love to sunbathe on rocks.

Leafy plants provide shade and good hiding spots.

1 Line your pond form with rocks.

2 Connect the pump to a hose.

Lizards are drawn to running water. Use a pond form and a pond pump, and be sure to build close to an electrical source.

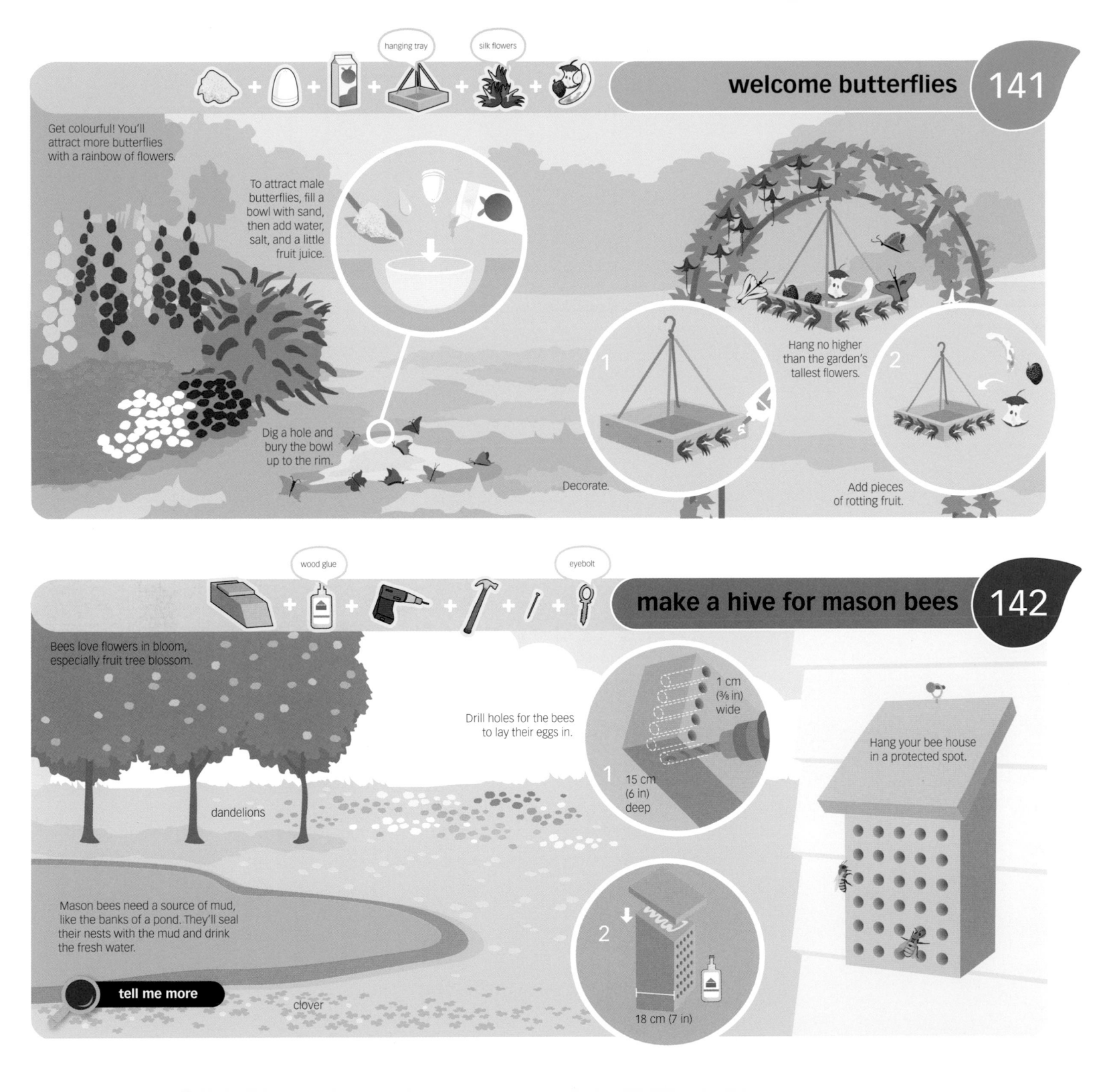

hanging tray

silk flowers

Get colourful! You'll attract more butterflies with a rainbow of flowers.

To attract male butterflies, fill a bowl with sand, then add water, salt, and a little fruit juice.

Dig a hole and bury the bowl up to the rim.

Hang no higher than the garden's tallest flowers.

1 Decorate.

2 Add pieces of rotting fruit.

wood glue

eyebolt

Bees love flowers in bloom, especially fruit tree blossom.

dandelions

Mason bees need a source of mud, like the banks of a pond. They'll seal their nests with the mud and drink the fresh water.

tell me more

clover

Drill holes for the bees to lay their eggs in.

1 cm (3/8 in) wide

15 cm (6 in) deep

1

2 18 cm (7 in)

Hang your bee house in a protected spot.

143 raise a butterfly

212 do the worm

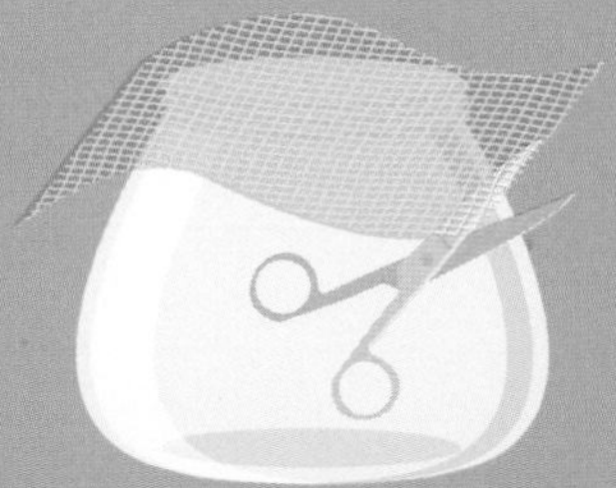

1 Trim mesh to fit over a jar.

2 Catch a caterpillar.

3 Add leaves from the plant she was on.

144 start an ant farm

1 Find two nesting jars. Poke holes in the big lid.

2 Find an ant hill and locate the queen. Avoid biting ants!

3 Funnel soil and worker ants into the large jar.

4 Add the queen and her eggs last.

4 Add fresh leaves and clean jar daily.

5 Spritz according to your guide and wait.

✻ You'll need a good field guide to help you identify your fuzzy friend, as well as tell you what she wants for breakfast, how damp she likes her jar and when she'll be ready to fly away.

6 Add fresh flowers and an orange slice.

7 Release her where you found her.

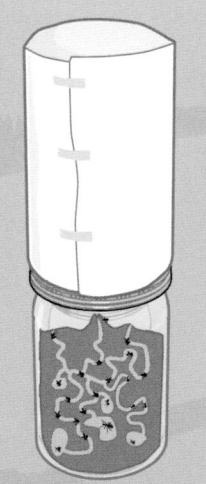

5 Soak a cotton-wool ball in water, and bread crumbs in honey.

6 Feed your new pets every ten days.

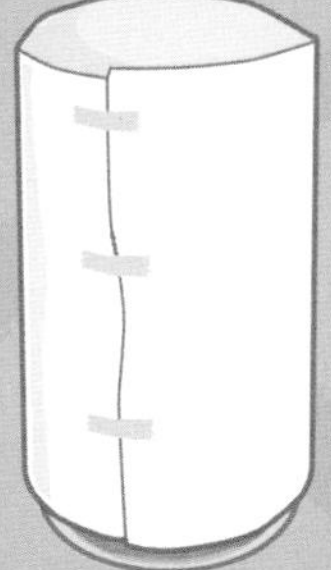

7 Cover. The ants will think they're underground and make tunnels.

8 Lift the paper to check out the ant-farm action, then re-cover.

spy on sea life

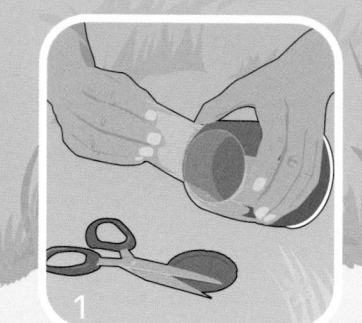

Cut the bottom off a cup. Tape the edges.

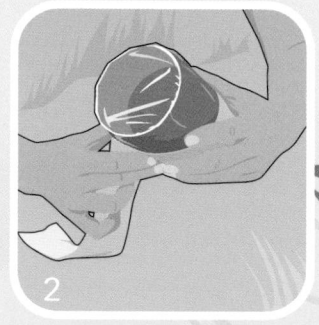

Tape plastic food wrap over the mouth.

If you want to see what's going on in deeper water, build the viewer with a PVC pipe instead of a cup.

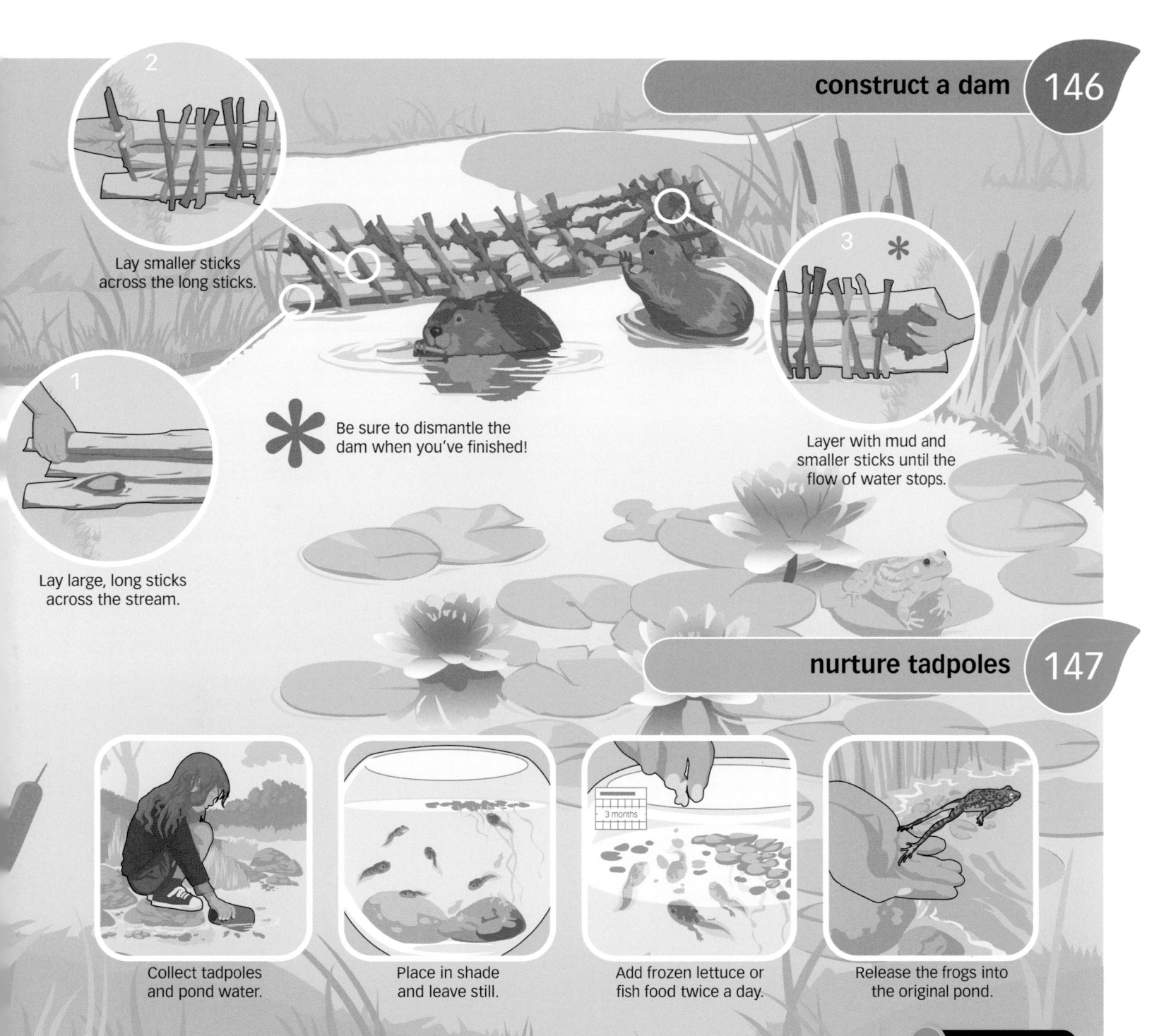

Lay smaller sticks across the long sticks.

3 *

Lay large, long sticks across the stream.

* Be sure to dismantle the dam when you've finished!

Layer with mud and smaller sticks until the flow of water stops.

Collect tadpoles and pond water.

Place in shade and leave still.

3 months

Add frozen lettuce or fish food twice a day.

Release the frogs into the original pond.

tell me more

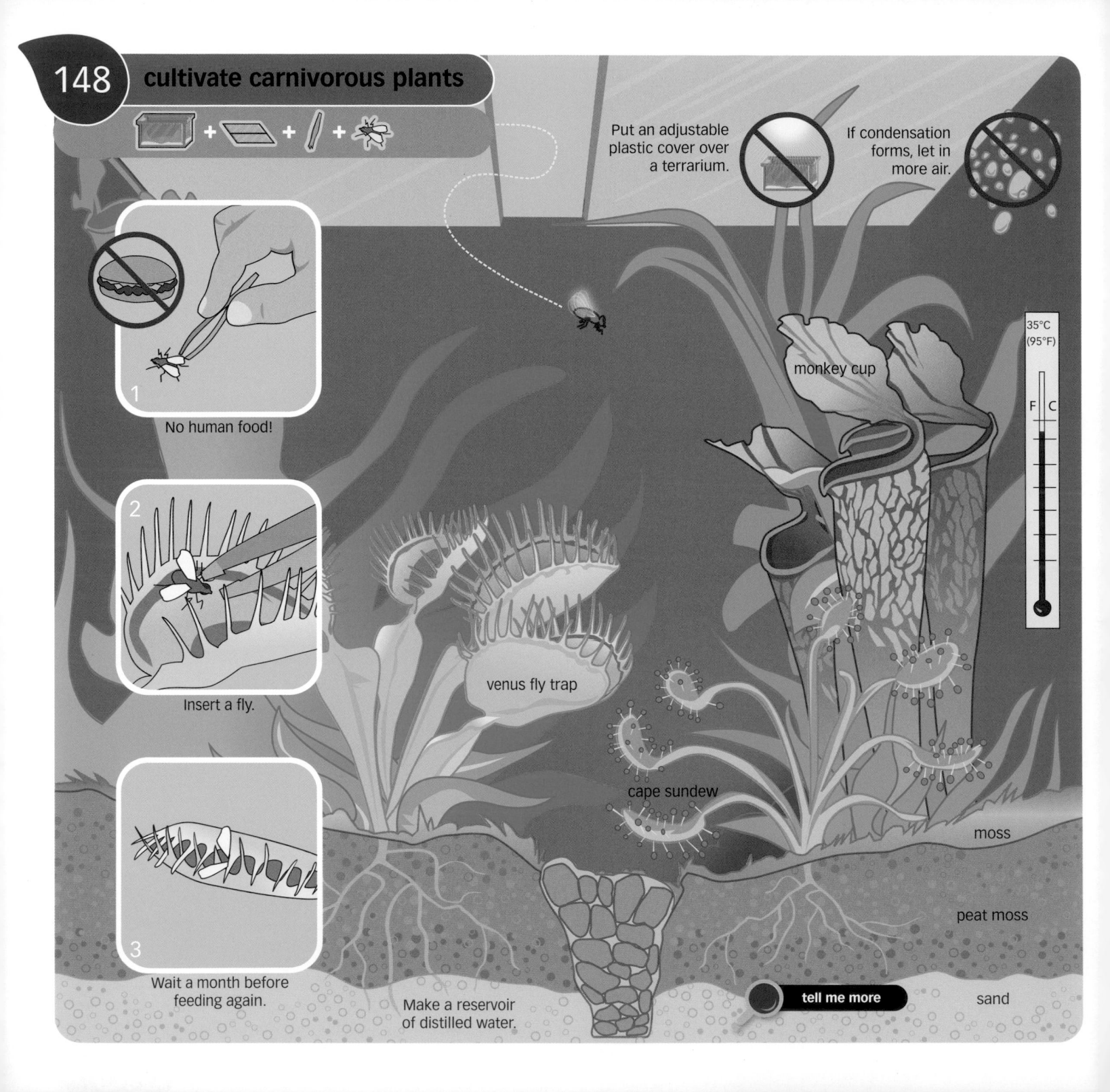

1 No human food!

2 Insert a fly.

3 Wait a month before feeding again.

Put an adjustable plastic cover over a terrarium.

If condensation forms, let in more air.

monkey cup

35°C (95°F)

F C

venus fly trap

cape sundew

moss

peat moss

Make a reservoir of distilled water.

tell me more

sand

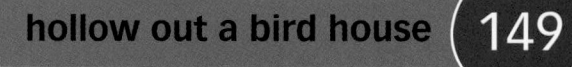 

wood glue · clothes line

1. Give your gourd a good scrub.

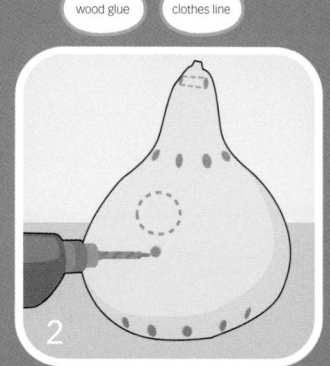

2. Drill holes. Cut a high entrance.

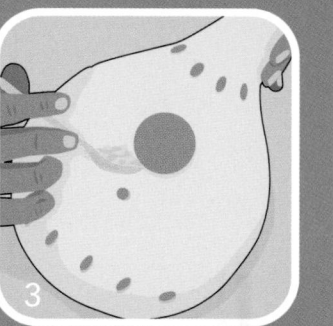

3. Scoop out the insides.

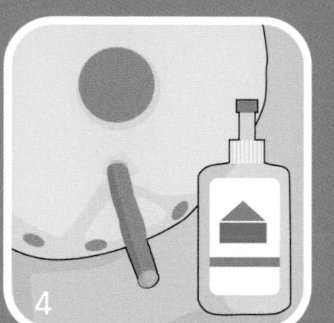

4. Glue a perch in place.

5. Thread a piece of clothes line.

6. Hang up in early spring.

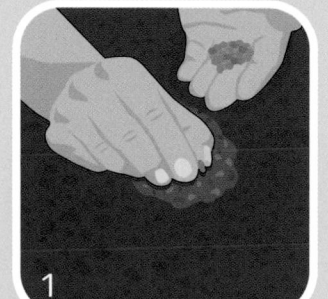

1. Plant the melon seeds.

2. Water regularly.

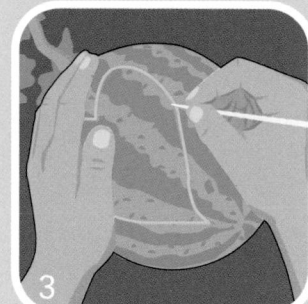

3. Etch lines with a wooden skewer.

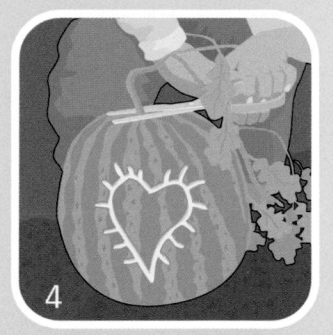

4. The melon will heal, revealing your art!

Pluck some pretty flowers, stem and all.

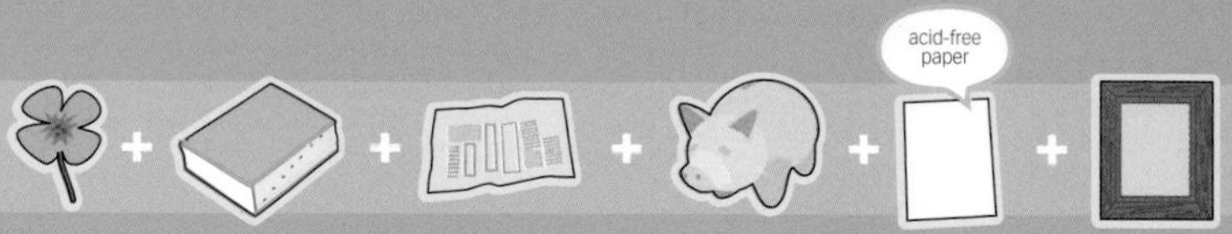

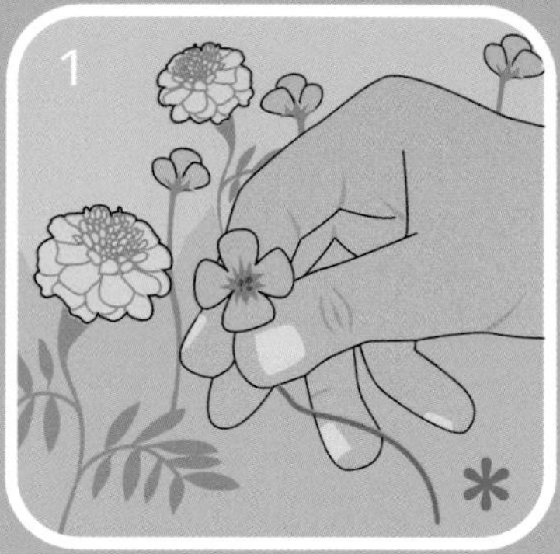

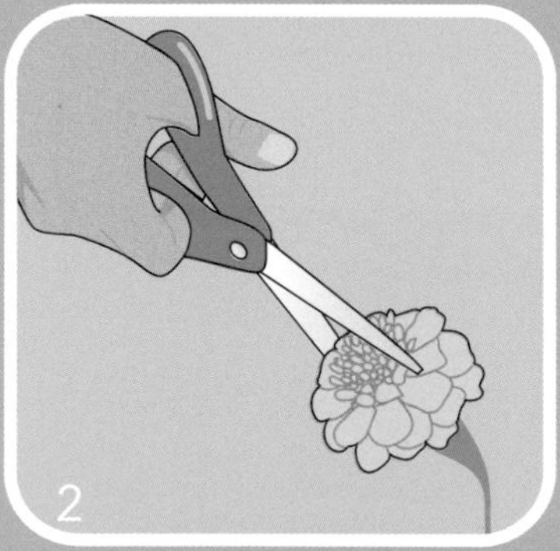

Slice thicker flowers in half.

If you want to preserve your bouquets but keep them looking full, hang them upside down to dry.

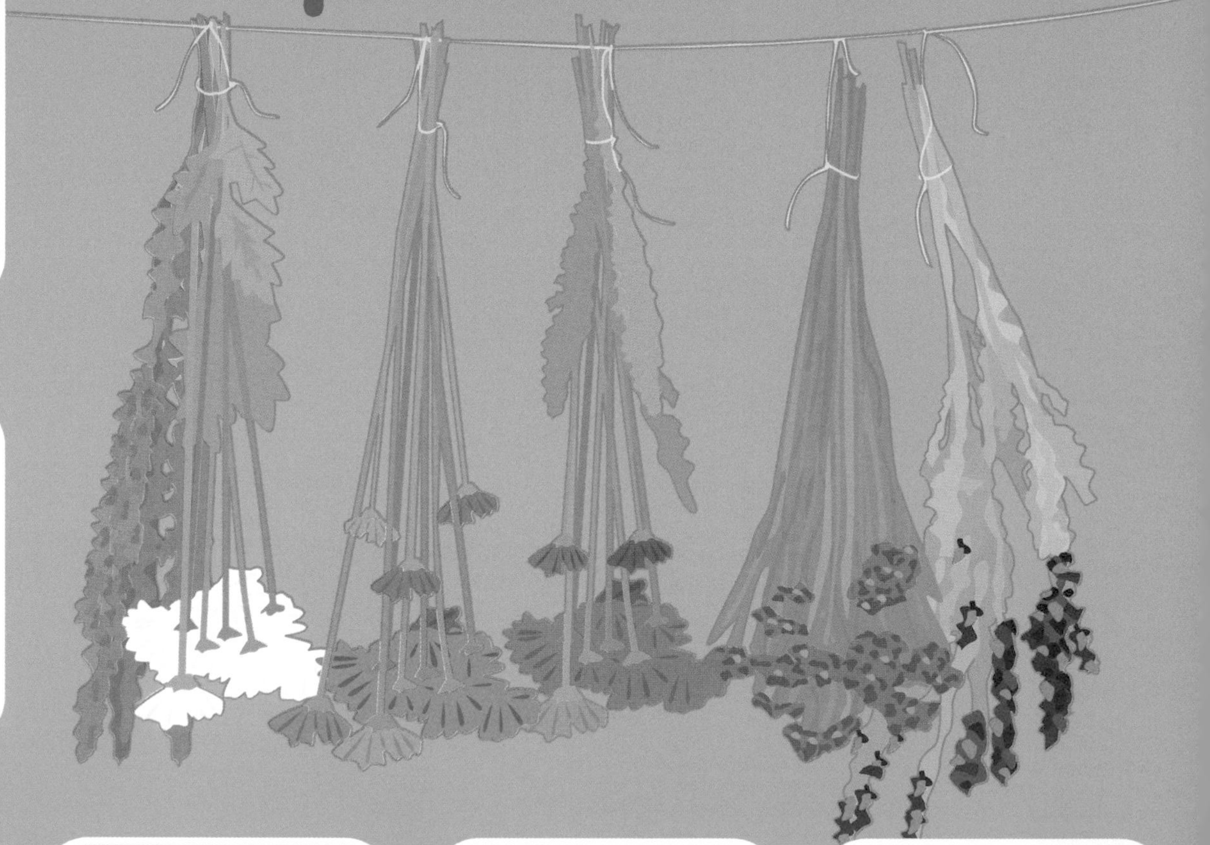

3 Place on newspaper in a heavy book.

4 Carefully fold the newspaper.

5 Close the book and add a weight. Wait!

6 Arrange on acid-free paper and frame.

acid-free paper

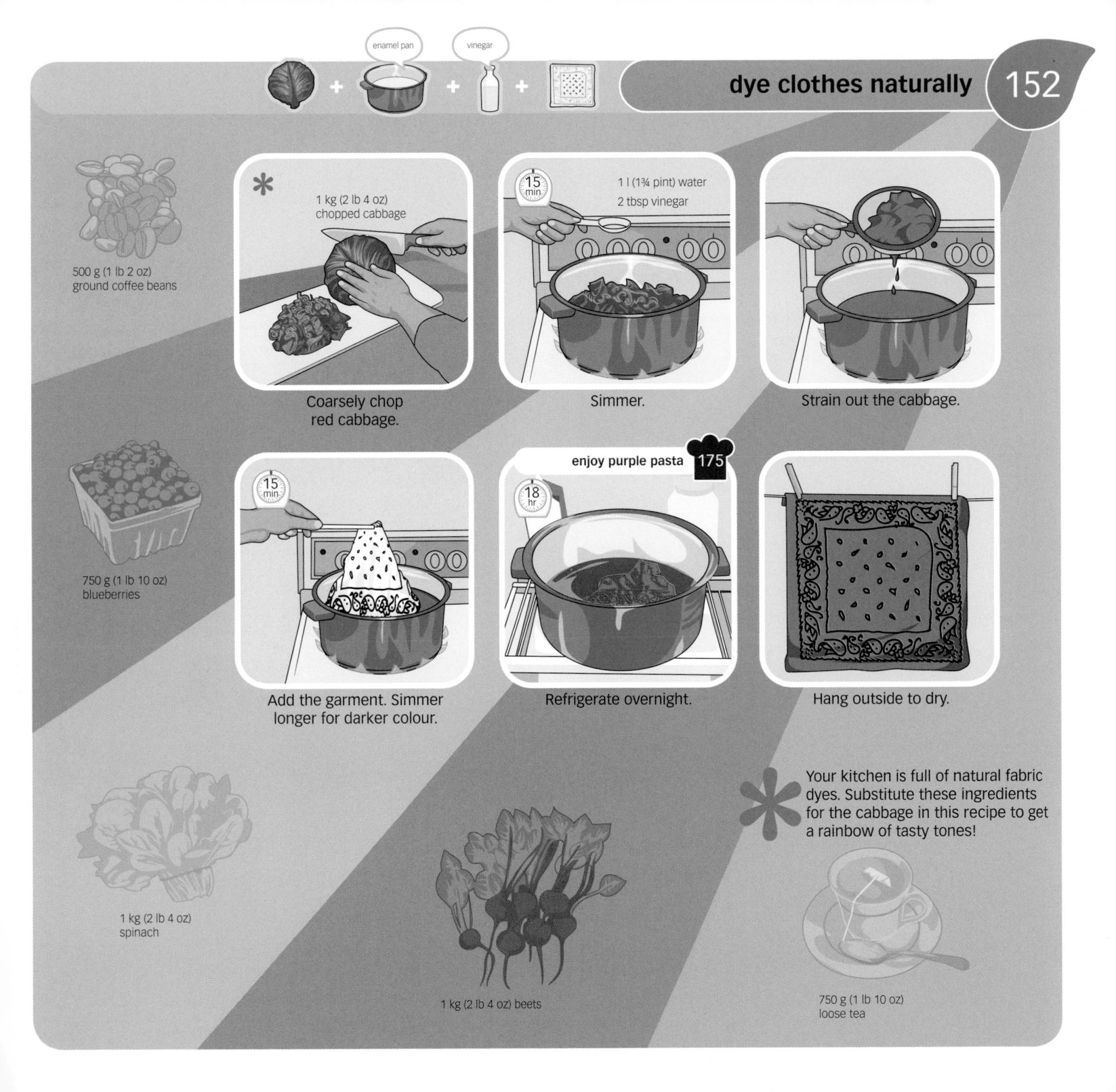

enamel pan

vinegar

500 g (1 lb 2 oz)
ground coffee beans

750 g (1 lb 10 oz)
blueberries

*

1 kg (2 lb 4 oz)
chopped cabbage

Coarsely chop
red cabbage.

15 min

1 l (1¾ pint) water
2 tbsp vinegar

Simmer.

Strain out the cabbage.

15 min

Add the garment. Simmer
longer for darker colour.

enjoy purple pasta 175

18 hr

Refrigerate overnight.

Hang outside to dry.

1 kg (2 lb 4 oz)
spinach

1 kg (2 lb 4 oz) beets

* Your kitchen is full of natural fabric
dyes. Substitute these ingredients
for the cabbage in this recipe to get
a rainbow of tasty tones!

750 g (1 lb 10 oz)
loose tea

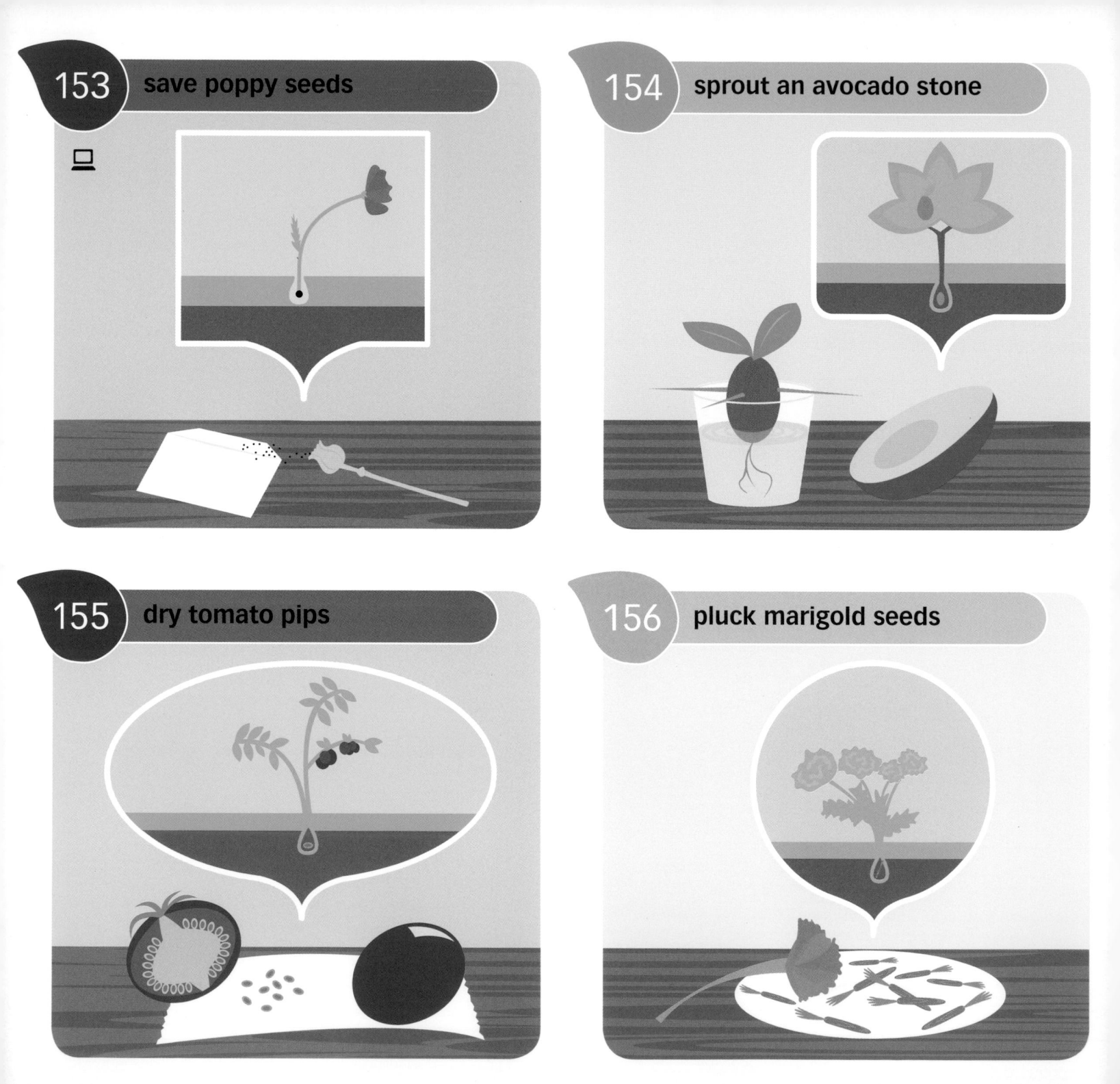

153 save poppy seeds

154 sprout an avocado stone

155 dry tomato pips

156 pluck marigold seeds

wire mesh

Shred paper.

Fill a blender with equal
parts paper and water.

Blend at low speed
until you have pulp.

Carefully stir in seeds.

Roll the pulp onto
the mesh screen.

Turn on a fan to make the
paper dry more quickly.

Gently peel off
the dry paper.

Why not send a plantable
greetings card?

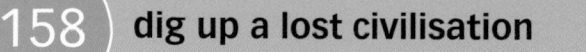

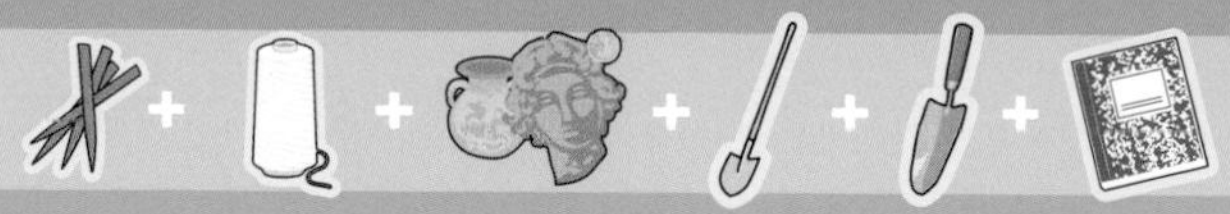

Choose (or invent!) a lost civilisation and bury objects in your garden that the society would have used. Then invite some friends to dig up your artefacts and piece together the life of your lost city, just like real archaeologists do!

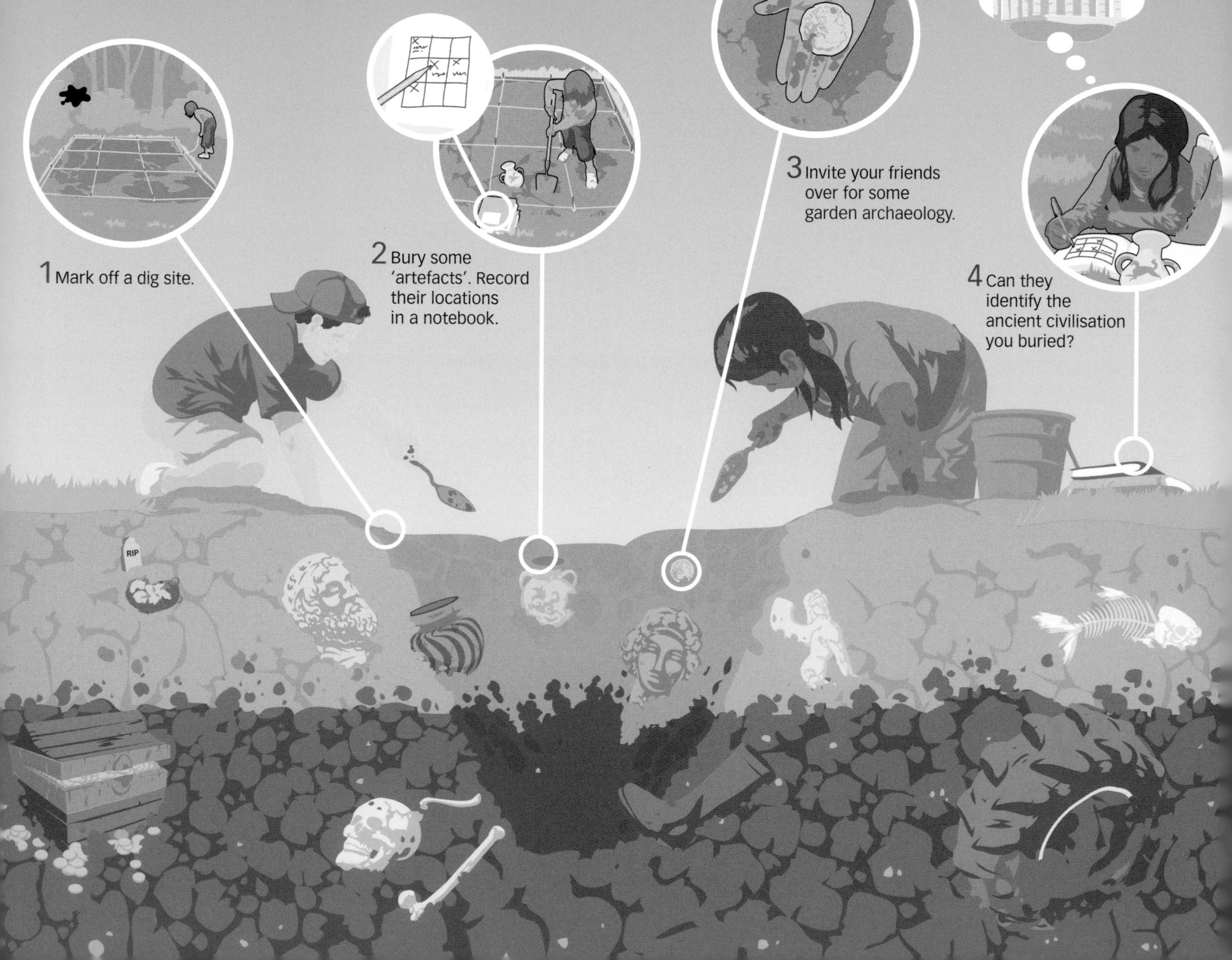

1 Mark off a dig site.

2 Bury some 'artefacts'. Record their locations in a notebook.

3 Invite your friends over for some garden archaeology.

4 Can they identify the ancient civilisation you buried?

RIP

plaster

Pick an area with
lots of foot traffic.

Prepare the plaster as
the package instructs.

Carefully fill
a footprint.

Let the plaster set
and then remove.

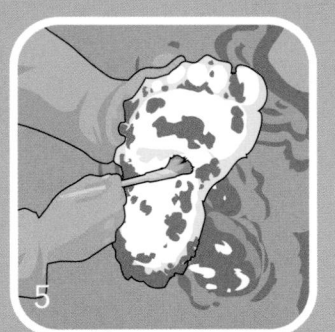
Brush off your fossil.

Try to work out
who made it!

160 roll sweet sushi

Use your favorite fruit jelly (and your imagination) to make your own sweet sushi. Fruit leather makes yummy nori, and gummy fish are great in nigiri. Keep it healthy with dried fruit stuffings (such as golden raisins or apricots), and get gooey with crisped rice treats for the rice rolls.

172 make chewy fruit leather

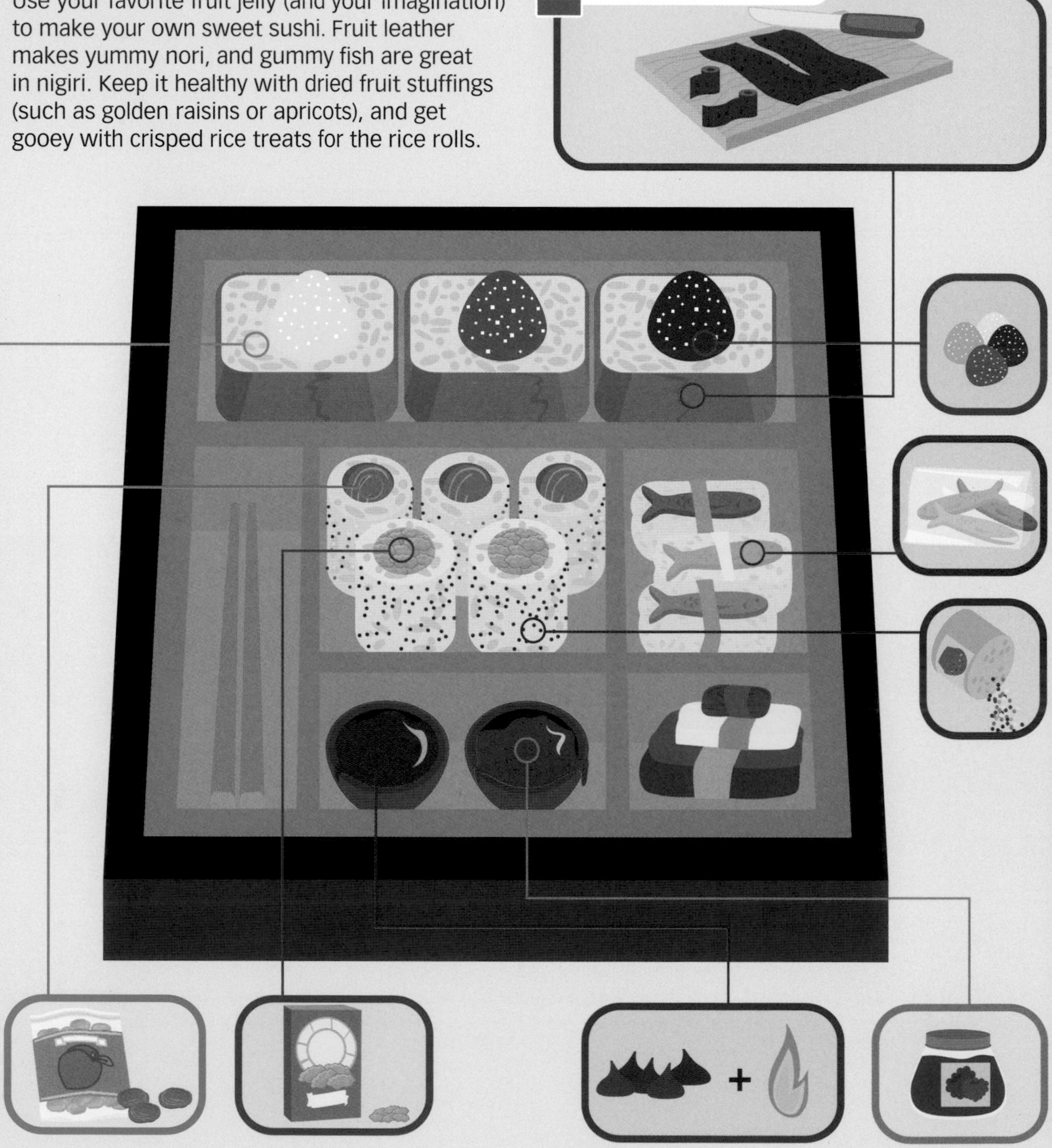

20 large marshmallows

3 tbsp butter

1

Melt together on medium-low heat.

2 700 g (1lb 9 oz) rice cereal

Stir in crisped rice cereal.

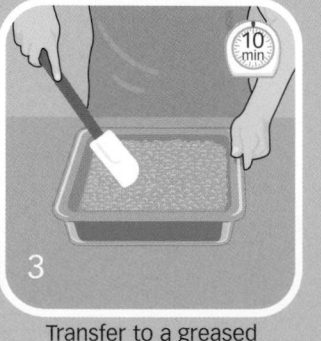

10 min

3

Transfer to a greased tin to cool.

golden syrup + + paper towel-wrapped fork + cooking thermometer + + vanilla extract + + waxed paper

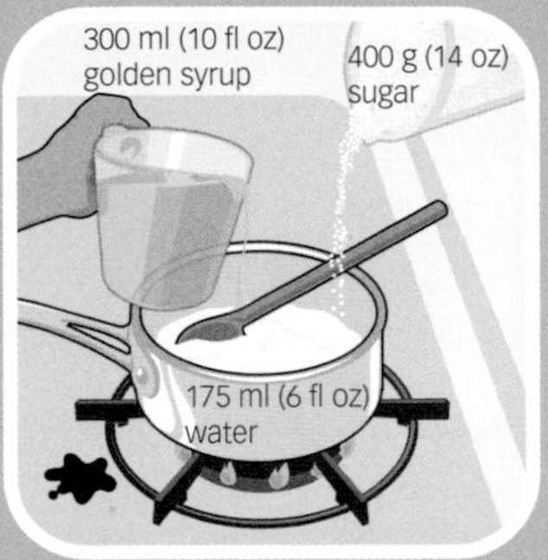

Stir over low heat until sugar dissolves.
- 300 ml (10 fl oz) golden syrup
- 400 g (14 oz) sugar
- 175 ml (6 fl oz) water

Raise heat. Wipe any crystals off the sides.
- 1 tsp salt

Remove when well heated. Add butter.
- 130°C (265°F)
- 2 tbsp butter

* To make other flavours, substitute peppermint, almond or lemon extract for the vanilla.

Divide. Wait until it's cool enough to handle.

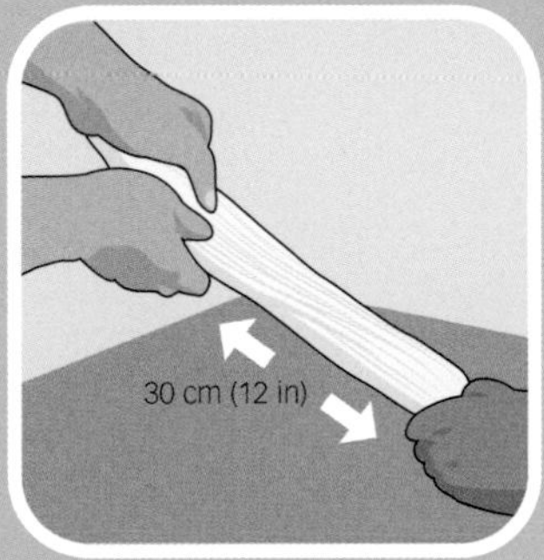

Stretch one part with buttered hands.
- 30 cm (12 in)

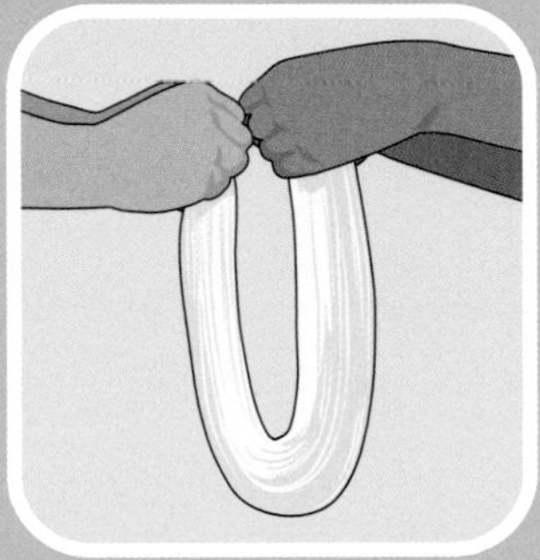

Bring the ends together.

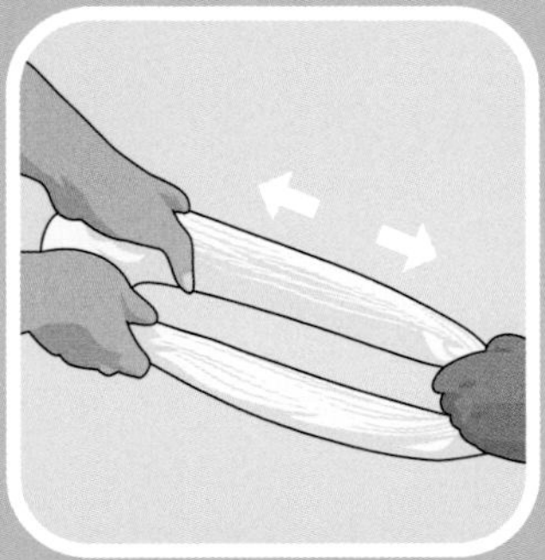

two flavours twisted together

Grab the ends and loop. Stretch again.

* Add flavour and colour. Pull until toffee is stiff.
- 3 drops food colouring
- 3 drops vanilla extract

Cut with buttered scissors. Wrap.

two flavours rolled in a pinwheel, then sliced

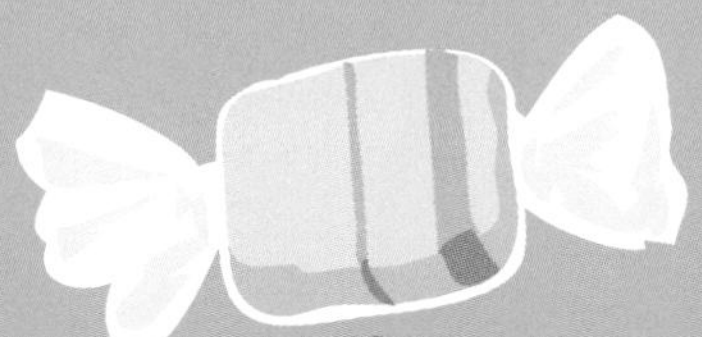

two flavours stacked, then sliced

whipping cream + vanilla extract + 450 g (1 lb) coffee can + 1.5 kg (3 lb) coffee can + rock salt

250 ml (8 fl oz)
milk

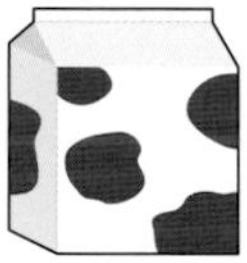

250 ml (8 fl oz)
whipping cream

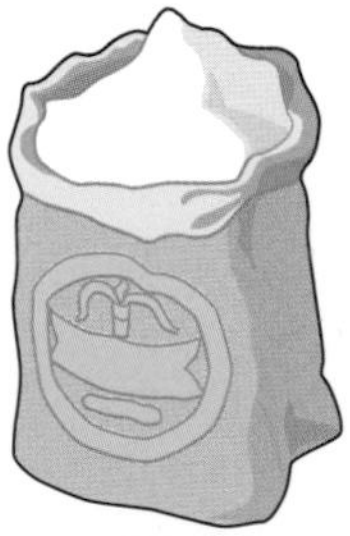

100 g (3½ oz)
sugar

*
½ tsp
vanilla extract

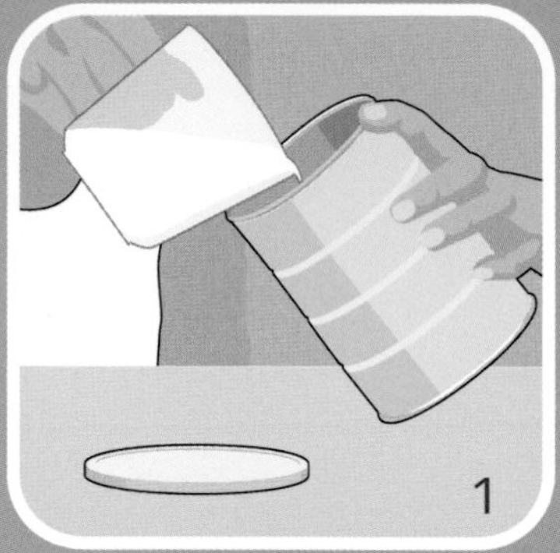

1
Pour the ingredients at left into the smaller can.

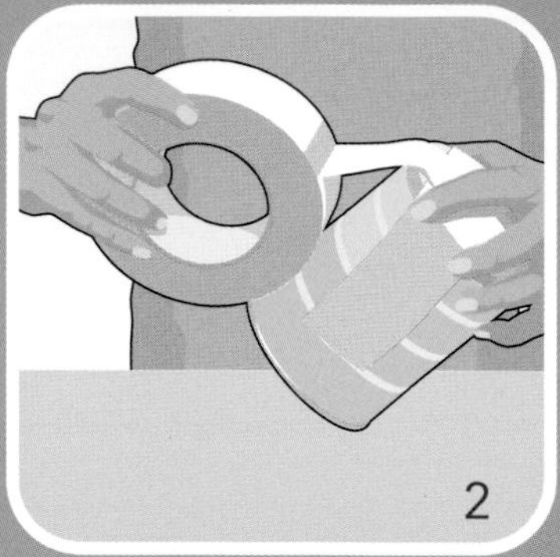

2
Duct tape the lid down securely.

3
Put the smaller can into the big can.

4
12:1
Pack with lots of crushed ice and a little rock salt.

5
Cover this lid with a lot of duct tape.

202 master goalie moves

6
10 min
Roll, shake or kick the can.

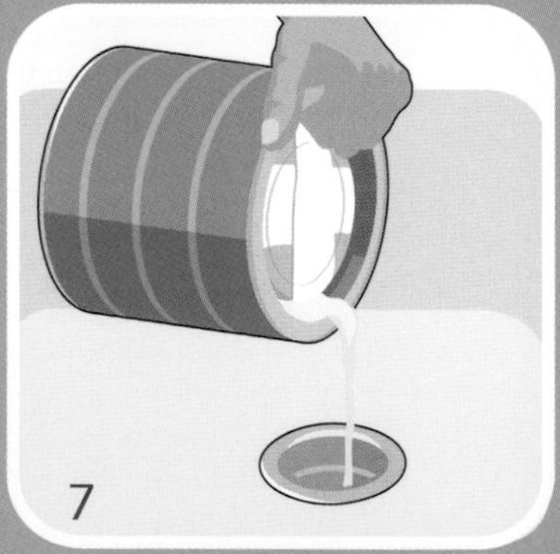

7
Open the big can and drain the melted ice.

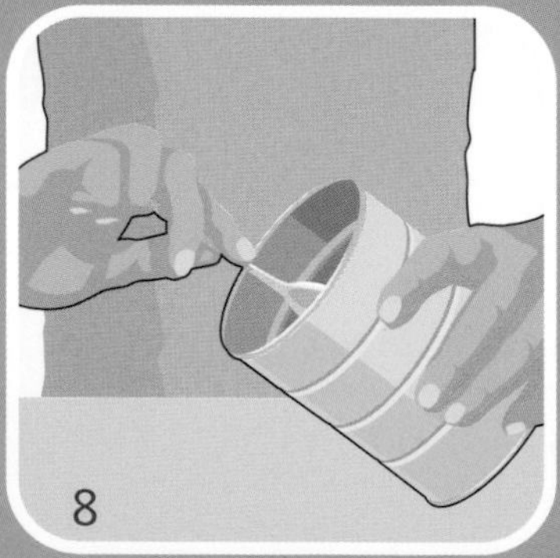

8
Open the small can. Stir and scrape the sides.

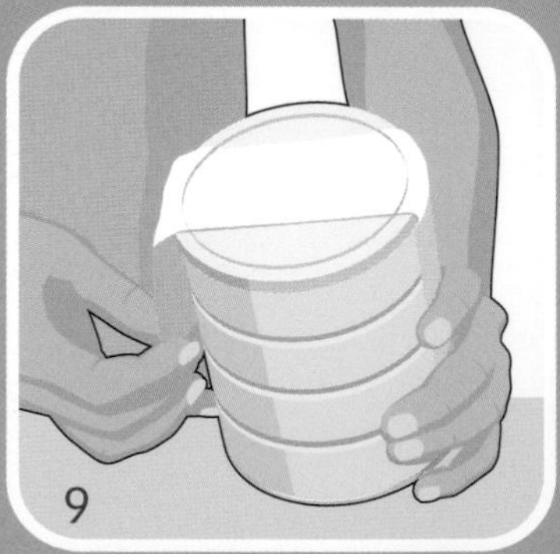

9
Tape. Repeat from step 3 until the ice cream is firm.

1

225 g (8 oz) berries

450 g (1 lb) sugar

475 ml (17 fl oz) water

Combine.

2

30 min ✳

Cook over low heat until the sugar dissolves.

3

Strain and let cool.

4

Add lemon juice to taste.

5

Add ice. Fill a third of the way with syrup.

6

Top off with sparkling water, then stir.

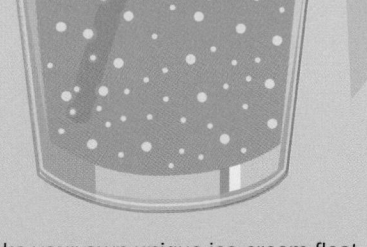

✳ To make your own unique ice-cream float concoction, try different flavour extracts in the ice cream and different fruits in the syrup.

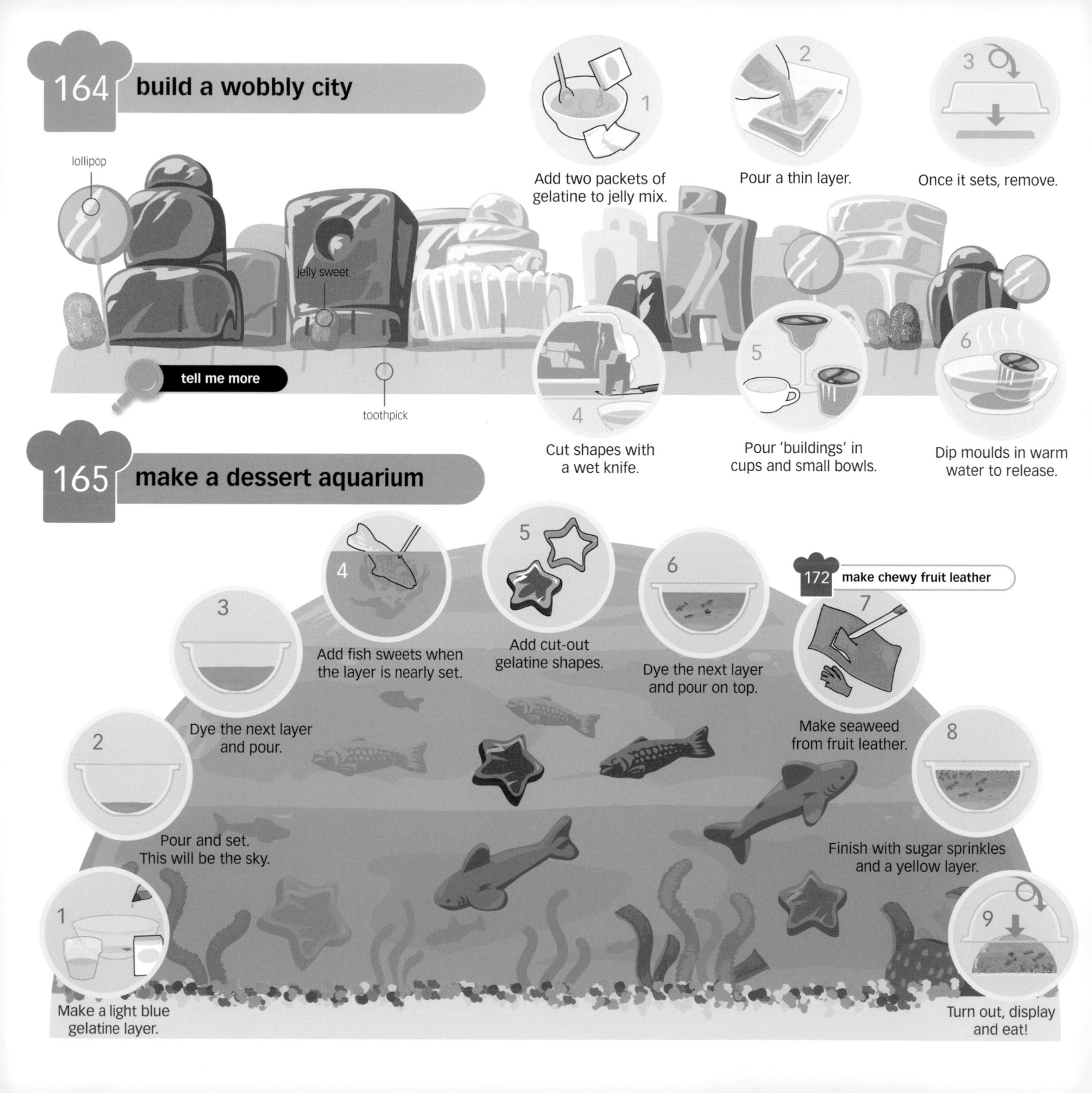

164 build a wobbly city

lollipop

jelly sweet

tell me more

toothpick

1. Add two packets of gelatine to jelly mix.
2. Pour a thin layer.
3. Once it sets, remove.
4. Cut shapes with a wet knife.
5. Pour 'buildings' in cups and small bowls.
6. Dip moulds in warm water to release.

165 make a dessert aquarium

172 make chewy fruit leather

4. Add fish sweets when the layer is nearly set.
5. Add cut-out gelatine shapes.
6. Dye the next layer and pour on top.
7. Make seaweed from fruit leather.
3. Dye the next layer and pour.
2. Pour and set. This will be the sky.
8. Finish with sugar sprinkles and a yellow layer.
1. Make a light blue gelatine layer.
9. Turn out, display and eat!

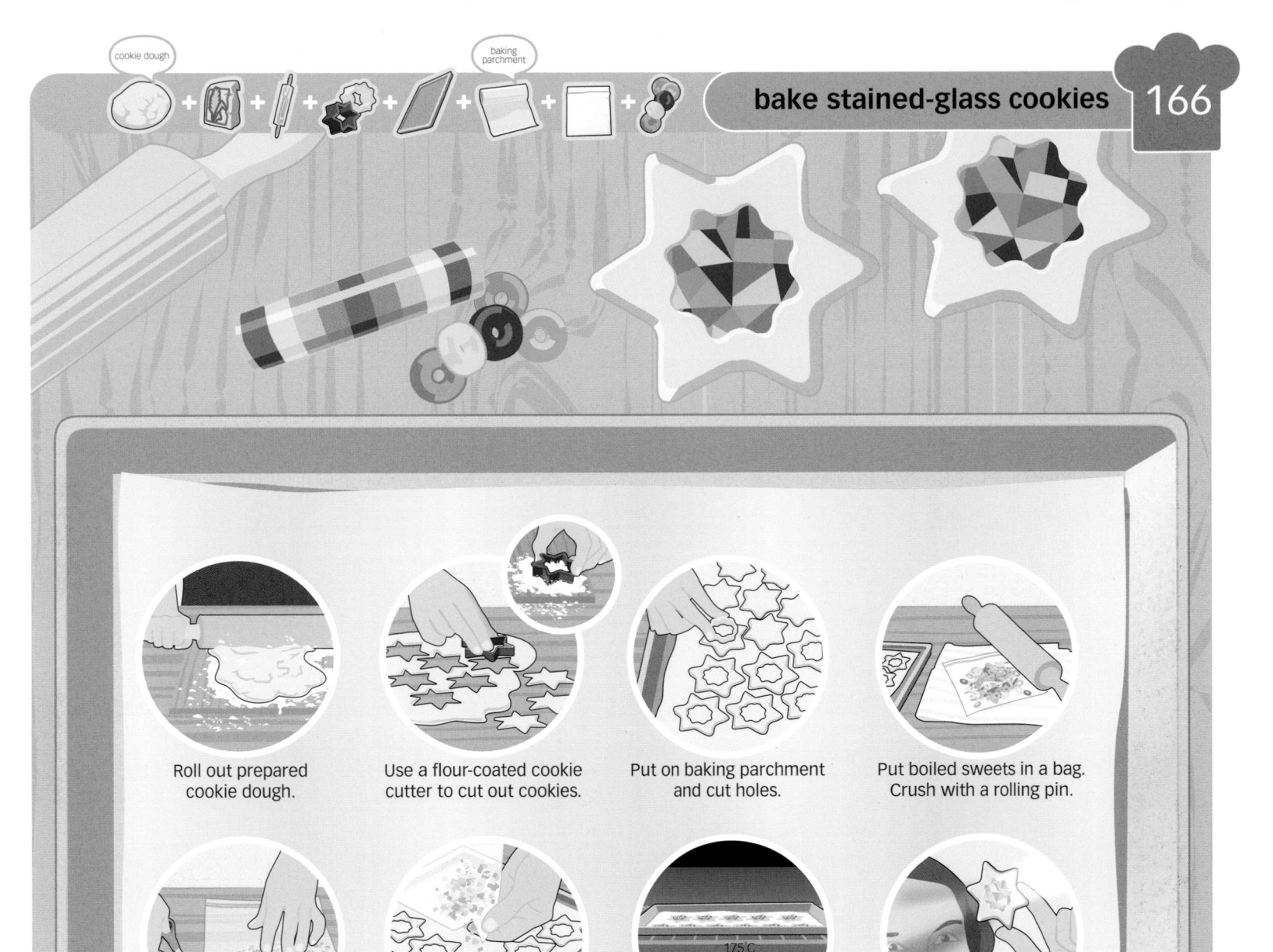

Roll out prepared cookie dough.

Use a flour-coated cookie cutter to cut out cookies.

Put on baking parchment and cut holes.

Put boiled sweets in a bag. Crush with a rolling pin.

Cut the tip off the plastic bag.

Sprinkle the crushed sweets into the holes.

Bake until light brown.

Let the sun shine through!

175 C (350 F)

8 min

tell me more

167 separate an egg

53 squeeze an egg into a bottle

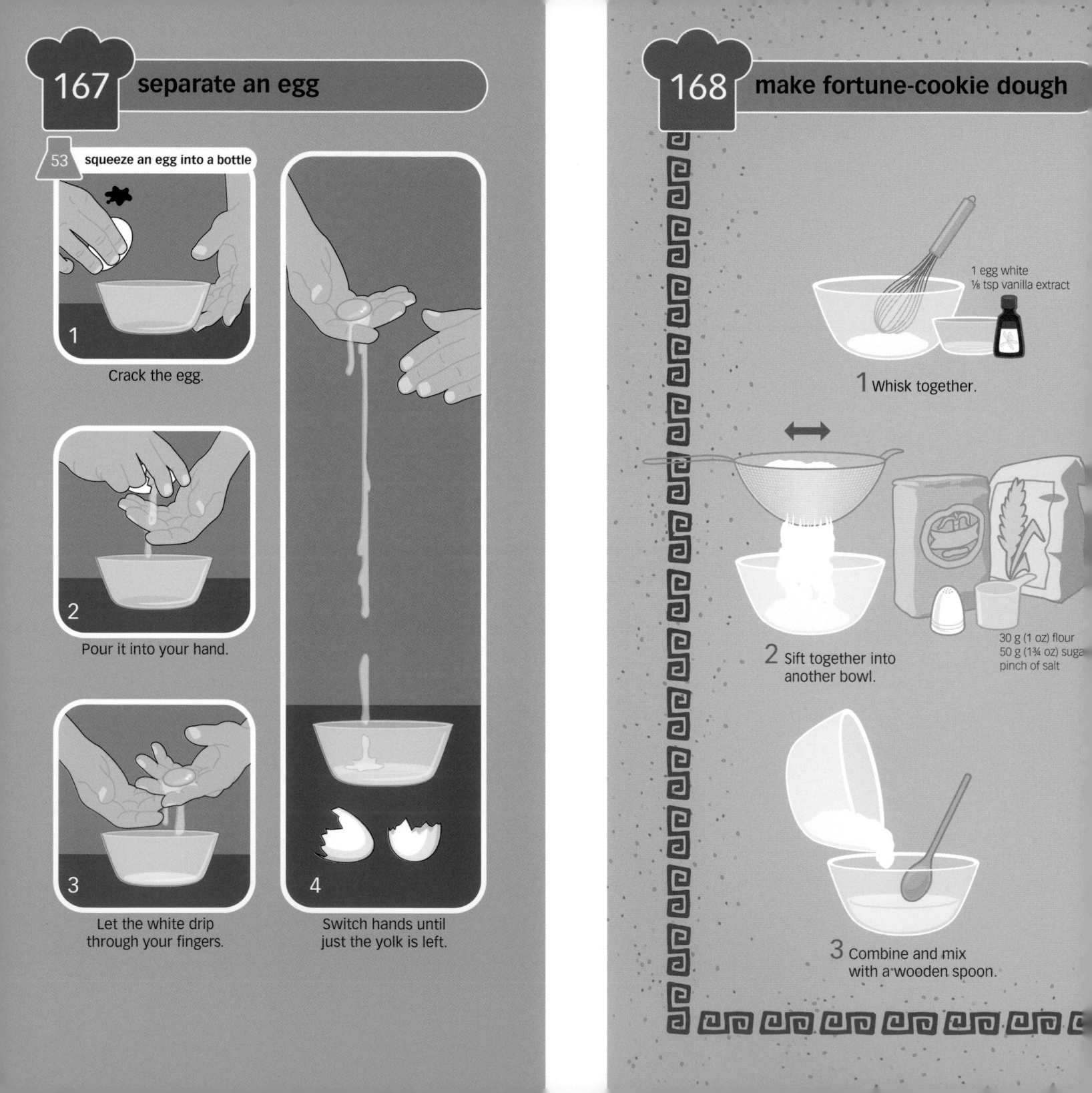

1 Crack the egg.

2 Pour it into your hand.

3 Let the white drip through your fingers.

4 Switch hands until just the yolk is left.

168 make fortune-cookie dough

1 egg white
⅛ tsp vanilla extract

1 Whisk together.

2 Sift together into another bowl.

30 g (1 oz) flour
50 g (1¾ oz) suga
pinch of salt

3 Combine and mix with a wooden spoon.

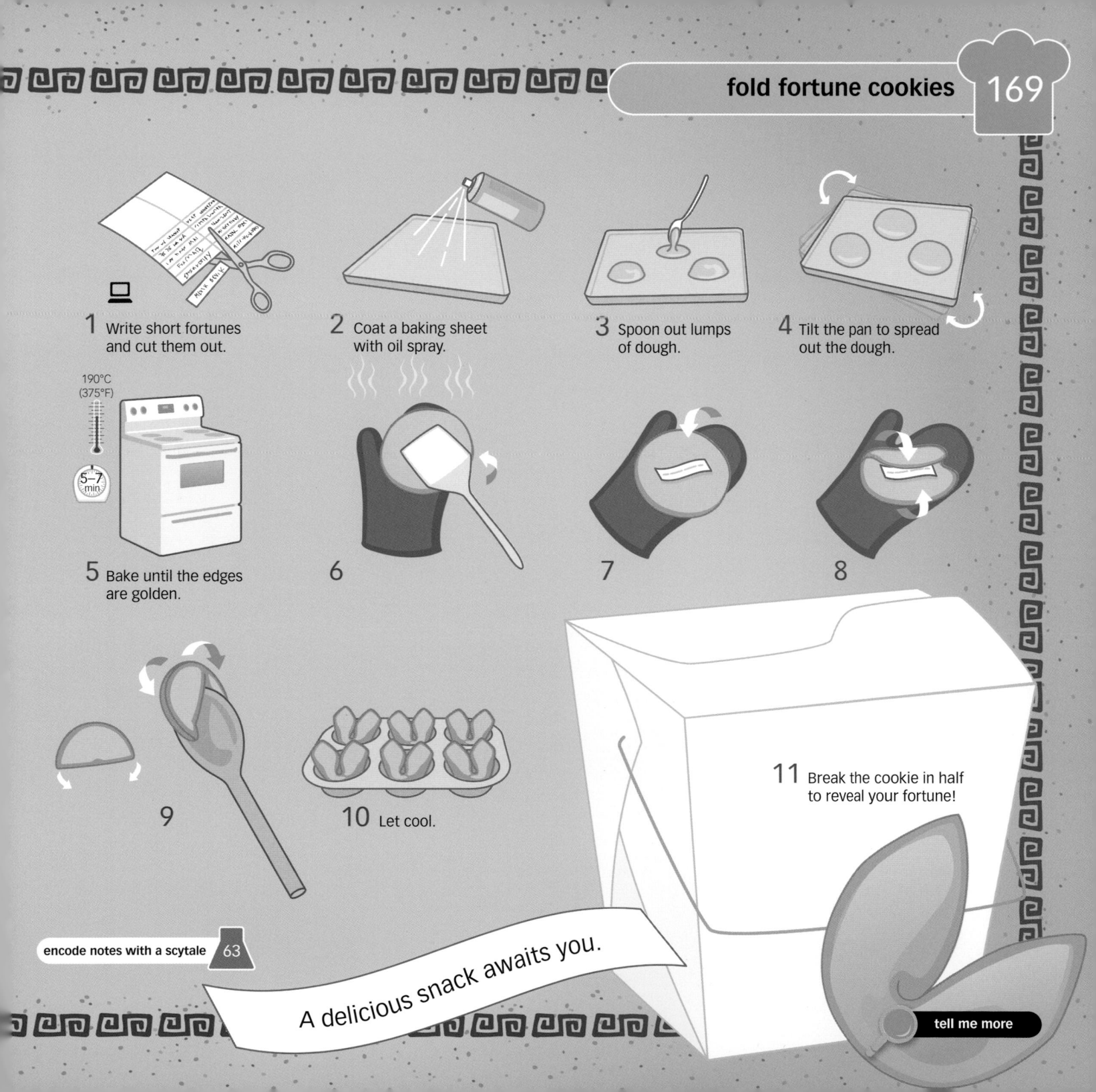

1 Write short fortunes and cut them out.

2 Coat a baking sheet with oil spray.

3 Spoon out lumps of dough.

4 Tilt the pan to spread out the dough.

190°C (375°F)

5–7 min

5 Bake until the edges are golden.

6

7

8

9

10 Let cool.

11 Break the cookie in half to reveal your fortune!

encode notes with a scytale 63

A delicious snack awaits you.

tell me more

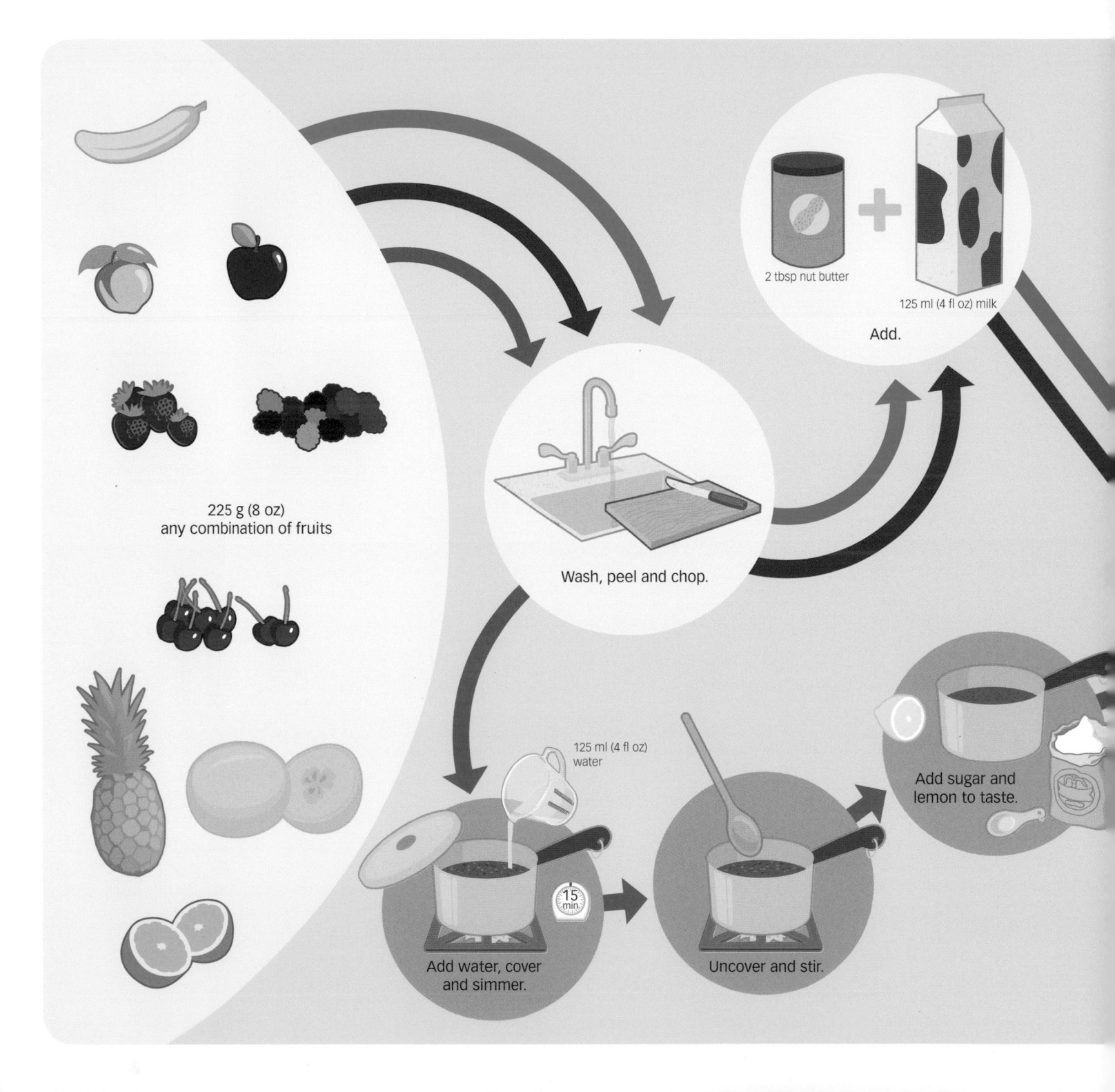

225 g (8 oz)
any combination of fruits

2 tbsp nut butter

125 ml (4 fl oz) milk

Add.

Wash, peel and chop.

125 ml (4 fl oz)
water

15 min

Add water, cover
and simmer.

Uncover and stir.

Add sugar and
lemon to taste.

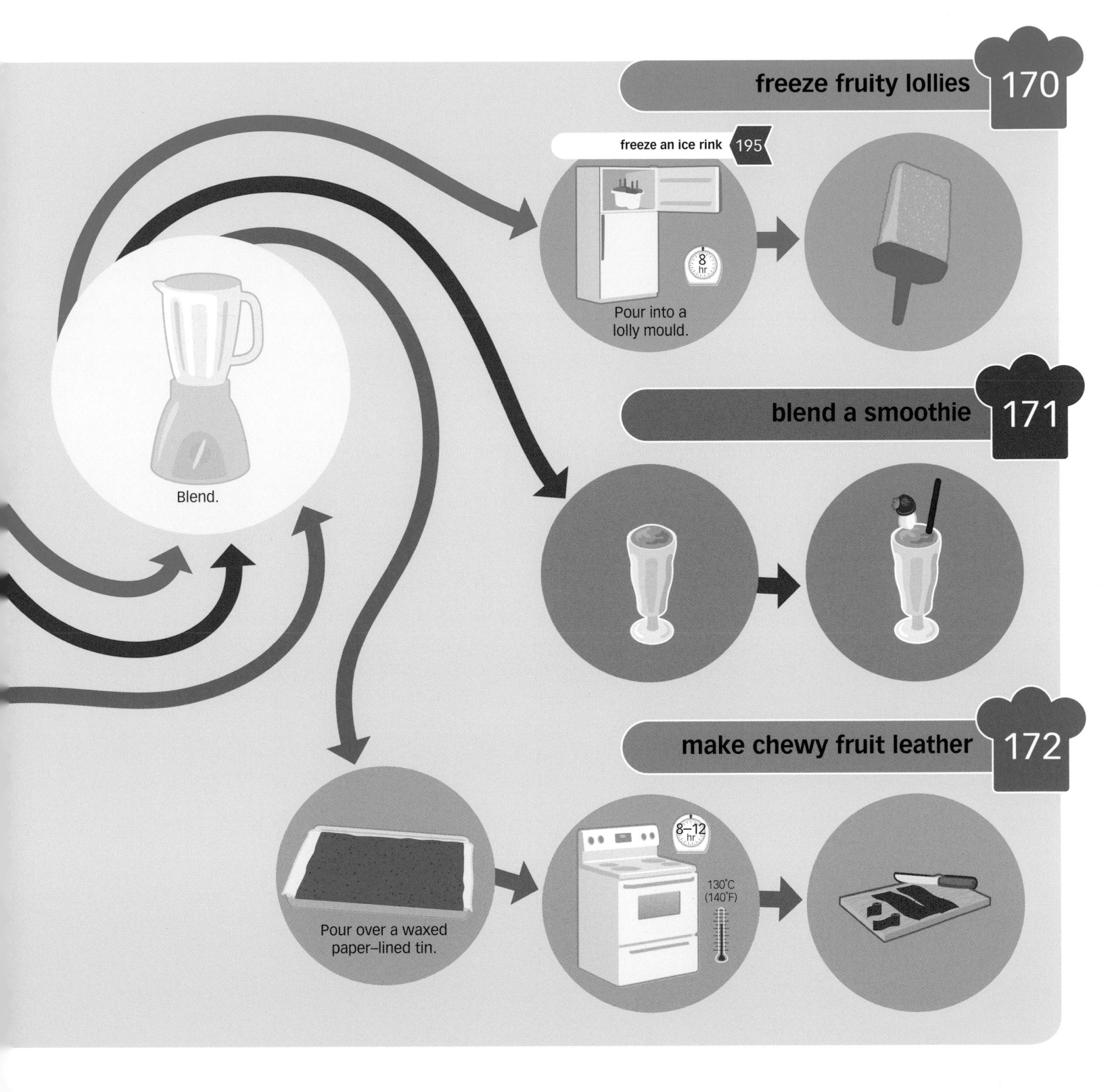

freeze fruity lollies 170

freeze an ice rink 195

Pour into a lolly mould.

8 hr

Blend.

blend a smoothie 171

make chewy fruit leather 172

Pour over a waxed paper–lined tin.

8–12 hr

130°C (140°F)

roll pasta dough

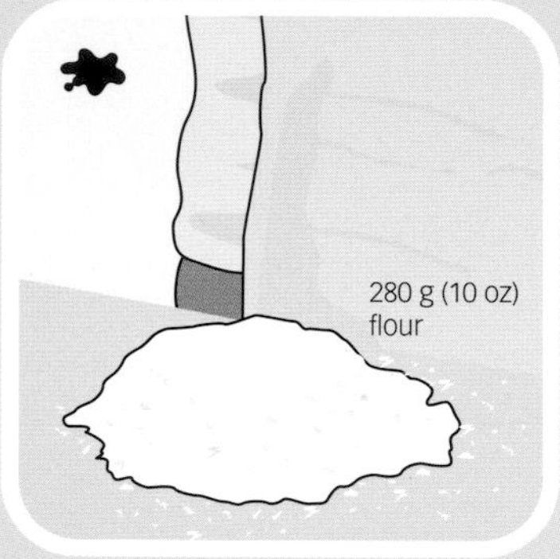

Pile the flour on
a clean surface.

Make a well in the centre.

167 separate an egg

280 g (10 oz)
flour

2 tsp olive oil
4 egg yolks

Whisk the egg yolks and
oil. Pour into the well.

Blend in the flour.

dough
scraper

fold tortellini

pasta filling

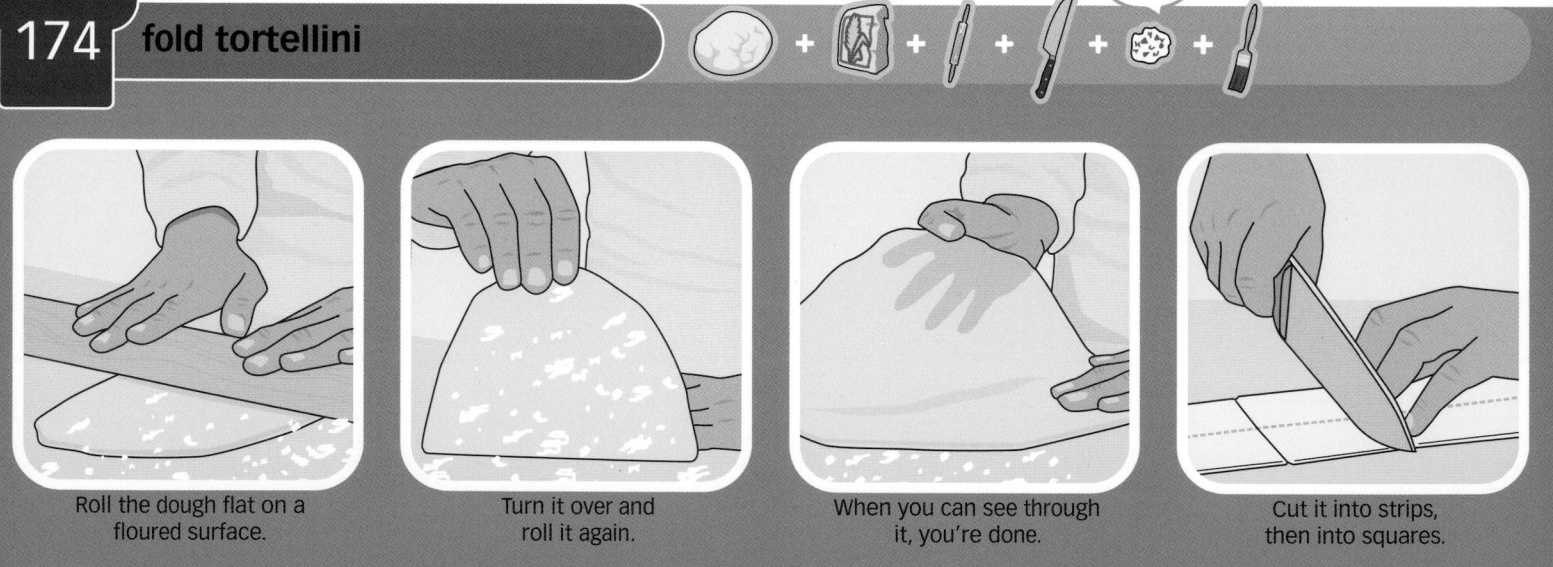

Roll the dough flat on a
floured surface.

Turn it over and
roll it again.

When you can see through
it, you're done.

Cut it into strips,
then into squares.

Roll all the flour into the dough.

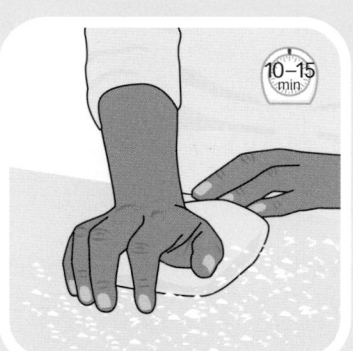

Knead on a floured surface until the dough is smooth.

Cut into quarters.

Roll each piece into a ball. Flatten.

Add a lump of filling. Wet the edges with water.

83 fold a paper aeroplane

Fold into a triangle. Press the edges to seal.

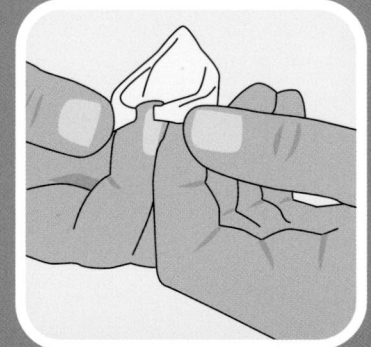

Wrap the corners around and press together.

Gently add to boiling water. Cook and serve.

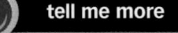

tell me more

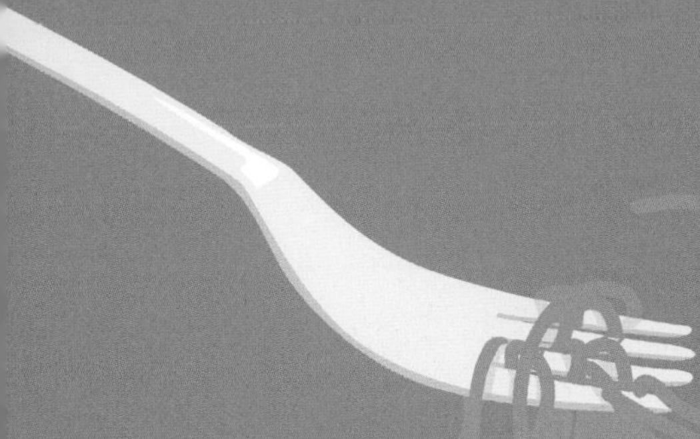

enjoy purple pasta

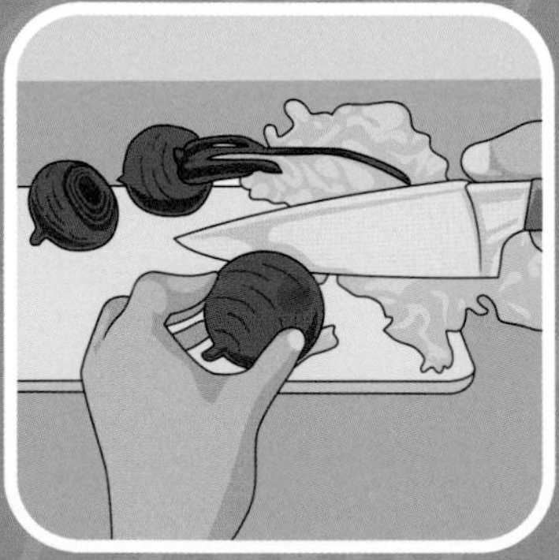

Cut the tops off the beetroot.

Put the beetroot top-down in a little water.

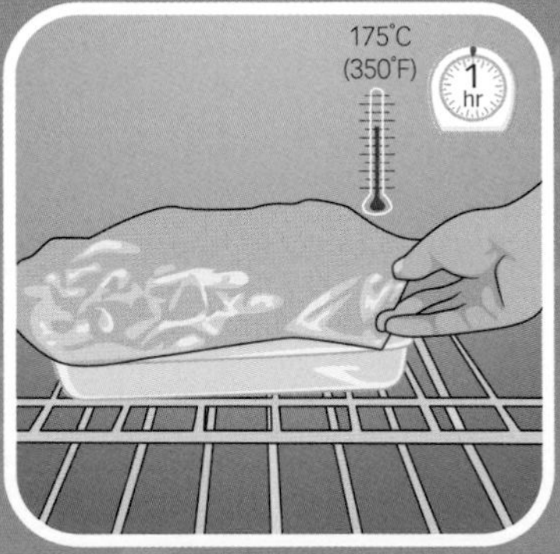

175°C
(350°F)
1 hr

Cover with foil and bake.

Let the beetroot cool, then peel. Keep the juice.

Dice one. Save the rest for another recipe.

10 min

Cook the pasta in boiling water.

Drain.

1 tbsp beet-root juice

Toss with diced beetroot, juice and butter.

dried pasta

Floppy celery snacks got you down? Cut the ends off your stalks and put them in coloured water. Place them in the fridge and check daily to see how much dye has travelled up the stems. Pretty soon, you'll have the brightest veggies on the block!

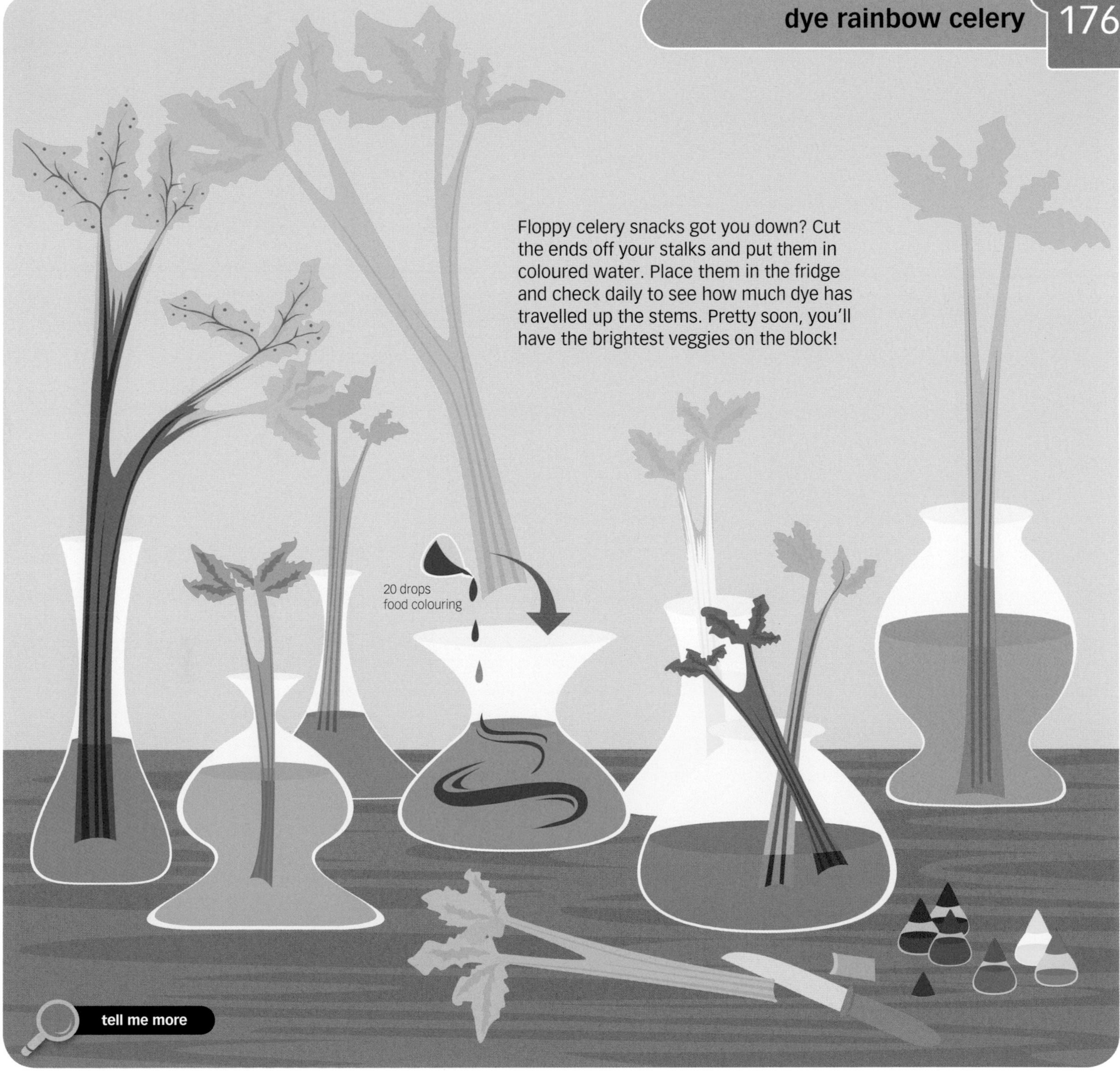

20 drops food colouring

tell me more

twist up soft pretzels

active dry yeast + + + + vegetable oil + plastic food wrap + + coarse salt

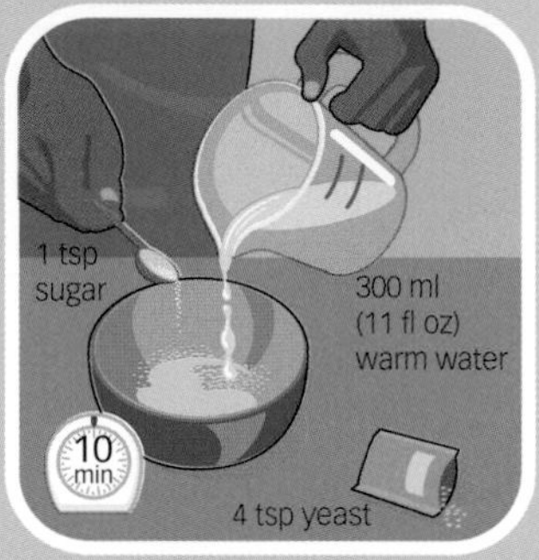

1 tsp sugar

300 ml (11 fl oz) warm water

10 min

4 tsp yeast

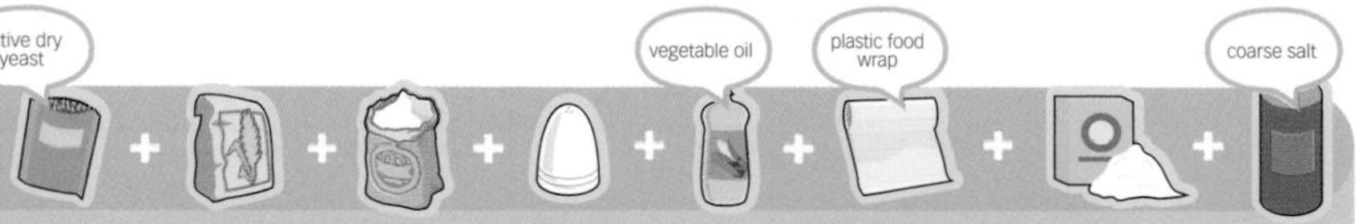

Mix yeast, sugar and warm water. Leave.

1½ tsp table salt

1 kg (2 lb 4 oz) flour
100 g (3½ oz) sugar

In another bowl, mix flour, sugar and salt.

1 tbsp vegetable oil

Make a well. Add the yeast mix and oil.

7 min

Knead into dough. Add water if it's dry.

Oil a bowl. Add dough and coat thoroughly.

1 hr

Cover and put aside to rise.

1 l (1¾ pt) hot water

(100 g) 3½ oz baking soda

Dissolve baking soda in hot water.

Turn risen dough onto a floured surface.

Roll it into ropes and twist to make shapes.

Dip each into the baking soda water.

Put on greased baking sheet. Add salt.

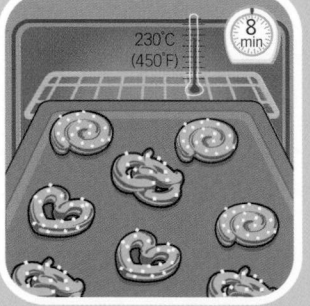

230°C (450°F)

8 min

Bake until golden brown.

clear vinegar | pickling spice

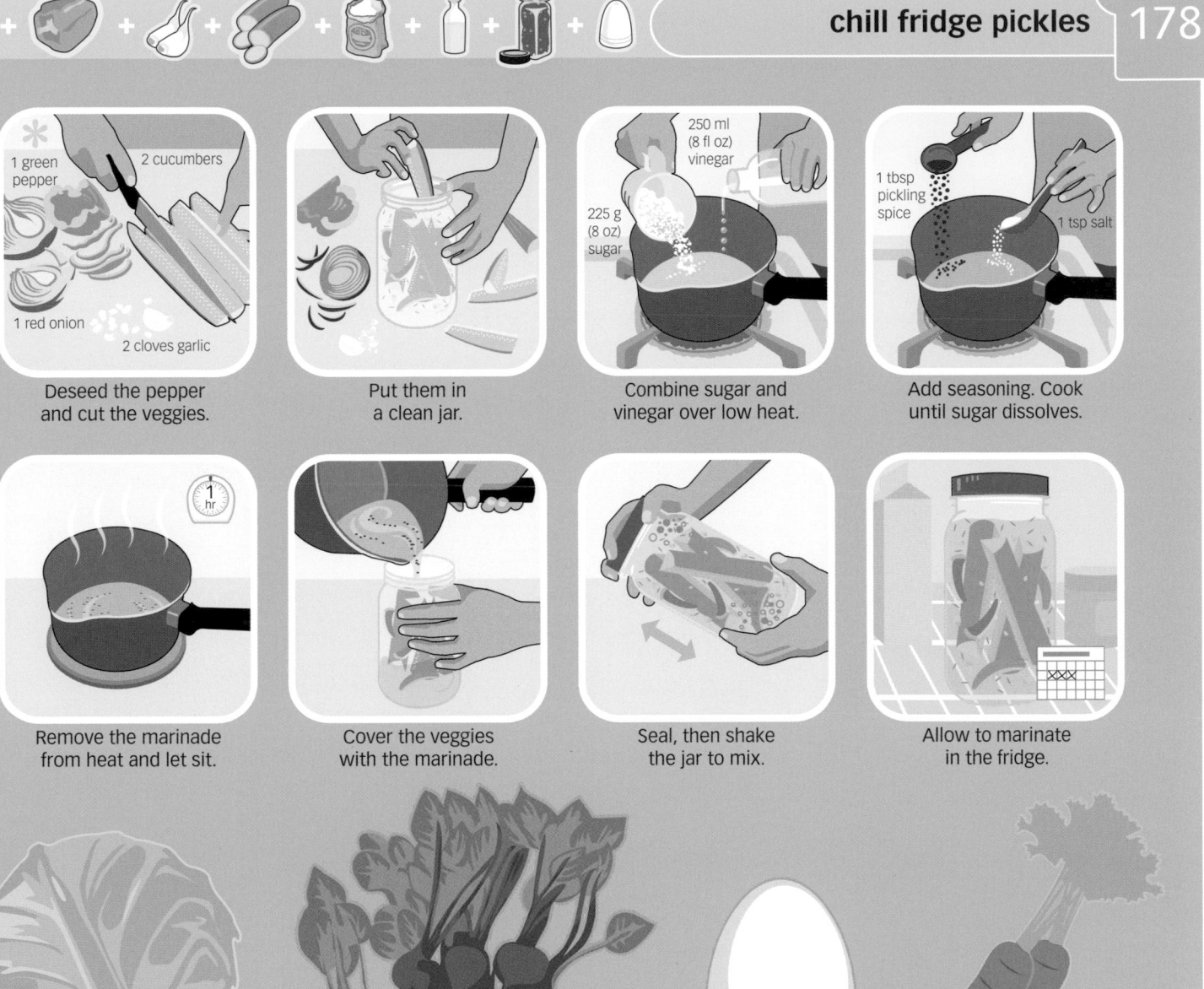

1 green pepper | 2 cucumbers
1 red onion
2 cloves garlic

Deseed the pepper and cut the veggies.

Put them in a clean jar.

250 ml (8 fl oz) vinegar
225 g (8 oz) sugar

Combine sugar and vinegar over low heat.

1 tbsp pickling spice | 1 tsp salt

Add seasoning. Cook until sugar dissolves.

1 hr

Remove the marinade from heat and let sit.

Cover the veggies with the marinade.

Seal, then shake the jar to mix.

Allow to marinate in the fridge.

Pickling isn't just for cucumbers! Try this recipe with other vegetables or even a hard-boiled egg.

Whoever said you shouldn't play with your food was wrong. You can turn that boring lunch into a team of crazy creatures, like a mouse made with scoops of steamed brown rice, or a hot-dog dog with a wagging bean-sprout tail. Use toothpicks or cocktail sticks to hold your edible creations together.

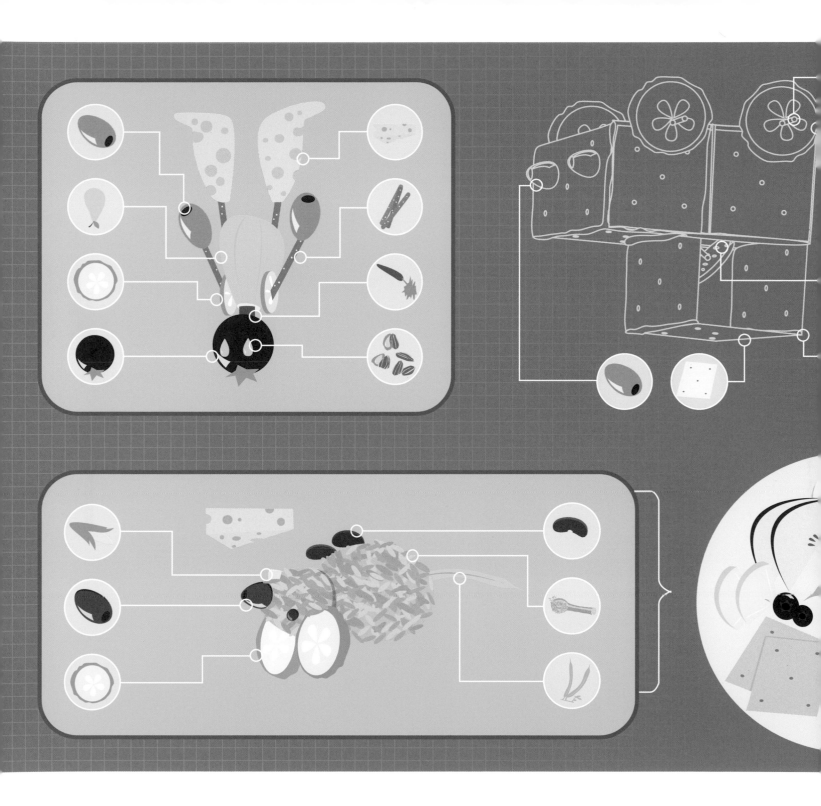

180   roast veggies in the wild

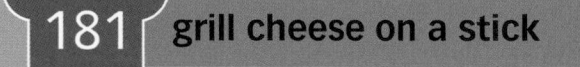

1
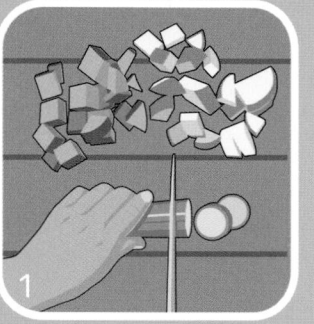
Cut the veggies into equal-sized pieces.

2

Toss with olive oil, salt and pepper.

3

Put the veggies on a square of tinfoil.

4
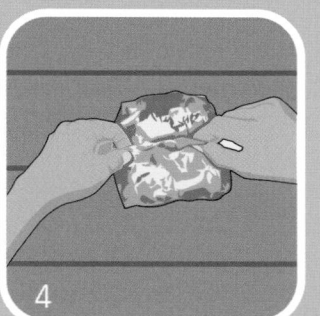
Fold into a packet.

5

Add to coals. Turn every five minutes.

6
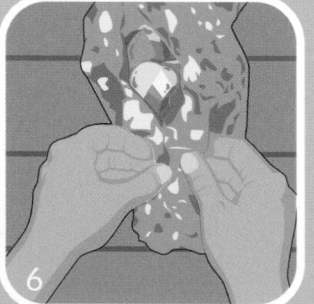
Unwrap and enjoy!

181   grill cheese on a stick

130   drink from a tree branch

1

Scrape the bark off part of a forked stick.

2
×2
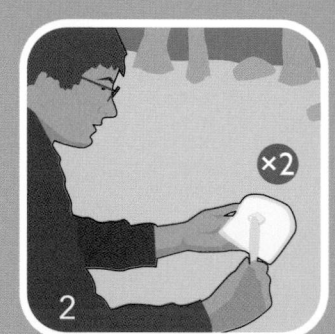
Butter one side of each bread slice.

3
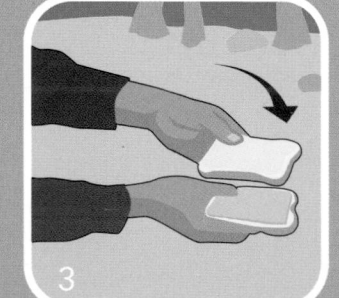
Put cheese between the unbuttered sides.

4
5 min

Hold over the fire.

5

When brown, remove from fire and turn.

6
5 min

Grill the other side.

bake a cake in an orange 182

1 Cut off the oranges' tops, then hollow out.

2 Prepare the cake mix.

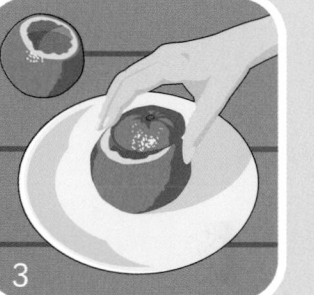

3 Fill each halfway with mix. Add the tops.

4 Wrap each orange in tinfoil.

5 Place them in coals and turn often.

35 min

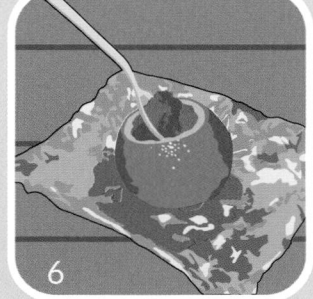

6 Unwrap and enjoy your campfire cake!

cook campfire toffee apples 183

cinnamon + peeler

1 Combine cinnamon and sugar.

1 tbsp cinnamon

100 g (3½ oz) sugar

2 Peel an apple.

3 Place the apple on the end of a stick.

4 Soften it over the fire, turning often.

3–5 min

5 Roll the apple through the sugar mix.

6 Heat until the sugar melts.

5–7 min

concoct chocolate anthills

chocolate + vanilla bean + crispy chow mein noodles + baking parchment

Melt chocolate in a double boiler.

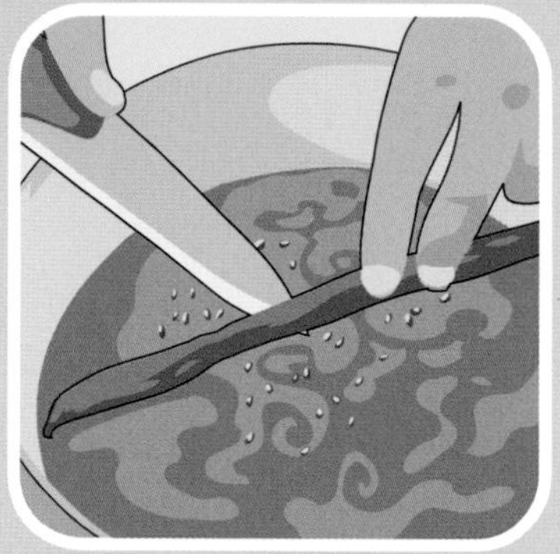

Add vanilla seeds.

144 start an ant farm

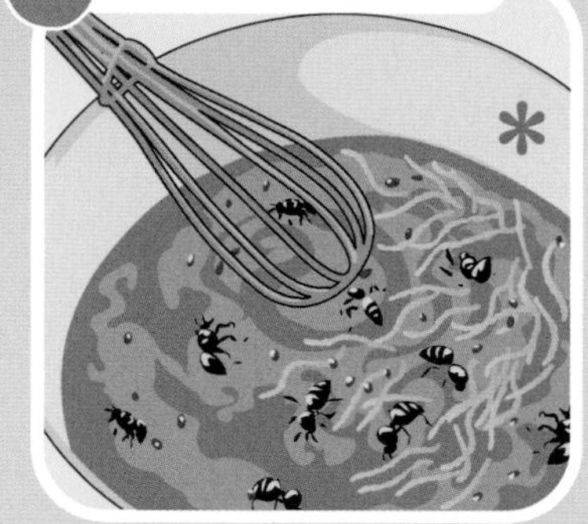

Stir in ants and noodles.

Spoon onto baking parchment. Refrigerate.

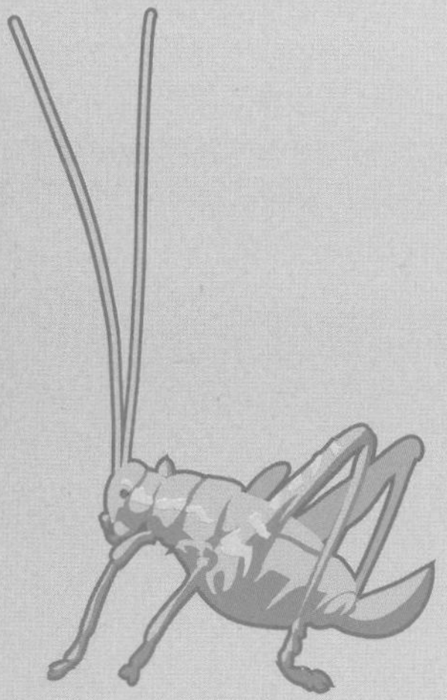

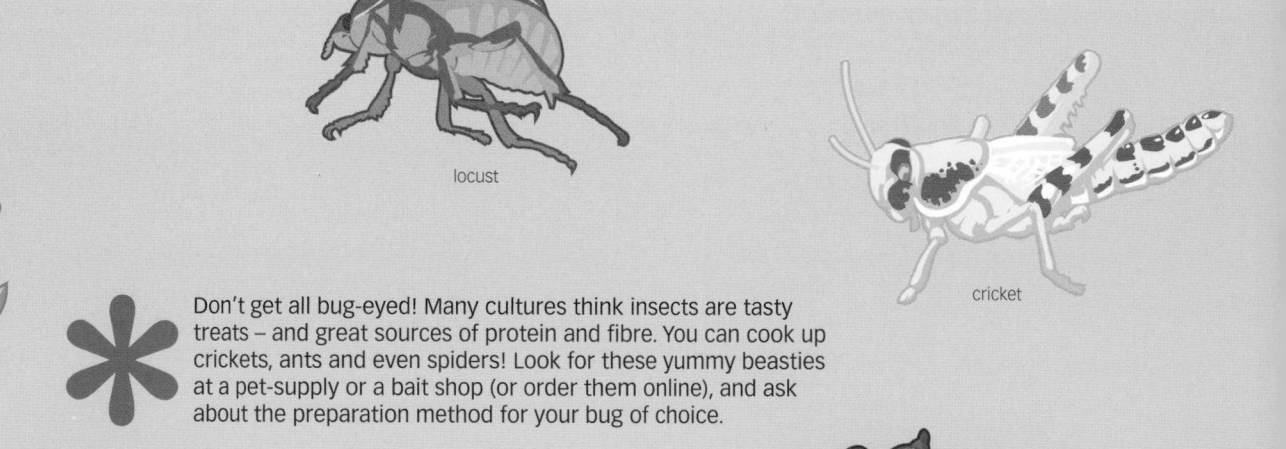

locust

cricket

grasshopper

Don't get all bug-eyed! Many cultures think insects are tasty treats – and great sources of protein and fibre. You can cook up crickets, ants and even spiders! Look for these yummy beasties at a pet-supply or a bait shop (or order them online), and ask about the preparation method for your bug of choice.

beetle

bird spider

gelatine + cocoa powder + porridge oats + raisins + cooking spray

1 package unflavoured gelatine
15 min

60 ml (2 fl oz) apple sauce

Mix over low heat.

Add two pinches cocoa powder.

Some oats and a few raisins add nasty texture.

Coat a large plate with non-stick cooking spray.

2 hr

Spoon the gross mixture onto the plate to cool.

booby trap a bathroom 43

Remove the 'vomit' and hide it somewhere clever.

move

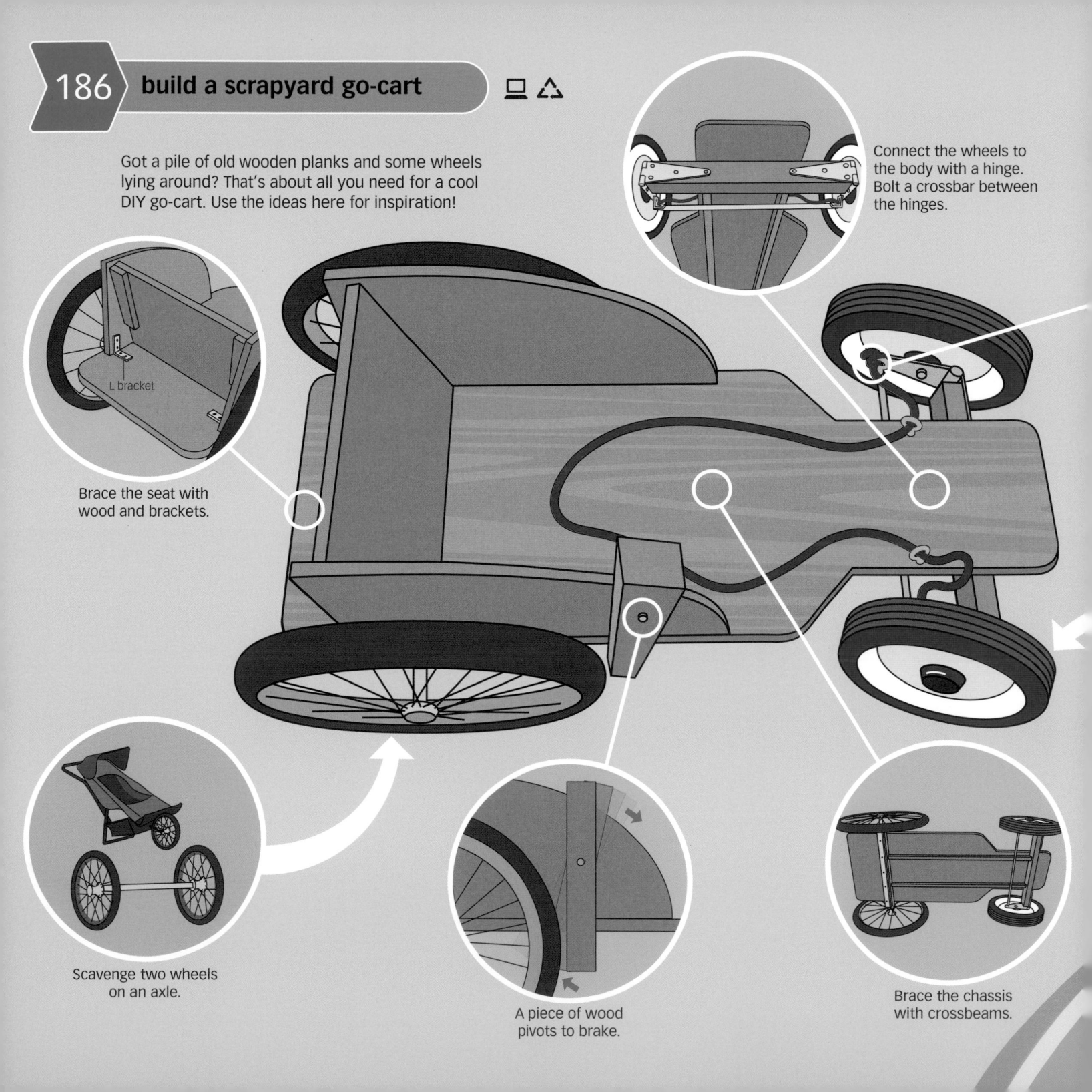

Got a pile of old wooden planks and some wheels lying around? That's about all you need for a cool DIY go-cart. Use the ideas here for inspiration!

Connect the wheels to the body with a hinge. Bolt a crossbar between the hinges.

L bracket

Brace the seat with wood and brackets.

Scavenge two wheels on an axle.

A piece of wood pivots to brake.

Brace the chassis with crossbeams.

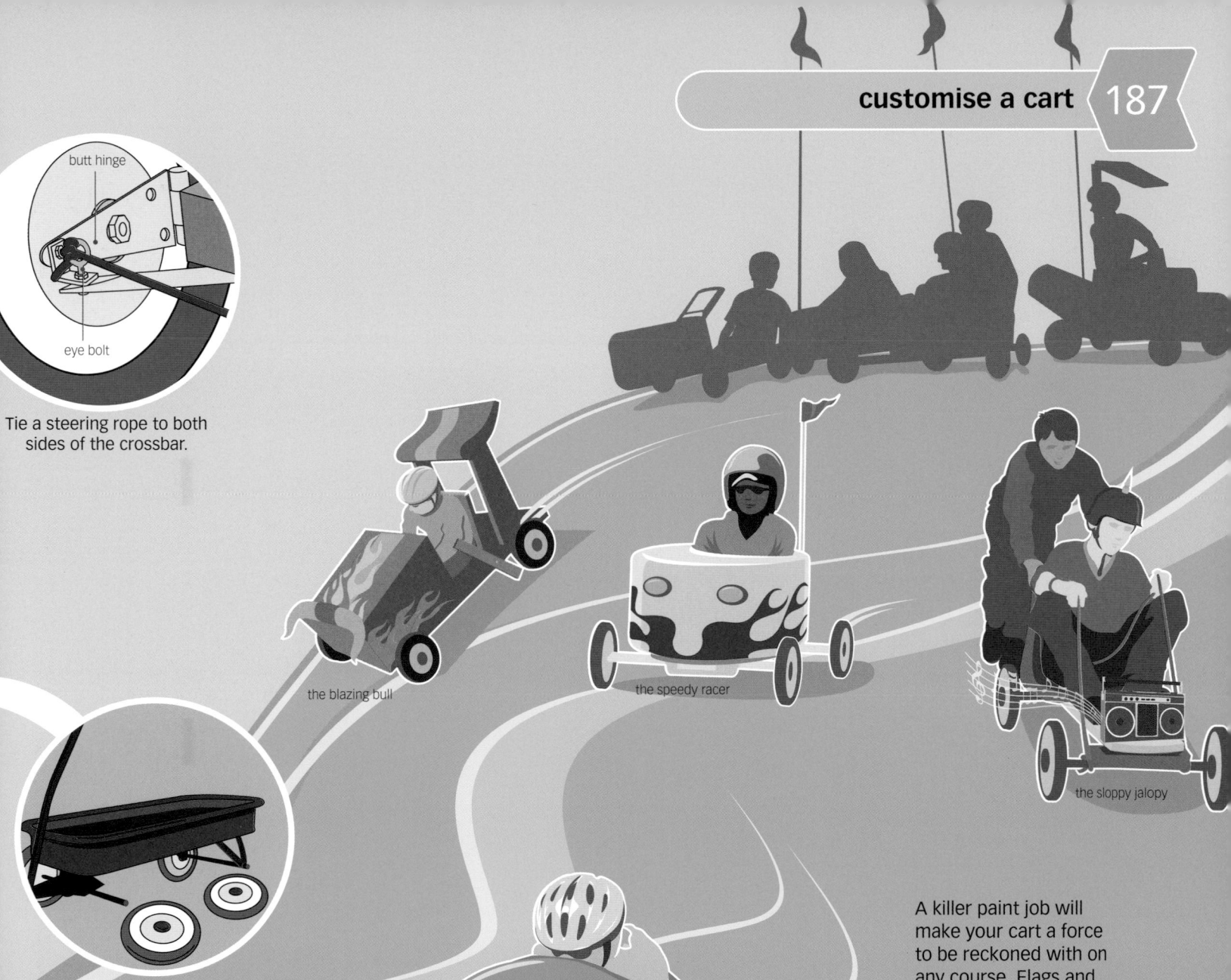

butt hinge

eye bolt

Tie a steering rope to both sides of the crossbar.

the blazing bull

the speedy racer

the sloppy jalopy

Remove two wheels from their axles.

the boastful bomber

A killer paint job will make your cart a force to be reckoned with on any course. Flags and streamers show off your speed, while a well-mounted radio serenades you across the finish line.

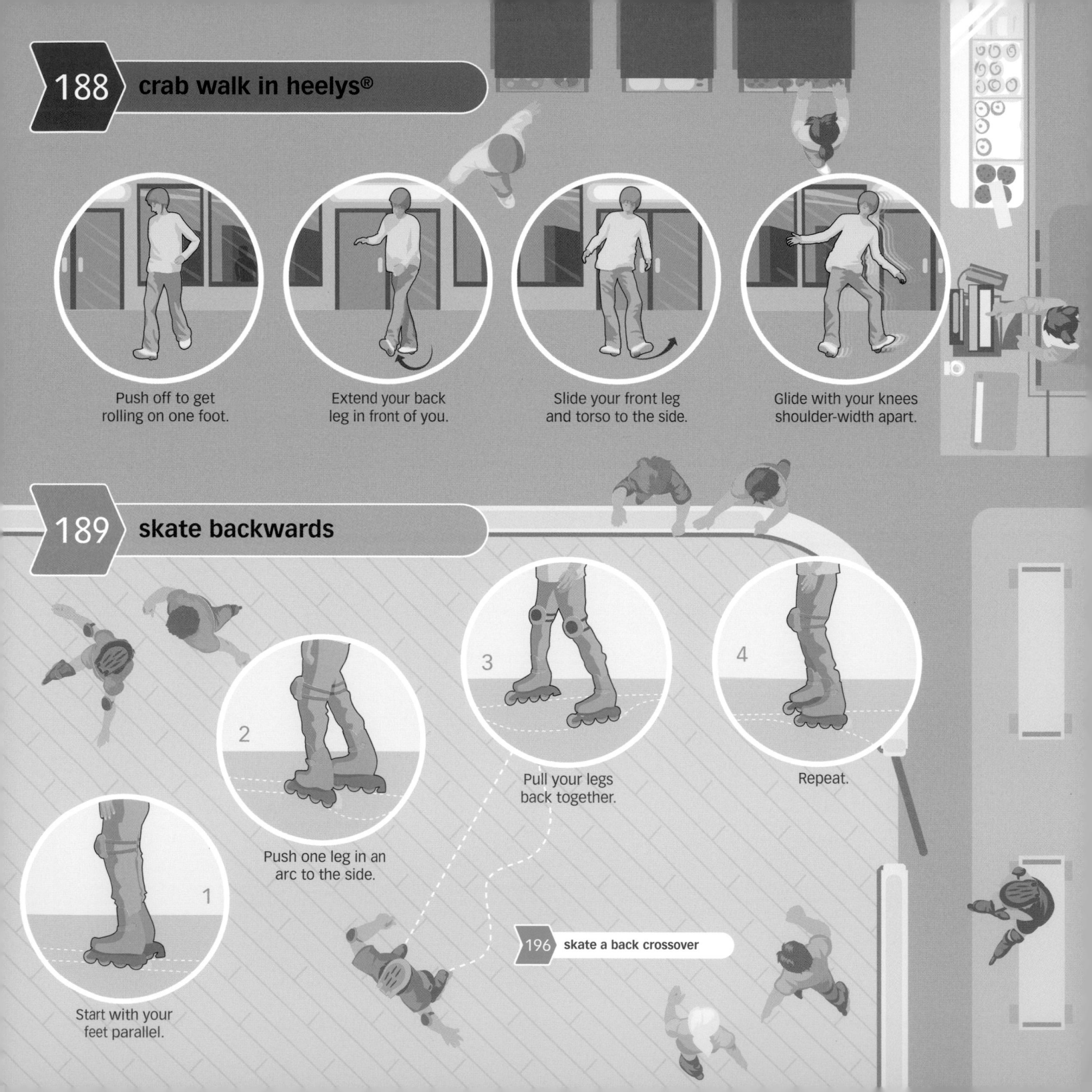

188 crab walk in heelys®

Push off to get rolling on one foot.

Extend your back leg in front of you.

Slide your front leg and torso to the side.

Glide with your knees shoulder-width apart.

189 skate backwards

1 Start with your feet parallel.

2 Push one leg in an arc to the side.

3 Pull your legs back together.

4 Repeat.

196 skate a back crossover

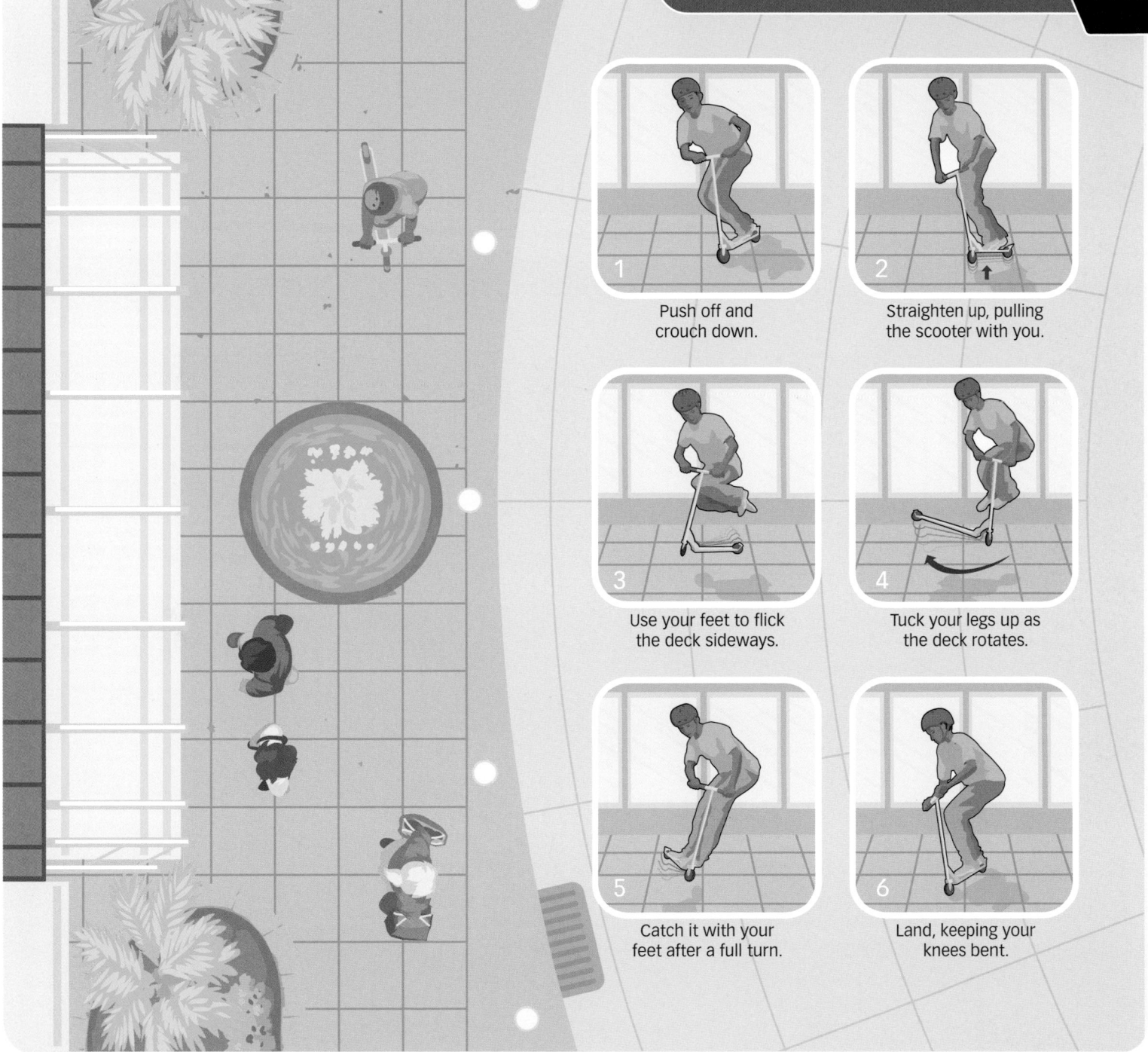

1. Push off and crouch down.

2. Straighten up, pulling the scooter with you.

3. Use your feet to flick the deck sideways.

4. Tuck your legs up as the deck rotates.

5. Catch it with your feet after a full turn.

6. Land, keeping your knees bent.

1 Ollie up onto a ramp.

2 Straddle the back truck over the edge. Point the nose to the far side.

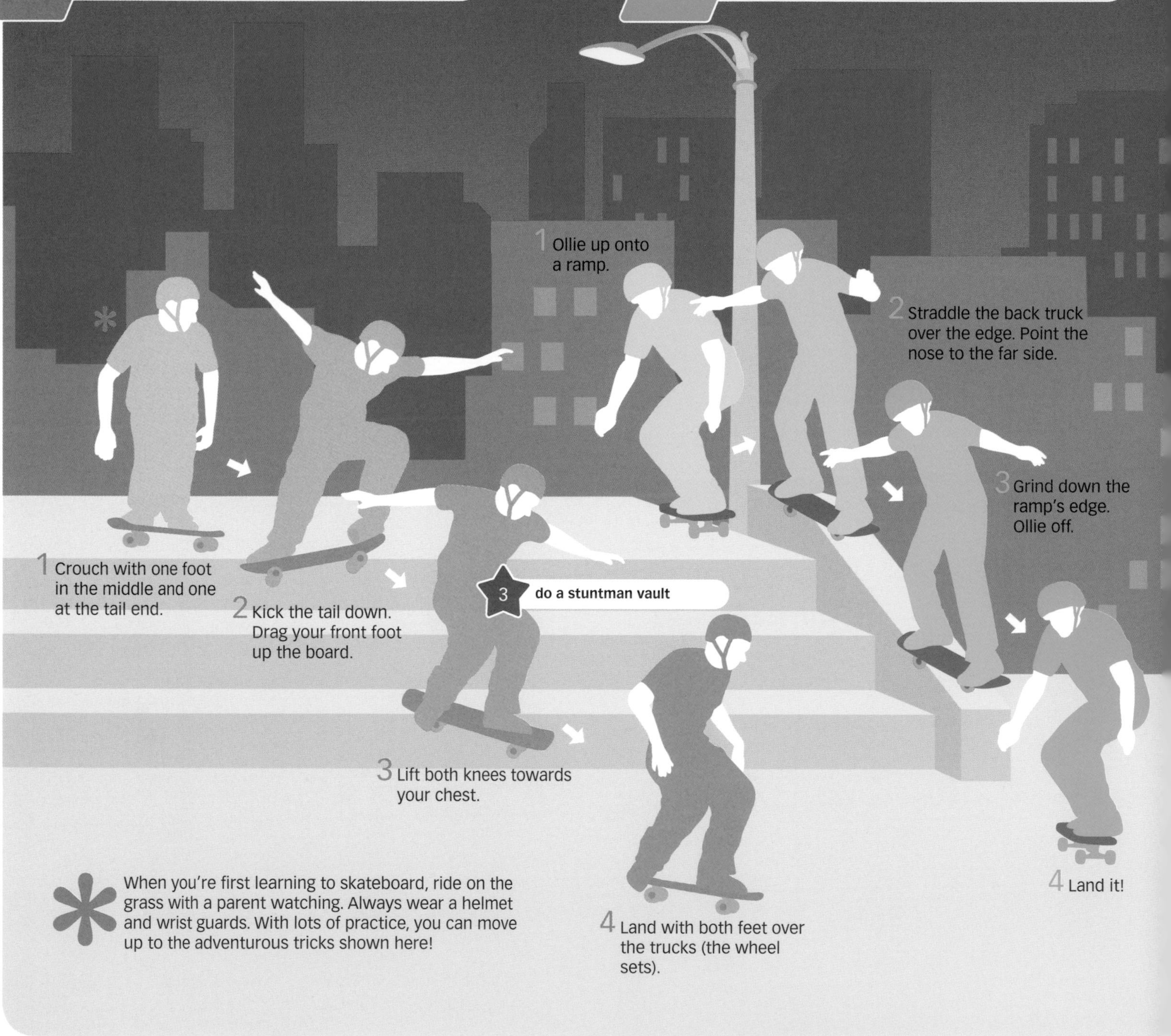

3 Grind down the ramp's edge. Ollie off.

4 Land it!

1 Crouch with one foot in the middle and one at the tail end.

2 Kick the tail down. Drag your front foot up the board.

3 do a stuntman vault

3 Lift both knees towards your chest.

4 Land with both feet over the trucks (the wheel sets).

When you're first learning to skateboard, ride on the grass with a parent watching. Always wear a helmet and wrist guards. With lots of practice, you can move up to the adventurous tricks shown here!

193 land a kickflip

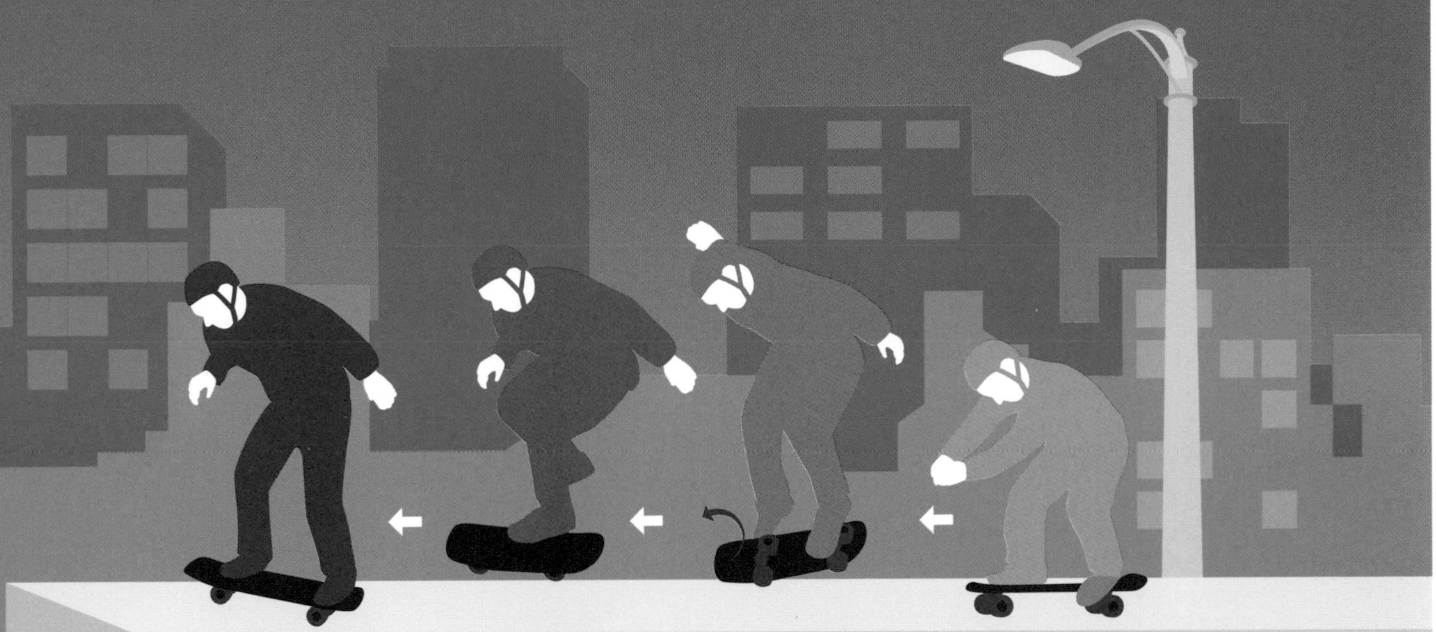

1 Squat down to gather momentum.

2 Leap. Kick the board into a sick spin.

3 Bring both feet above the board as it turns.

4 Land with your feet over the trucks.

194 nail a handstand fingerflip

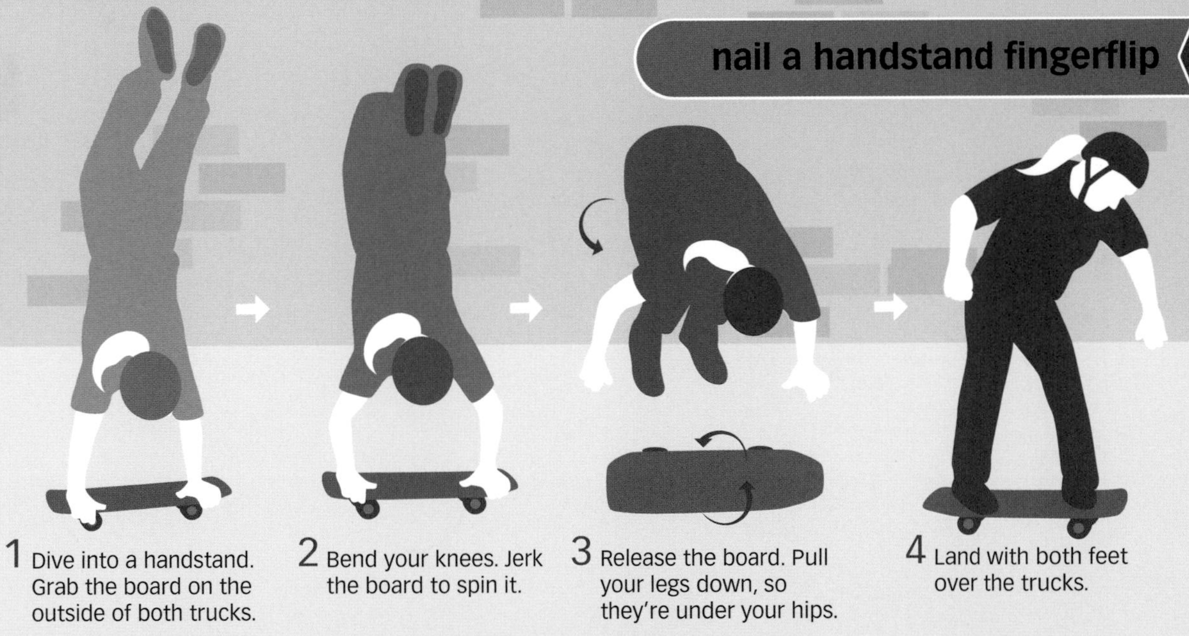

1 Dive into a handstand. Grab the board on the outside of both trucks.

2 Bend your knees. Jerk the board to spin it.

3 Release the board. Pull your legs down, so they're under your hips.

4 Land with both feet over the trucks.

195 freeze an ice rink

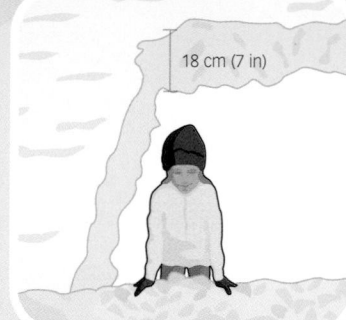
Find a level spot and pack snow into walls.

18 cm (7 in)

Pour water over walls and leave to freeze.

12 hr

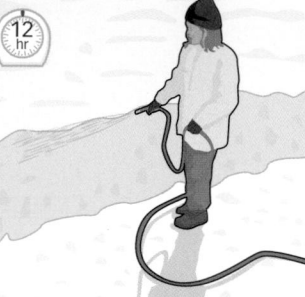
Cover walls and base with a large tarpaulin.

60 cm (2 ft)

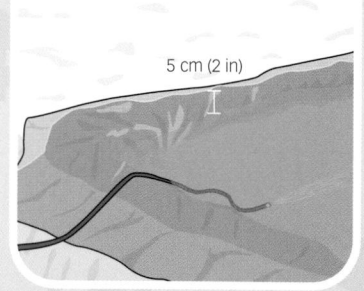
Add water. Leave to ice up for a few freezing nights.

5 cm (2 in)

196 skate a back crossover

Start skating backwards. Gather momentum.

Cross your right foot in front of your left.

Bring your left foot to the side.

Repeat, starting with your right foot.

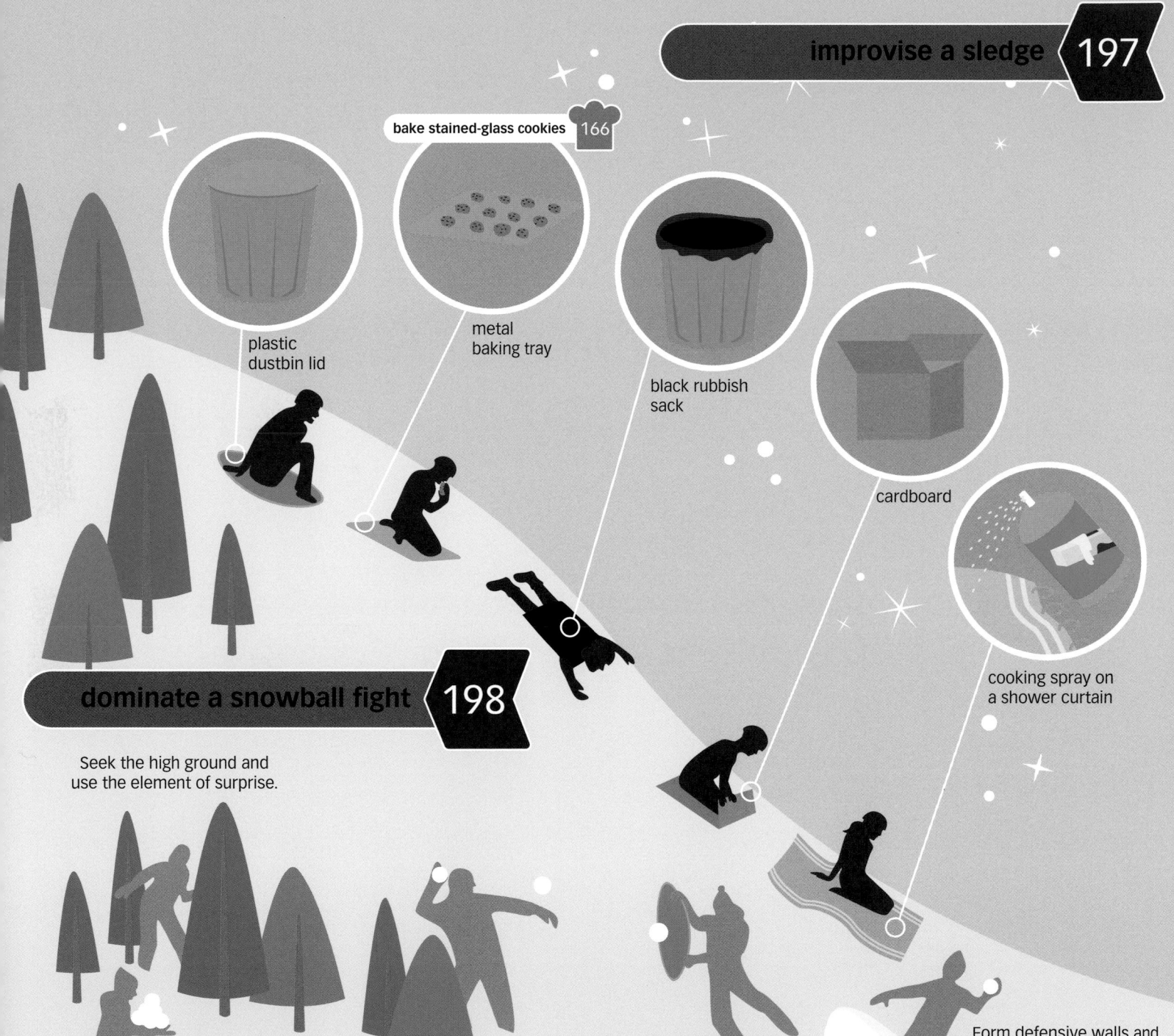

improvise a sledge 197

bake stained-glass cookies 166

plastic
dustbin lid

metal
baking tray

black rubbish
sack

cardboard

cooking spray on
a shower curtain

dominate a snowball fight 198

Seek the high ground and
use the element of surprise.

Stockpile ammo so you're
always ready to reload.

Many sledges can double
as shields.

Form defensive walls and
keep your ammo mobile.

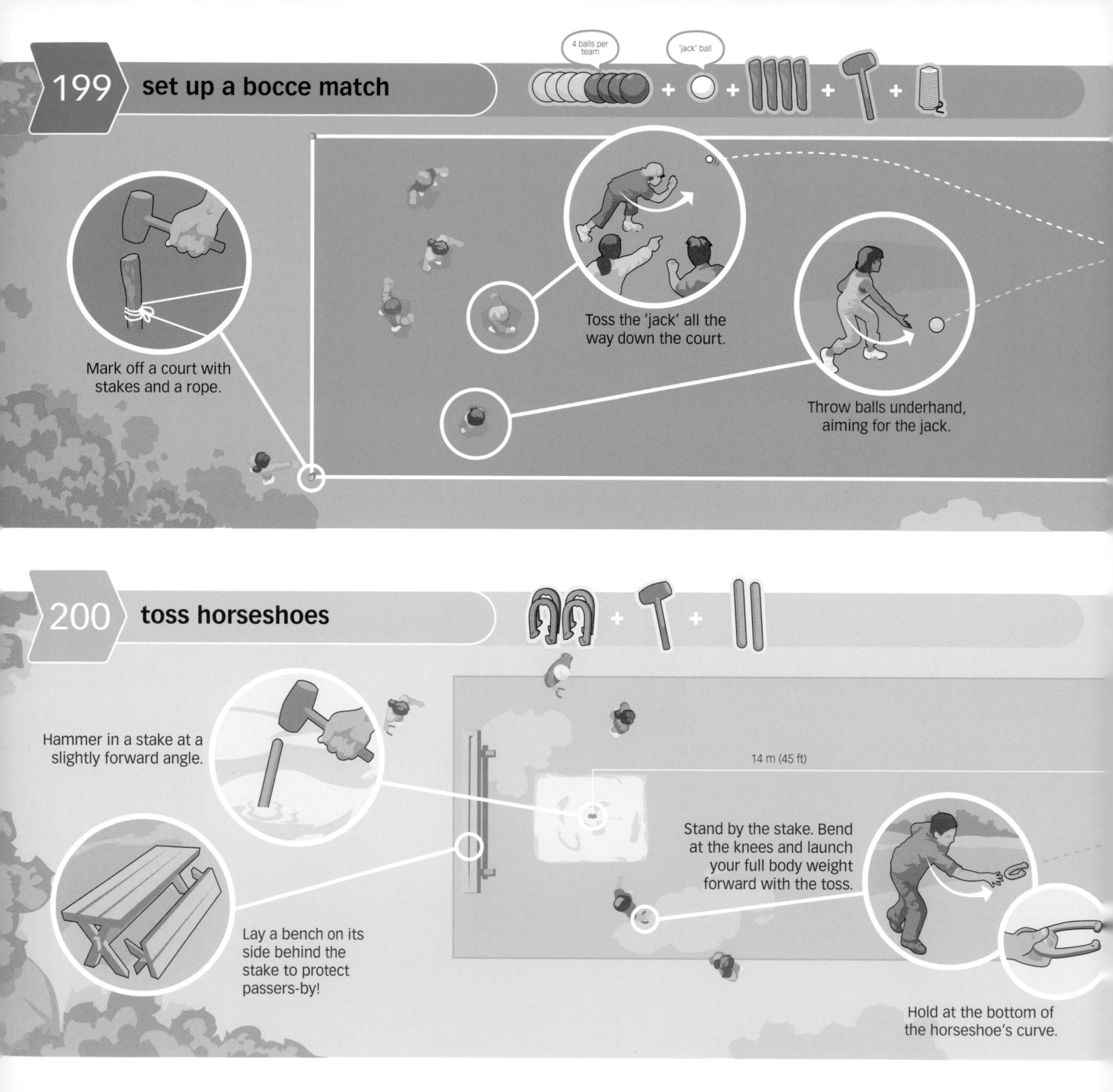

199 set up a bocce match

4 balls per team + 'jack' ball + ◫ + ⬒ + ⬒

Mark off a court with stakes and a rope.

Toss the 'jack' all the way down the court.

Throw balls underhand, aiming for the jack.

200 toss horseshoes

Hammer in a stake at a slightly forward angle.

Lay a bench on its side behind the stake to protect passers-by!

14 m (45 ft)

Stand by the stake. Bend at the knees and launch your full body weight forward with the toss.

Hold at the bottom of the horseshoe's curve.

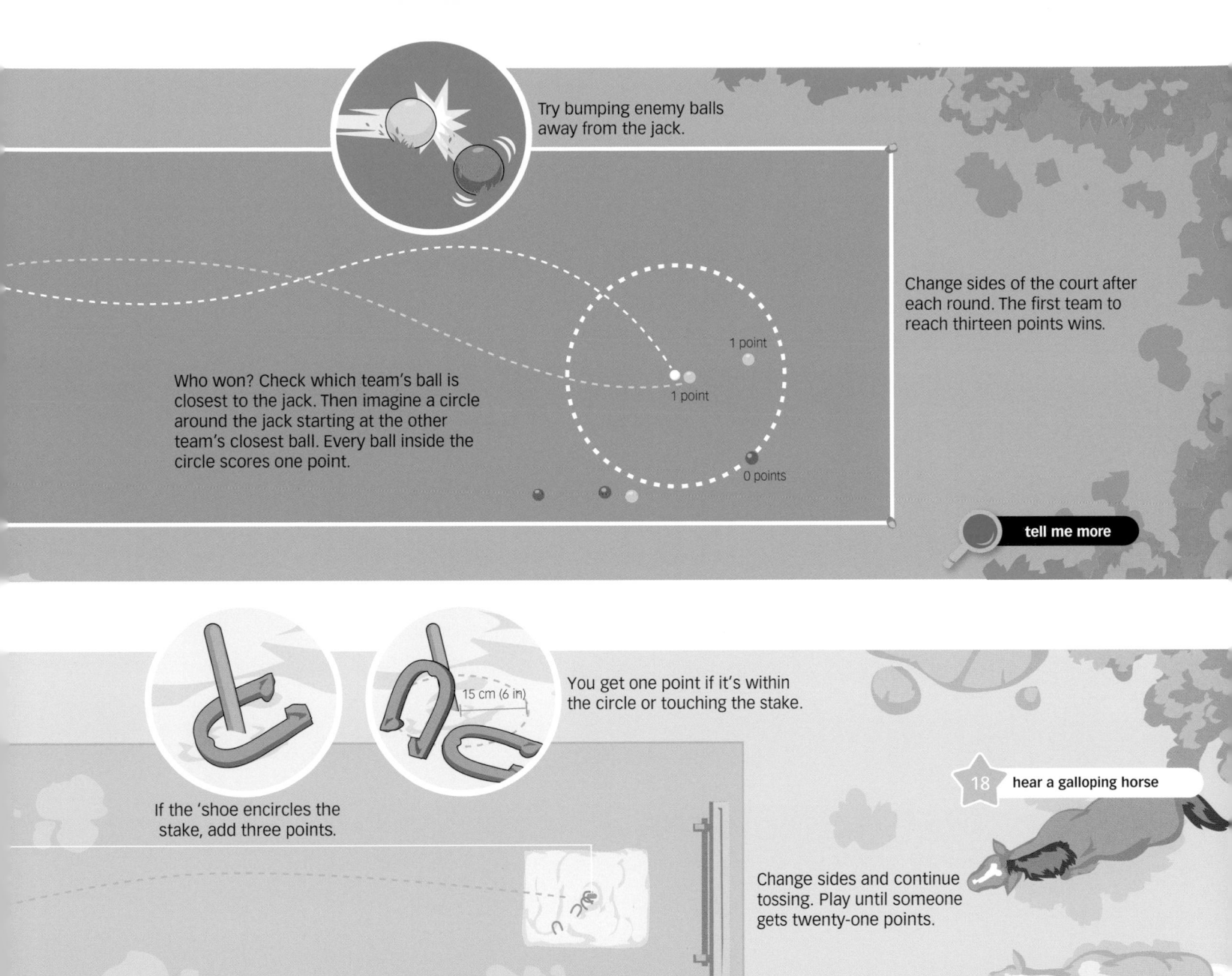

Try bumping enemy balls away from the jack.

Change sides of the court after each round. The first team to reach thirteen points wins.

1 point

1 point

0 points

Who won? Check which team's ball is closest to the jack. Then imagine a circle around the jack starting at the other team's closest ball. Every ball inside the circle scores one point.

tell me more

You get one point if it's within the circle or touching the stake.

15 cm (6 in)

If the 'shoe encircles the stake, add three points.

18 hear a galloping horse

Change sides and continue tossing. Play until someone gets twenty-one points.

tell me more

Hit the lower part of the ball to send it up.

Bend from the waist. Close your mouth and hit squarely.

Hit the top part of the ball to send it down.

202 master goalie moves

Make a diamond with your hands.

Start in the basic goalkeeper position.

Dive to make the catch.

Pull to your chest.

Scoop up the ball with both hands.

Hug the ball to your chest.

Cover the ball.

1 2.5 cm (1 in)

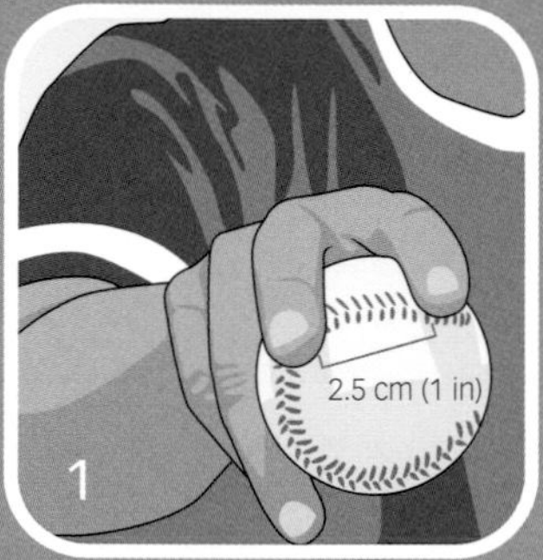

Put index and middle
fingers on the seam.

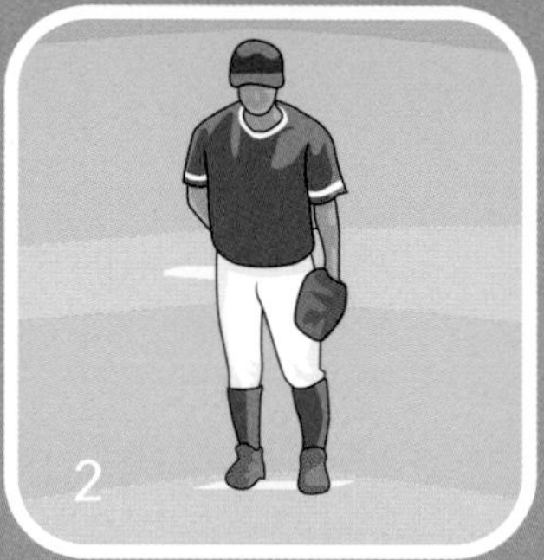

2

Hide your hand to
conceal your grip.

3

Shift to your back
foot. Angle your front.

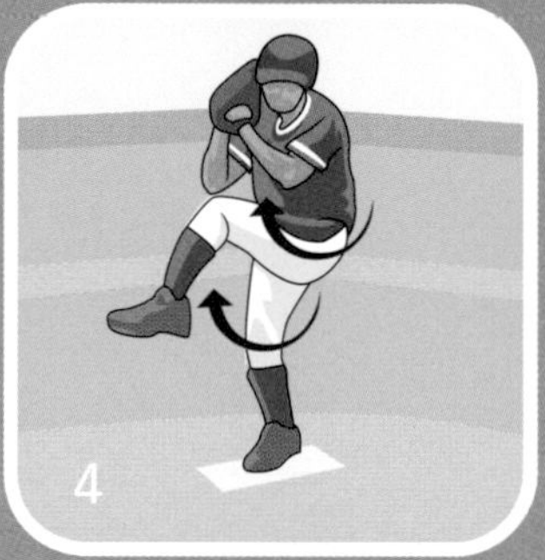

4

'Wind up', using your
front leg and arm.

5

Release with your
fingers over the ball.

6

Follow through
after you throw.

1

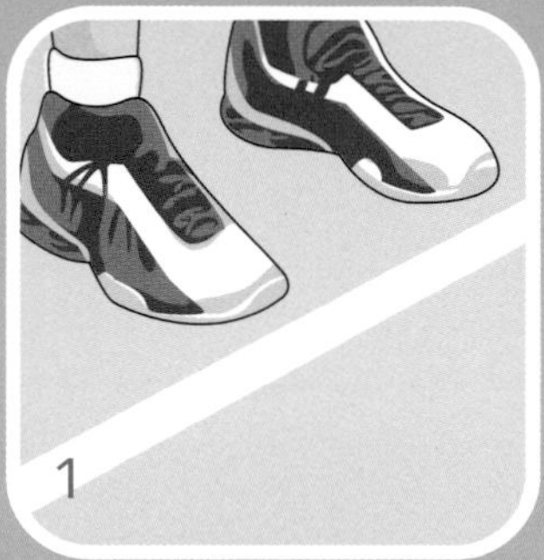

Stand at the
free-throw line.

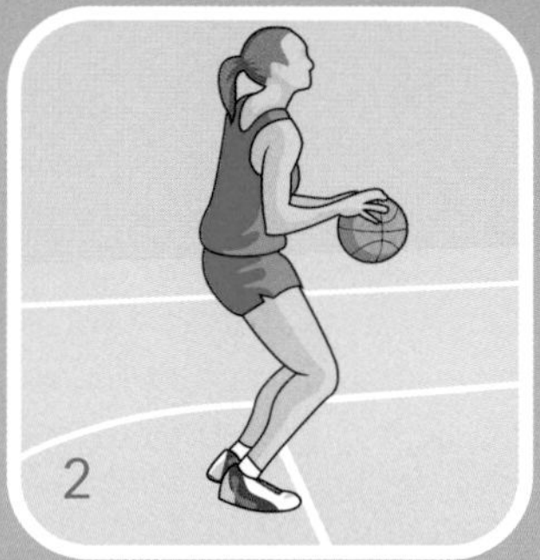

2

Crouch down. Keep
your knees loose.

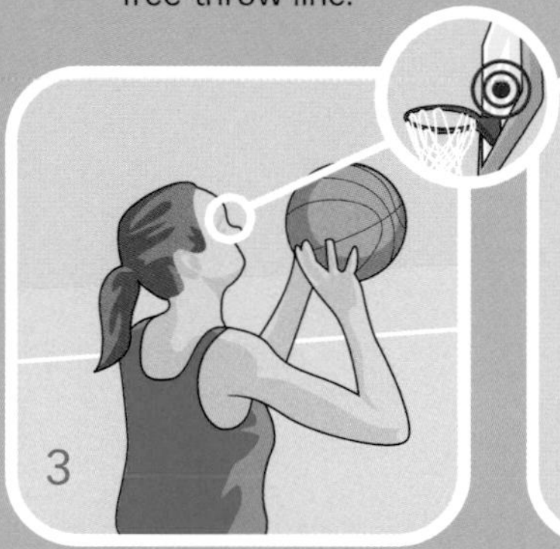

3

Focus on the
backboard.

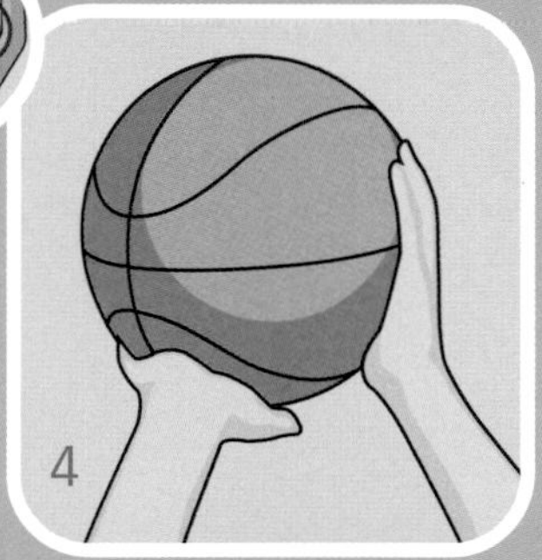

4

Put one hand on the
ball's side to guide it.

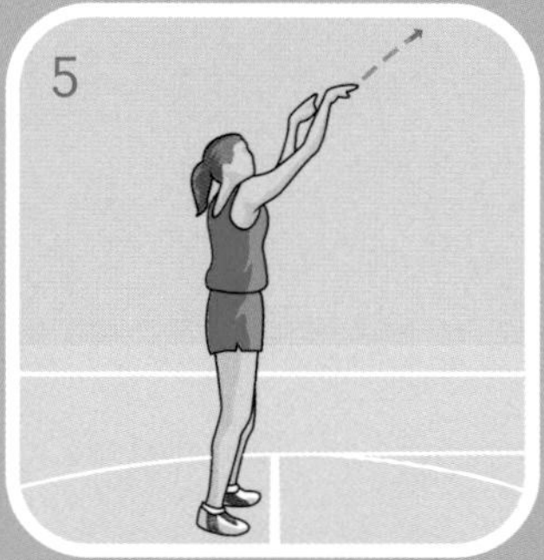

5

Straighten up. Flick
your wrists.

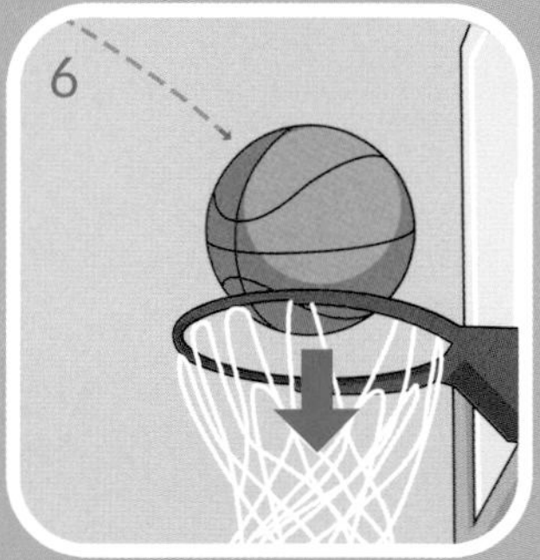

6

Swish!

205 ride a boogie board

1 Wear flippers for speed.
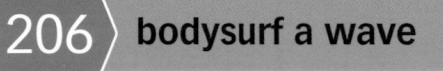

2 Swim past the wave break.

3 Watch for a perfect wave.
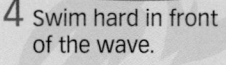

4 Swim hard in front of the wave.

206 bodysurf a wave

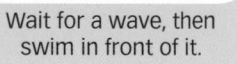

Swim out beyond the wave break.

Wait for a wave, then swim in front of it.

Swim to the side of the break.

Take a deep breath. Steer with your arms.

5 Use your hands and shoulders to steer.

6 Ride the curl!

Gnarly!

 Riding in the curl (at right angles to the direction the wave is heading) takes practice! Start by riding the wave straight into the beach.

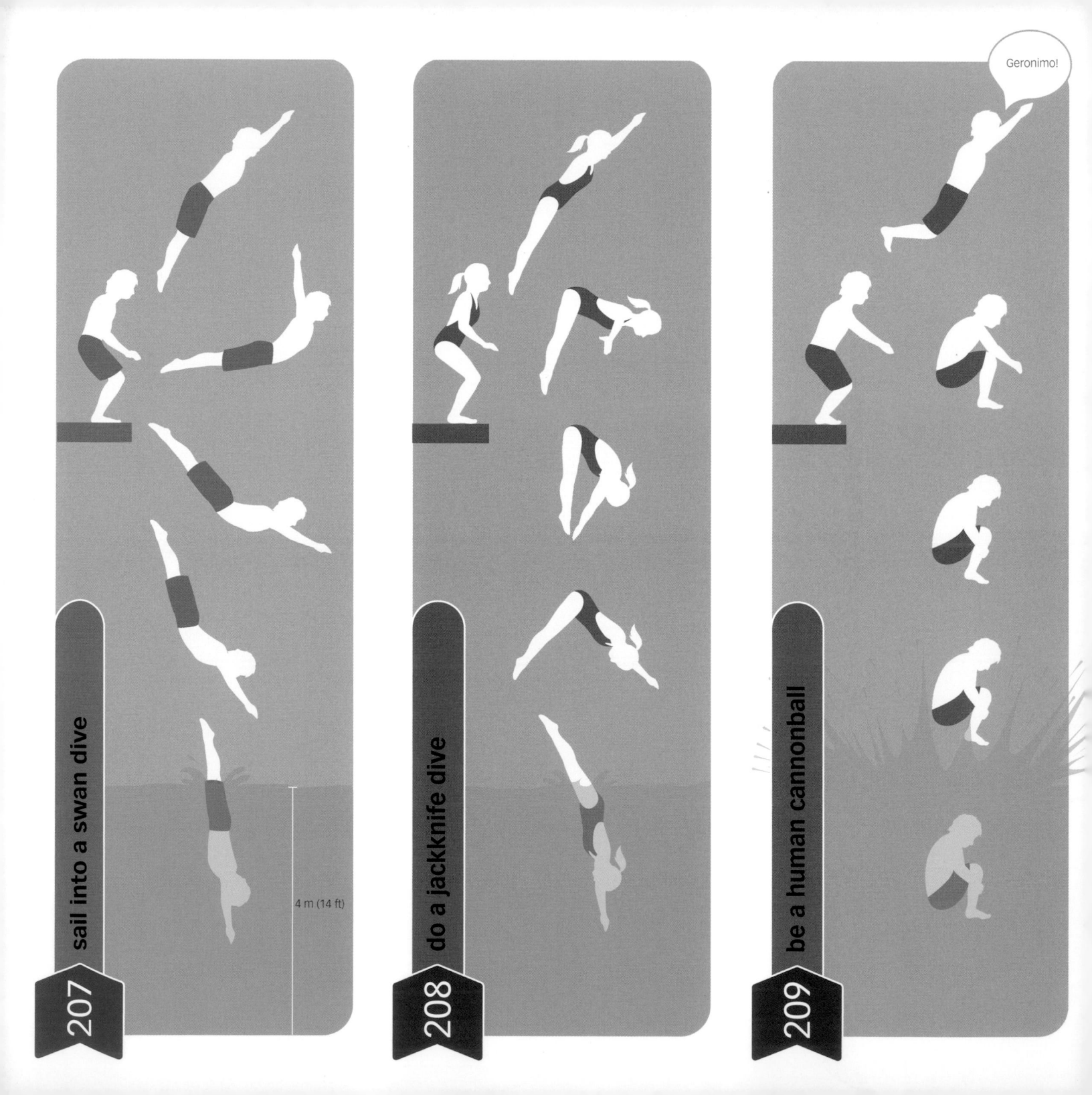

Geronimo!

207 sail into a swan dive

4 m (14 ft)

208 do a jackknife dive

209 be a human cannonball

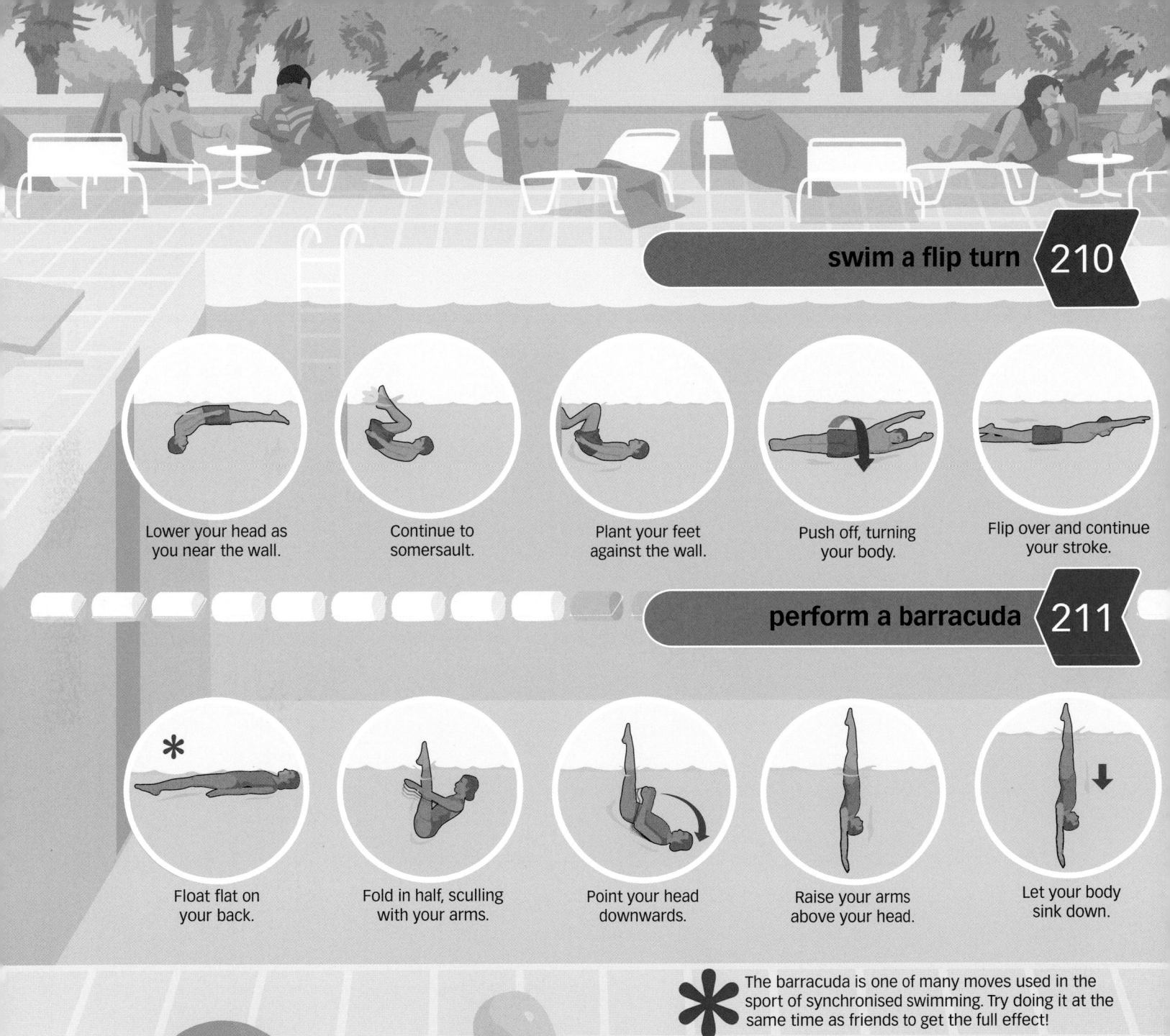

Lower your head as you near the wall.

Continue to somersault.

Plant your feet against the wall.

Push off, turning your body.

Flip over and continue your stroke.

perform a barracuda 211

Float flat on your back.

Fold in half, sculling with your arms.

Point your head downwards.

Raise your arms above your head.

Let your body sink down.

* The barracuda is one of many moves used in the sport of synchronised swimming. Try doing it at the same time as friends to get the full effect!

212 do the worm

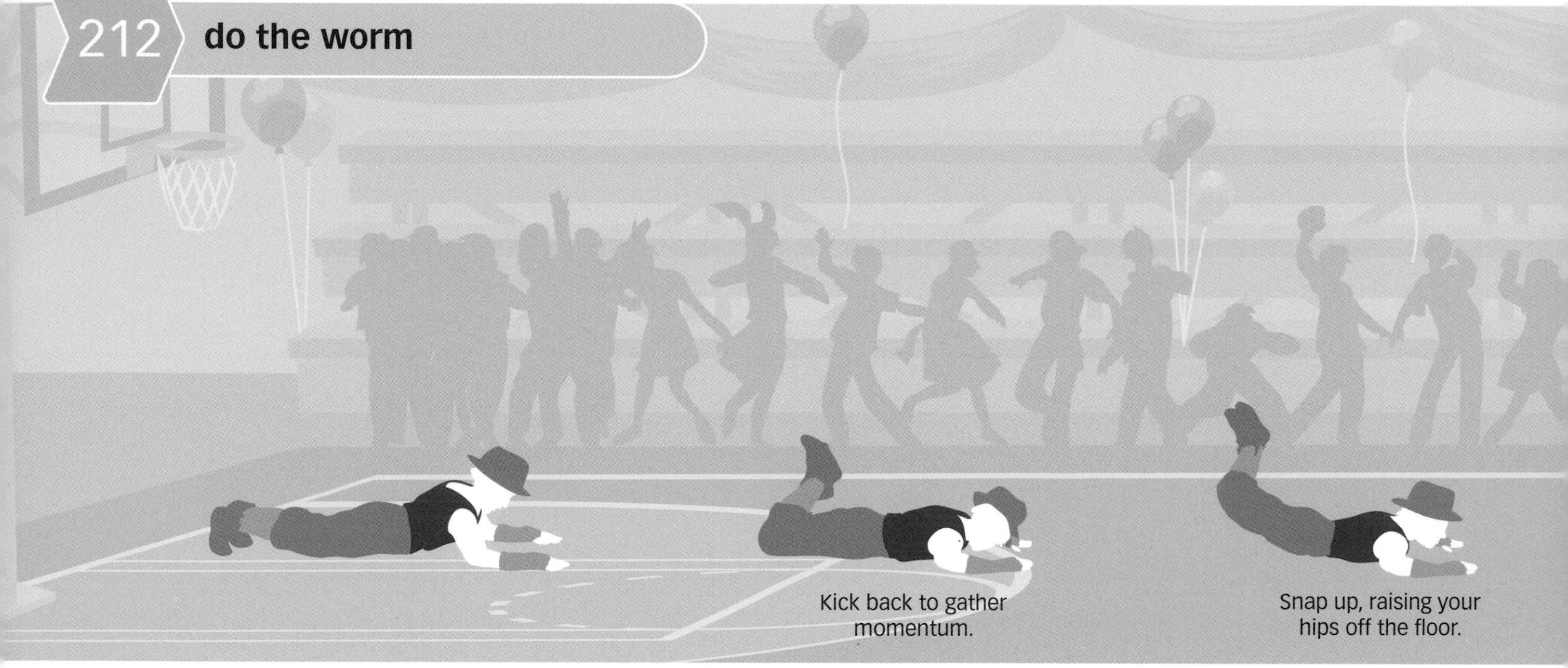

Kick back to gather momentum.
Snap up, raising your hips off the floor.

213 moonwalk in style

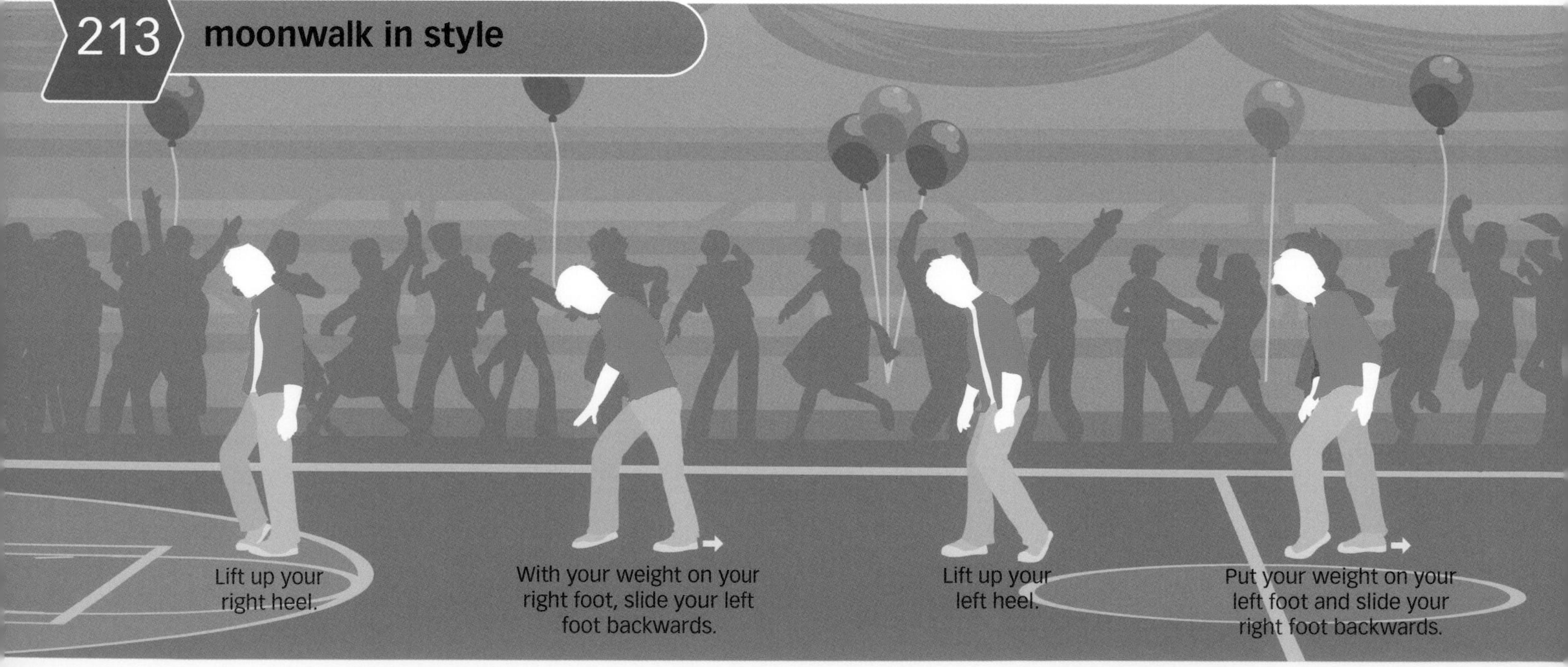

Lift up your right heel.
With your weight on your right foot, slide your left foot backwards.
Lift up your left heel.
Put your weight on your left foot and slide your right foot backwards.

Land on your toes
and push up.

50 do a rock-star jump

Repeat, starting with
your right heel up.

Slide your left foot
back. You've got it!

Pivot and...

...moonwalk back the
other way.

214 ▷ stand on your head

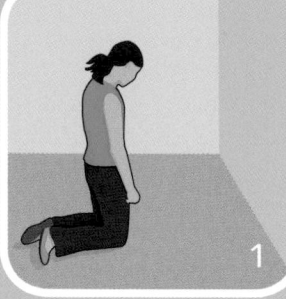

Clear away furniture.
Kneel down.

Put your head and
hands down.

Straighten your legs.

Put one knee on
your elbow.

Put the other knee
on the other elbow.

Raise both legs
into the air.

215 ▷ walk on your hands

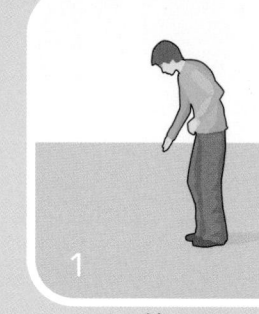

Stand in an open,
flat area.

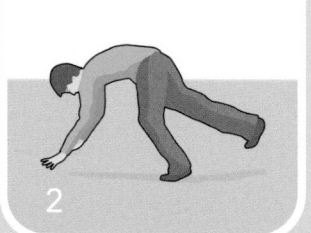

Dive forwards. Kick
one foot in the air.

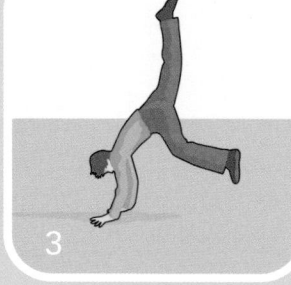

Kick off with your
other foot.

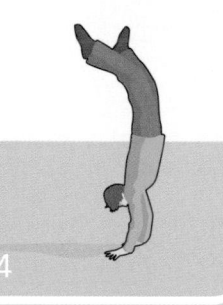

Swing both legs up.
Bend your knees.

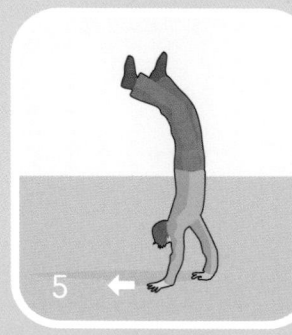

'Step' one
hand forward.

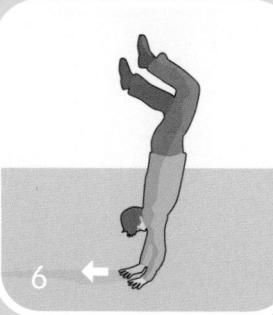

Bring the other
hand forward.

Want to turn head over heels? Practise each phase until you're confident, then move to the next. Don't rush!

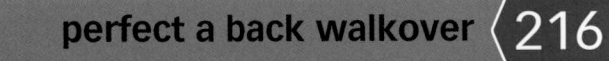

twist up soft pretzels 177

1

Gently stretch into a bridge position.

2

'Walk' your hands down a wall into a bridge. Then try it without the wall.

3

Walk up the wall and then kick over.

4

Practise kicking over without the wall. Tighten your stomach muscles.

5

Put it all together and tumble off into the distance.

ace a cherry drop

Grab the bar. Bring your
toes up to touch the bar.

Place your legs
over the bar.

Hang from the bar
by your knees.

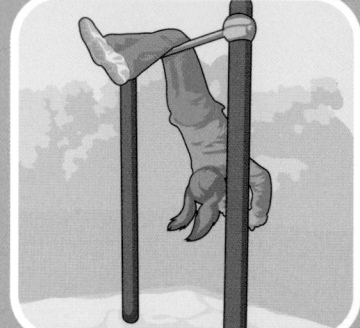

Start swinging back and
forth to build momentum.

 When you're looking for a perfect high bar, make sure there's a soft
surface underneath. You'll also need a spotter to help you practise
these moves – they're more fun with an audience anyway!

---

218 **skin the cat**

Seize the bar and kick
back to build momentum.

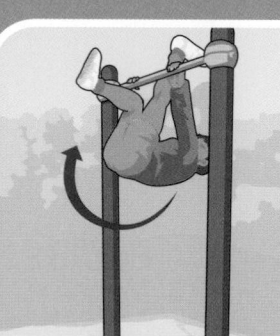

Swing your legs up. Bring
both under the bar.

Let your legs drop down.

Let go and land with
your knees bent.

Keep swinging – you want to have a lot of speed!

Release the bar by unbending your knees.

Tuck your legs underneath you.

Land with your knees bent. No wobbling!

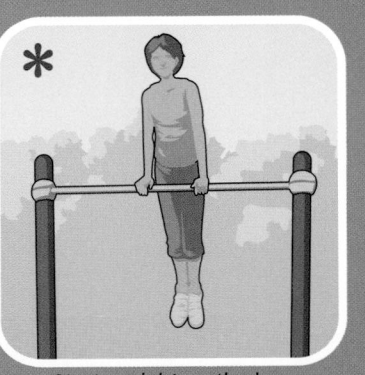

* Start upright on the bar.

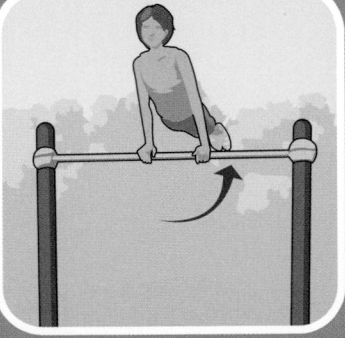

Keeping your arms locked, swing your legs back.

Sweep your legs around the bar in a circle.

Hey presto! You're right back where you started.

bunny-hop a bike

Crouch low.

Hop up, pulling the handlebars with you.

Point your toes down. Keep pulling up!

Tuck your legs up to raise the back wheel.

Land it!

Don't have a dirt-bike course nearby? Practise on the grass to avoid skinned knees. When you feel confident, move up to the pavement!

Start pedalling slowly.

Push one pedal down hard and lean backwards.

Lean back farther and pull up on the handlebars.

Rock out! Keep your balance.

Lean forward and push the handlebars down.

Set the front wheel down.

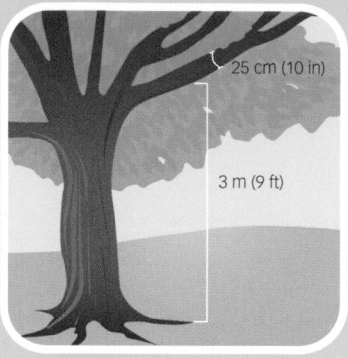

Start with a sturdy tree.

25 cm (10 in)

3 m (9 ft)

Clean an old tyre.

Drill three holes
for drainage.

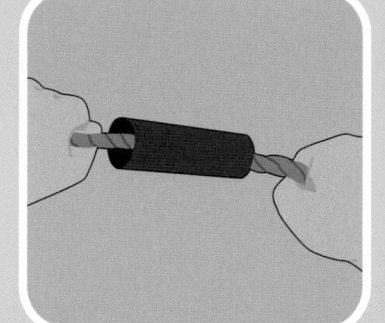

Add tubing to protect the
tree and prevent fraying.

Ask an adult to
place the rope.

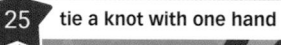

25 | tie a knot with one hand

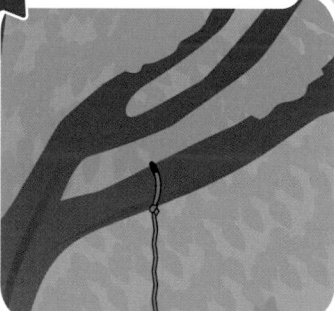

Ask an adult to tie
the rope securely.

Hang with the drainage
holes at the bottom.

Add some bark chippings
for soft landings.

tell me more

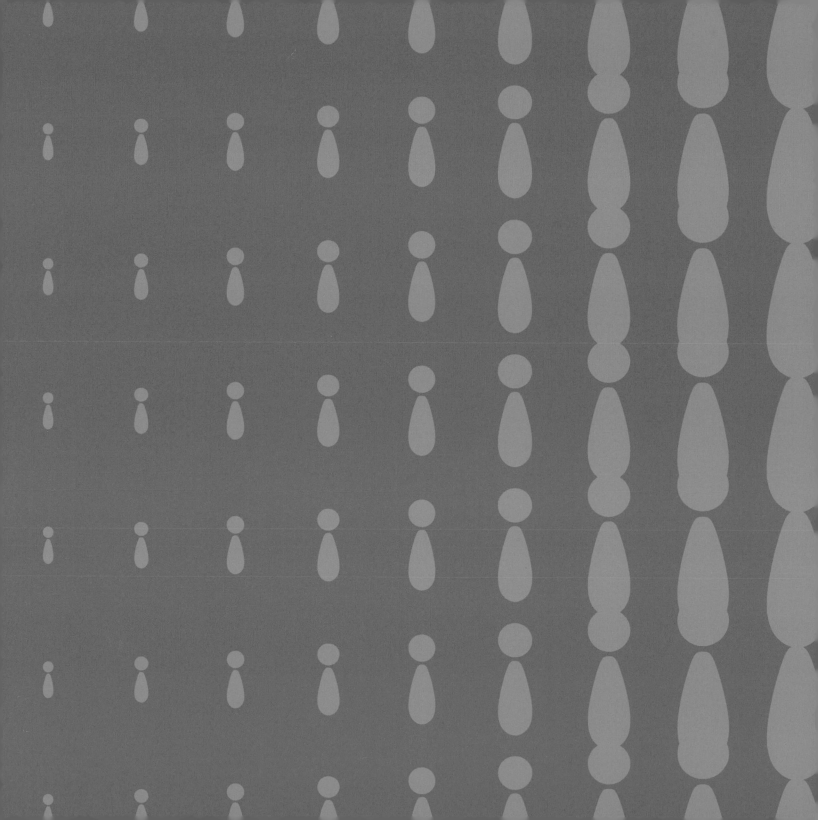

tell me more

Pssst! Want to know more about a project in this book? This handy section is full of trivia, history and extra expert advice that will help you tackle certain activities or better understand what's so awesome about them.

18 hear a galloping horse

Before television, people listened to drama or comedy shows on the radio. To make these stories sound realistic and action-packed, radio shows hired 'soundmen'. These technicians used common objects to improvise noises, which brought the action of a story to life.

Here are a few more classic radio tricks for you to try.

Sprinkle rice on metal.

Tap a metal lid.

Stab a watermelon.

Crunch cat litter.

8 make a floating finger

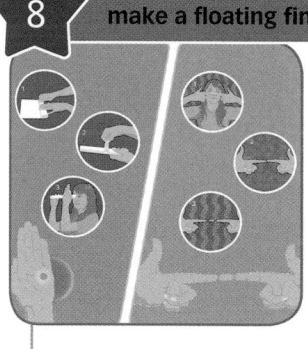

Think your eyes are playing tricks on you? You're right. As both of your eyes focus on your fingers, their paths of vision converge at one point. But then your eyes must make their paths of vision nearly parallel to focus on a distant object. While both your eyes can still see your fingertips, they see slightly overlapped images. This illusion is called a trick of perspective.

10 fake mummy organs

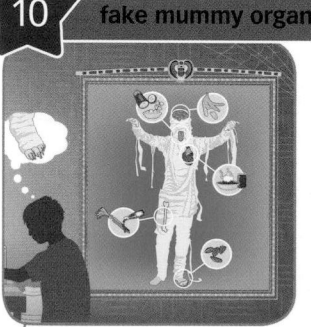

Before placing deceased loved ones' bodies in sarcophagi, ancient Egyptians would 'mummify' them by wrapping their bodies in linen strips. They'd also remove some of the bodies' organs, which were then washed, dried, bandaged and placed in special jars. It sounds like a lot of trouble, but the Egyptians believed that this process ensured a pleasant afterlife for the deceased.

29 dowse for water

People all around the world have practised dowsing, also known as 'water witching', for centuries. Dowsers claim to be able to locate water, oil, mineral deposits and lost objects using just their minds and a stick that twitches when the goods are found. Is it for real? Scientists tend to say no, but farmers and miners around the world continue to pay top rates for dowsers' services.

read a love line 30

To read a friend's palm, start with her dominant hand (the hand she writes with). The lines on this hand will show you behaviours and attitudes that are firmly set in this person, as well as her past actions. Next read her other hand (the passive hand). These lines will tell you her potential in the future. Remember, palm reading is just for fun – don't take it too seriously!

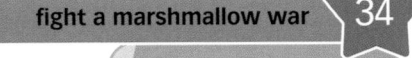

fight a marshmallow war 34

Can't find these exact marshmallow creatures in your local shop? Don't worry – you can make your own 'mallow monsters. Stack a few marshmallows and arm them with cocktail sticks. Then let them fight it out in the microwave.

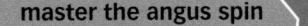

master the angus spin 51

When you try this move, you may look idiotic – but you'll be in good company! The invention of the Angus Spin is credited to vaudeville performer Curly Howard, one of the original Three Stooges. The move became a part of rock 'n' roll history when it was adopted by Angus Young of the band AC/DC (thus earning its name). Homer Simpson is another famous practitioner.

squeeze an egg into a bottle 53

How does this trick work? When the lighted match heats up the air in the bottle, the air molecules move around and spread apart. When the fire goes out, the molecules cool down and move closer together. Normally, this would suck in air from outside, but the egg blocks the entry. The pressure of the air molecules outside the bottle is so great that it forces the egg into the bottle.

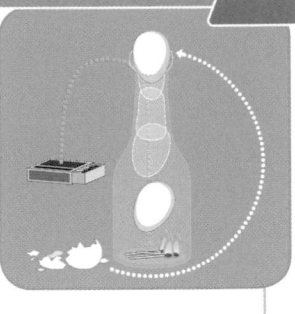

bend water with static 54

Everything in the world is made of atoms, and atoms are made of positive, negative and neutral electric charges. These are known as protons (positive), electrons (negative) and neutrons (neutral). When certain objects, like your hair and a comb, come into contact, the electrons jump from one to the other. This leads to a build up of negative charges on one object – in this case, on the comb.

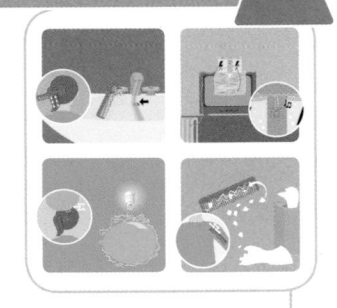

Because opposites attract, these electrons will be drawn to positive charges (a state called static electricity). That's why the electrons on the negatively charged comb can tug other positively charged objects (like the torn tissue or stream of water) towards the comb. This attraction is also why the electrons on the television screen can jump to the tinfoil and why the electrons move from the balloon to the light bulb: these negative charges want to take over positively charged areas! And when they do, the static electricity they generate can set off sparks or even make a little music.

Want to try one more static trick? Use static to separate salt and pepper! Make a small pile of salt and pepper on a flat surface. Rub a balloon vigorously against a woollen jumper, then slowly bring the balloon near the salt and pepper pile – the pepper will fly up and stick to the balloon, leaving the salt.

58   tell the time with a potato

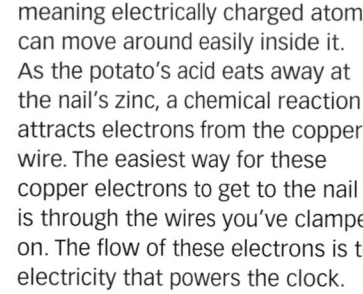

The acid in a potato is conductive, meaning electrically charged atoms can move around easily inside it. As the potato's acid eats away at the nail's zinc, a chemical reaction attracts electrons from the copper wire. The easiest way for these copper electrons to get to the nail is through the wires you've clamped on. The flow of these electrons is the electricity that powers the clock.

61   lift a friend's fingerprint

For more than a thousand years, people have known that fingerprints are special. In ninth-century China, business people put their stamped fingerprints on documents instead of their signatures. By the 1500s, scientists had worked out that no two people had the same fingerprint. However, it wasn't until 1892 that the first criminal was caught as a result of fingerprint identification.

63   encode notes with a scytale

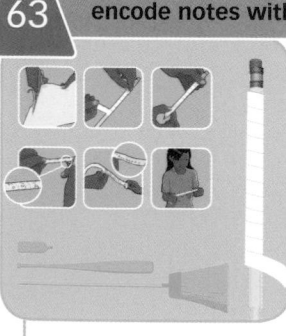

This spy device (pronounced 'skee-ta-lee') was invented by the ancient Romans for use during war. Each general had an identical rod and would write messages on leather strips wound around the rod, then unwind the strips and send them with a messenger. If the messenger carrying the unwound strips was captured, the message would be hard for the enemy to read. Sneaky!

64   send secrets by morse code

In the days before phones and radio, it could take people months to send a message across a long distance. In 1844, Samuel Morse popularised the telegraph – a device for sending electric signals across miles of cable. Messages were written in Morse code: a system of dots and dashes that symbolise letters and punctuation. It was very handy during World Wars I and II.

66   write in invisible ink

You can write disappearing messages with other common liquids that have been diluted with water, including milk, honey, vinegar and even wee! Spies used all of these methods during World Wars I and II, and may continue their use today. If you have a special black light handy, you can reveal invisible messages written in milk, liquid soap or washing powder.

67   turn the world upside down

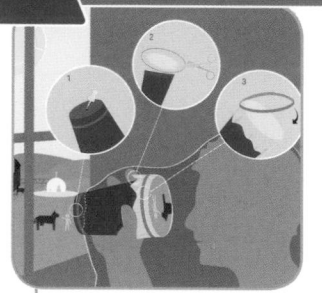

This device is known as a camera obscura. Why does the image flip upside down, exactly?
As light passes through the tiny hole, the light that is coming up from the bottom of the scene continues going up and the light shining down from the top of the scene continues travelling down. These separate light waves hit the paper screen, and the top and bottom are reversed.

Sun prints are also known as cyanotypes (cyan is a deep shade of blue). The paper is coated in a chemical that turns blue after exposure to sunlight. By placing objects over parts of the paper, you block the sunlight from reaching the surface beneath them, so those parts don't turn blue. When you rinse the paper in water, the parts of the chemical that haven't turned blue are washed away, and the paper gets bluer as it dries. Cyanotypes, invented in 1842, were popular with engineers and architects, who needed to reproduce notes and plans in the days before photocopiers. They called their cyanotypes 'blueprints'.

You can make beautiful sun prints by cutting shapes out of thick paper and arranging them into scenes.

What causes this awesome explosion, you ask? When vinegar, which is an acid, combines with baking soda, a base, the resulting chemical reaction creates carbon dioxide gas. As the gas tries to rise into the air, it gets caught in the murky red liquid inside the volcano, creating foamy red bubbles. These gas-filled bubbles tumble out, erupting like lava from a volcano.

While marbleising your masterpiece, did you see how the paint floats on top of the water instead of mixing into it or sinking? That's because water is denser than paint. The atoms of water are packed together tightly, while oil paint's atoms are held together more loosely.

Now that you know how marbleising works, here are a few advanced techniques for you to try:

Blow across the paint's surface with a drinking straw. Try changing your angle and position for different designs.

Drag a feather across the paint for hundreds of tiny, delicate lines, or use a large fork to make bolder lines.

Remove leftover paint by drawing newspaper strips across the water. Add more paint and start again.

Spanish for 'perforated paper', this festive artwork originates in Mexico, where it's hung up during religious, national and family celebrations. Experienced artists there make designs by laying out a thick stack of tissue papers, setting down a stencil, then whacking a chisel through the papers with a mallet. Their designs usually feature birds, flowers, skeletons or lattice patterns.

87 paste up a piñata

Think you might want to keep your piñata rather than burst it open? Then you'll need to adjust your papier-mâché recipe beforehand to keep the piñata from sprouting mould – gross! Mix one part flour with two parts water to get a thick, gluey consistency. Add more flour if it seems runny, or more water if it's too thick to dip the paper in. Then mix in 4 tbsp salt.

104 draw awesome manga

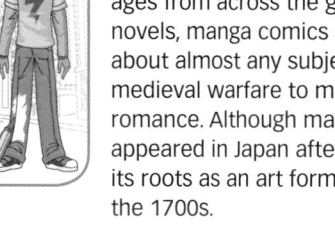

Manga is a type of Japanese comic that has attracted avid fans of all ages from across the globe. Like novels, manga comics can be written about almost any subject, from medieval warfare to modern romance. Although manga originally appeared in Japan after World War II, its roots as an art form go back to the 1700s.

114 ink a fake tattoo

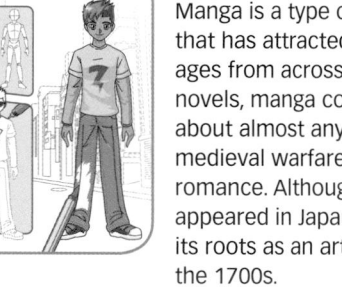

Humans have tattooed themselves since prehistoric times – the tradition is thought to be more than 12,000 years old. The oldest mummy ever found in Europe, Otzi the Iceman (who lived way back around 4,000 BC), was found to have 57 tattoos. Back then ink or soot was poked into the skin with a stick or rubbed into a design cut into the skin. Ouch!

118 screen-print a T-shirt

Screen-printing is sometimes called silk-screening. That's because when the Chinese first popularised this art form during the Song Dynasty (AD 960–1279), they used screens made of silk to transfer their images. Now we use polyester screens.

Here are some screen-printing tips.

 Simplify multiple tones into bold, high-contrast shapes.

Use half-tone dots to show gradual shifts in tone.

Avoid using thin lines, which can clog and smear easily.

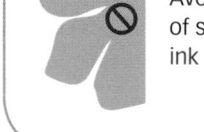 Avoid very large areas of solid colour where ink might pool.

Print colours one at a time. Layer them for a cool effect.

122 make a magnetic compass

Your leaf-and-needle compass works on a familiar premise: that opposites attract. The Earth's poles are magnetised, so the magnetised needle is attracted to them and aligns itself with the north-south axis. It's important that there are no other magnetised items near the leaf – they can interfere with your compass's reading. It also helps to keep the leaf out of the wind.

collect water in damp sand 129

Even in desert-like areas that appear totally dry, water seeps into the ground when it rains. The heat and sun warm only the ground's surface, but below the surface, the water never evaporates. When you dig your mini well below this saturation point, water will slowly seep into the hole, seeking equilibrium. Remember, don't drink collected water unless you strain and boil it.

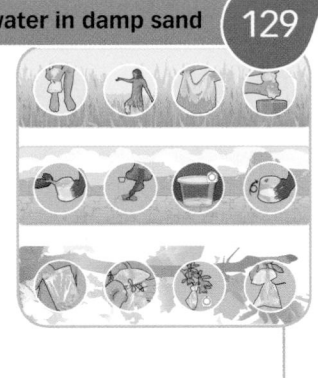

identify clouds 131

Earth isn't the only place with clouds. These atmospheric features also appear over all the other planets, with the exception of Mercury. Jupiter and Saturn have some clouds made of water, just like ours, but most of the other planets in the solar system have clouds made up of highly poisonous gases. Think of that next time you're fed up with a cloudy day!

blaze a trail 133

This trail-marking system has been around for a while. It's based on similar codes first invented by the San Bushmen in the Kalahari Desert to communicate silently while hunting. More recently, pioneers and hikers have relied on this system to mark (or blaze) new trails in the days before GPS, using painted symbols, flags, stone piles or sticks to point others in the right direction.

build a bat house 139

Bats, when they're not living in caves, prefer to sleep and raise young in trees – ideally in a place where bark has split off a tree trunk. Deforestation means many bats have nowhere to live, so the best thing you can do for them is to offer a warm, secluded spot that mimics these tree homes. Your bat house should be tall and narrow, with a tiny entrance slot at the bottom and a scratchy interior surface that the bats can climb up and cling to.

So why go to all this trouble? A bat eats hundreds, sometimes thousands, of insects per hour, keeping your garden free from pests that munch on your plants. Plus, bats are pollinators, which means they spread pollen between plants, causing new plants to grow that other creatures can eat. So these dark-winged mammals play a crucial part in our ecosystem: when bat populations decline, other local creatures will suffer as well.

While pre-made bat houses are available at garden centres and online, making them isn't hard. Our instructions are a good start; you can also check with a local conservation group to find out what homes will be popular with your local bats.

make a hive for mason bees 142

Unlike common honeybees, Mason bees don't live in hives or work together – each bee flies solo. These bees make their own private homes, usually in hollow reeds or small holes in wood. Although they won't make you any honey, Mason bees will come in very handy in your garden. Like bats, they're excellent pollinators, carrying pollen from flower to flower.

147 nurture tadpoles

When raising your tadpoles, don't overcrowd your tank. Each tadpole needs 3.75 l (1 gallon) of water. After a few weeks, the tadpoles will stop eating the food you give them, and their tails will start to disappear. Don't freak out! They are growing normally. As soon as little legs appear, place some large rocks in the tank so the tadpoles can climb out of the water to breathe.

148 cultivate carnivorous plants

Carnivorous plants use various methods of trapping insects, from the dramatic snap of the Venus flytrap and the drowning pool of the pitcher plant to the more common (but less exciting) sticky leaves of the 'flypaper' plants. These plants are very ancient. They probably first appeared in the Early Cretaceous Period (145 million years ago), when dinosaurs roamed the Earth.

164 build a wobbly city

If you'd like to make your buildings more transparent, use more gelatine and less coloured jelly mix. This extra gelatine will also help your creations stand up firmly on their own. When removing the 'buildings' from their moulds, turn them over and shake gently – a slapping sound means that they're ready to come out. If you don't hear it, let the moulds set longer.

166 bake stained-glass cookies

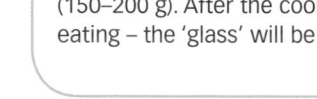

Want to make these cookies from scratch? You can skip the shop-bought stuff and make the cookie dough at home with an adult using this easy recipe.

350 g (12 oz) butter, softened
400 g (14 oz) white sugar
4 eggs
1 tsp vanilla extract
550 g (1 lb 3½ oz) plain flour
2 tsp baking powder
2 tsp salt

In a large bowl, mix the butter and sugar together until smooth. Beat in the eggs and vanilla. Add the flour, baking powder and salt, then mix thoroughly. Cover and leave dough in the fridge for 1 hour or longer.

Preheat the oven to 200°C (400°F). Sprinkle flour and a little sugar on a surface, then roll out the dough until it measures 1.25 cm (½ in) thick.

Follow the illustrated steps for cutting out the shapes, adding the crushed sweets and baking the cookies. If you use the recipe here, you should need between thirty and forty sweets (150–200 g). After the cookies have baked, let them cool before eating – the 'glass' will be very hot!

169 fold fortune cookies

These famous after-dinner treats are served in Chinese restaurants throughout the Western world, but they aren't Chinese at all. Several bakers in the U.S. state of California claimed to have invented the delicate cookies around the turn of the nineteenth century, and some theories trace their inspiration to either Chinese mooncakes or Japanese *sembei* crackers.

If you're feeling really gourmet, go ahead and make the filling for your tortellini yourself! Here are two simple, delicious recipes for cheese-and-veggie fillings:

Basil-Ricotta Filling
225 g (8 oz) ricotta cheese
3 tbsp Parmesan cheese, grated
3 basil leaves, finely chopped
2 pinches salt

Combine the ricotta, Parmesan, basil and salt in a small bowl, then mix well. Cover and refrigerate, or fold into the tortellini immediately.

basil

Spinach-Ricotta Filling
225 g (1 c) mozzarella, shredded
265 g (9 oz) breadcrumbs
2 eggs
285 g (10 oz) frozen spinach
225 g (8 oz) ricotta cheese
1 clove garlic, chopped

spinach

Thaw and drain the spinach. Put all the ingredients into a food processor and blend until smooth. If the mixture is dry, add more egg; if it seems runny, add a few more breadcrumbs. Cover and refrigerate, or add to the tortellini at once.

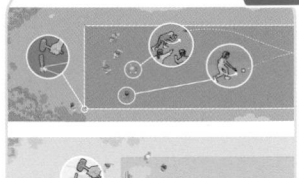

The rules shown here are from a version of the game called open bocce. Because this game has been popular all over the world since the time of the ancient Romans, there are plenty of small, international variations. So when you travel, be sure to try *pétanque* or *boules* in France, bowls in England, *bolas criollas* in Venezuela and *kloolschieten* in the Netherlands.

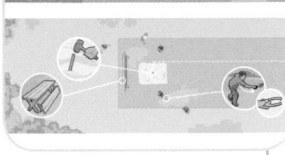

Horseshoes is another game with roots in ancient Rome; it is probably based on the Olympic sport of discus. Before the age of mechanised transport, it was a popular pastime for soldiers during many wars. When soldiers went home, horseshoes became a family game, then an official sport with famous players. Horseshoes is related to quoits, a Scottish game.

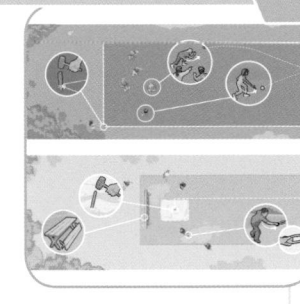

Plants breathe using a process called transpiration. In the case of celery, the plant 'inhales' water through tiny canals in its stem called xylem and then 'exhales' the water through pores in its leaves. When the celery sucks up dyed water, the xylem absorbs some dye from the water. Transpiration keeps the plant cool and transfers nutrients from its roots to its stalk and leaves.

The word 'ninja' is derived from a Japanese word meaning 'stealthy'. As you might expect, the history of these ancient, secretive and deadly warriors is tough to pin down! In ancient Japan, both boys and girls trained to be ninjas. One favourite trick was to wear sandals with bottoms carved to look like animal prints so that the ninja could sneak around without leaving footprints.

index

about the authors

Sarah Hines Stephens first learned to cook in order to get out of doing the washing up, and she still prefers making messes to cleaning them. One of three creative sisters, Sarah hails from generations of do-it-yourselfers: quilters, artists, writers and gardeners. When Sarah is not facilitating semi-explosive science experiments and kid-friendly crafts, she writes books for kids. She has written more than sixty books. She lives with her husband and two children in a home filled with glitter, fabric scraps, glue and power tools.

Bethany Mann is Sarah's sister and partner in creative mess-making. With a rallying cry of, "Hey, we could totally make that ourselves!" she has fearlessly led her family and friends in numerous craft adventures. These days Bethany channels her artistic powers for good by using recycled materials and growing vegetables. Her projects have been featured in craft books for adults and on DIY TV. She lives with her husband, teenage son and a menagerie of rescued pets in the mountains near Santa Cruz, USA. Read her blog at www.bitterbettyindustries.blogspot.com.

BONNIER PUBLISHING

Group Publisher John Owen

WELDON OWEN INC.

CEO, President Terry Newell

Senior VP, International Sales Stuart Laurence

VP, Sales and New Business Development Amy Kaneko

VP, Publisher Roger Shaw

VP, Creative Director Gaye Allen

Associate Creative Director Kelly Booth

Executive Editor Mariah Bear

Associate Editor Lucie Parker

Project Editor Frances Reade

Senior Designer Stephanie Tang

Designer Delbarr Moradi

Illustration Coordinator Sheila Masson

Production Director Chris Hemesath

Production Manager Michelle Duggan

Colour Manager Teri Bell

A TEMPLAR BOOK

First published in the UK in 2009 by Templar Publishing, an imprint of The Templar Company Limited, The Granary, North Street, Dorking, Surrey, RH4 1DN www.templarco.co.uk

Conceived and produced by
Weldon Owen Inc.
415 Jackson Street
San Francisco, California 94111
Copyright © 2009 Weldon Owen Inc.

ISBN 978-1-84011-759-2

10 9 8 7 6 5 4 3 2 1

Printed in China by SNP Leefung

Typeset in Vectora LH

SHOW ME NOW

A Show Me Now Book.
Show Me Now is a trademark of Weldon Owen Inc.

Special thanks to:

Storyboarders

Esy Casey, Julumarie Joy Cornista, Sarah Lynn Duncan, Chris Hall, Paula Rogers, Jamie Spinello, Brandi Valenza

Illustration specialists

Hayden Foell, Raymond Larrett, Ross Sublett

Editorial and research support team

Marc Caswell, Mollie Church, Elizabeth Dougherty, Alex Eros, Justin Goers, Emelie Griffin, Sarah Gurman, Susan Jonaitis, Peter Masiak, Grace Newell, Jennifer Newens, Paul Ozzello, Ben Rosenberg, Hiya Swanhuyser

Most excellent kid-reviewer panel

Emma Arlen, Leah Cohen, Sally Elton, Whitman Hall, Tesserae Honor, Nami Kaneko, Emily Newell, Eloise Shaw, Georgia Shaw

Illustration credits

Front cover

Liberum Donum (Juan Calle, Santiago Calle, Andres Penagos): manga **Hank Osuna**: pretzels **Vincent Perea**: tattoo designs **Bryon Thompson**: cyclist **Otis Thomson**: go-cart **Gabhor Utomo**: guitarist **Tina Cash Walsh**: back walkover

Back cover

Joshua Kemble: robot **Liberum Donum**: vault **Raymond Larrett**: hat trick

Key: bg = background; bd = border; fr = frames; ex = extra art

Kelly Booth: 30–32 **Henry Boyle**: 115 **Esy Casey**: 70 bg **Hayden Foell**: 23 bd, 24 bd, 36 bg, 38, 144, 163 ex **Britt Hanson**: 18–21, 23–25 bg, 34, 35 bg, 43–44, 54–57, 64, 67, 74, 89, 93, 100, 112, 143, 153–156, 160 bg, 176, 179, 196 bg, 197–198 **Gary Henricks**: 78, 90 **Joshua Kemble**: 76, 152, 175 fr, 203–204 **Vic Kulihin**: 37, 39 fr, 41, 75, 79–80, 116, 223, 224 **Raymond Larrett**: 26–29, 33, 35 fr, 36 fr, 59–60, 72, 81–82, 86, 88, 166 **Liberum Donum**: 1–4, 11, 15–17, 39 ex, 40, 42, 52, 58, 73, 101–104, 107, 113, 133–134, 147 fr, 158, 159 fr, 161, 164–165, 184, 188 bg, 189 bg, 190 bg, 199–200, 205–206, 212–213, 217–219 **Christine Meighan**: 5, 23, 83–84, 92,

162–163, 180, 182–183, 188 fr, 189 fr, 190 fr **Hank Osuna**: 160 fr, 177–178 **Vincent Perea**: 9–10, 68, 114, 135, 137–138, 148 **Ross Sublett**: 111 bg, 113 bg, 141 fr **Bryon Thompson**: 53, 98–99, 106, 120, 127, 139–142, 167–172, 191–194, 207–209, 220–221 **Otis Thomson**: 105, 186–187 **Wil Tirion**: 123, 126 **Taylor Tucek**: 70–71, 117 **Gabhor Utomo**: 7–8, 12–14, 22, 45–51, 61–63, 65–66, 69, 77, 85, 87, 91, 94–95, 108–110 bg, 118, 119 bg, 122, 124–125, 128–132, 145–146, 147 bg, 175 bg, 185, 201–202, 210–211 **Tina Cash Walsh**: 24 fr, 25 fr, 96–97, 108–110 fr, 111 fr, 119 fr, 136, 149–151, 157, 159 bg, 173–174, 181, 195–196 fr, 214–216, 222 **Mary Zins**: 6, 121

get involved!

your picture here!

SHOW ME TEAM

Want to be world famous? We probably can't help. But if you'd like to see your name in a book and show the world how clever, talented or just plain weird you are... that we can do. Is there something that you think should have been in this book? Something you or your friends know how to do really well and want to show off? If so, we want to hear about it! Send us your best ideas along with photos or a video of you showing them off, and you could be featured in the next **Show Off** book.

💻 www.showoffbook.com

ATTN: SHOW ME TEAM
Weldon Owen Inc.
415 Jackson Street
San Francisco, California 94111